SOS MGY

Titanic

The Ship, The Disaster, and why most of what you know about them is wrong.

F.L. Miller

Table of Contents

A Note to the Reader

In this book, you will find the following conventions observed:

The twenty four hour clock is used and times shown are local. Distances are in feet, inches, and nautical miles- as they were at the time. For the same reason, engine specifications are listed in horsepower, steam pressures are shown in pounds per square inch and liquid measures are in gallons.

Speed will be measured in knots, which is how many nautical miles a vessel covers in an hour.

Obviously, because the bulk of this discussion will involve *Titanic*, nautical terms- where they are appropriate- will be used to denote locations aboard and about the ship.

The left side of the ship is the "port" side and the right side is the "starboard" side.

The front of the ship is called the "bow" and it is located "forward."

The back of the ship is called the "stern" and is located "aft"

"Ahead" means in front of the ship, "astern" means behind. Engines ordered "astern" are asked to be run in reverse.

An object directly to the side of the ship is located on the "beam" or "abeam" of the ship. Beam also indicates the width of the vessel.

An object located off to either side of the bow of the ship is either on the "port bow" or the "starboard bow."

An object located off to either side of the stern is said to be on the port or starboard "quarter."

The center of the ship is known as "amidships." Objects within the ship are "inboard" and objects outside the ship are "outboard." For instance, a lifeboat is stowed inboard and swung outboard for launching.

A deck is any floor on the ship, except in the engine room where the decks are called "floor plates."

The "bridge" is the control center of the ship, and is sometimes called the "wheelhouse"- although the latter word actually refers to the location of the ship's wheel- or "helm."

The “watch” is a four hour shift of duty aboard a ship.

Chapter One- Introduction

In 1912, newspapers were the unchallenged source of daily news. Every town, burg, and hamlet had at least one, and larger cities usually had several- all fiercely fighting for readers.

The papers were always looking for exclusive information or angles that they could play to their advantage, but all of them shared a common objective- to sell papers- a *lot* of papers. And because of the intense competition, it was unusual if all of them in a given area carried a story about the same subject and gave it equal weight.

But early in the morning of April 15, 1912, the telegraph repeaters in newsrooms in Europe and North America began to chatter with such a story- a big one, with multiple perspectives that would cut across any differences in editorial policy, content, or viewpoint. Everyone would carry it on the front page.

Something had happened in the North Atlantic involving the brand new flagship of the White Star Line, *RMS Titanic*.

The ability to report any event at sea, much less an accident that involved the largest vessel in the world, was somewhat of a novelty, made possible by a new invention, the wireless telegraph- or simply the "wireless."

At the morning papers, the news was a source of mixed emotions. Although the story of any misfortune to *Titanic* would be a surefire story, guaranteed to sell copies, the news came at the worst possible time. Morning runs had already started and early editions were on the streets- or soon would be.

The story, as it was, was almost nothing. Early reports stated that *Titanic* had collided with ice somewhere southeast of Newfoundland. Details were sparse, and those received were contradictory, based entirely on intercepted ship-to-ship radio traffic originating at sea. Sending conditions during the night had been good, but ironically, this created a problem. The numerous transmitters working to relay the news about *Titanic* were interfering with one another- making the reception of a clear message difficult, and frequently garbling those that got through.

The fact that the news was arriving via wireless created another problem, at least for the large newspapers. Many that had taken years to build and develop strong newsgathering teams, and exclusive sources, found them to be no advantage, as everyone was receiving the same information.

The first priority would be to find some hard news to print. Senior editors were sent for or, if they had telephones, called at home. Reporters were summoned and given assignments. The majority of papers stopped their presses and replated their front pages. Copies that could be called back were.

Many editors now came face to face with the fact that their knowledge of maritime affairs, and *Titanic* herself, was somewhat limited. There were more questions than answers- and they had better get the answers before the other papers did.

What circumstances warranted a distress call? Did it indicate something serious or would it be sent as just a precaution? Was *Titanic* damaged and if she were, would it delay her scheduled arrival in New York?

Who was aboard? Who was in command?

Reporters fanned out and editors began hovering over their telegraph repeaters. Copyboys or junior reporters were sent to search the paper's "morgues"- their files- to bring back anything they found that could possibly relate to the story.

A few minutes of investigation revealed some items of interest. *Titanic's* almost identical older sister, *Olympic*, had been in a collision with a Royal Navy ship in Southampton just the previous September, under the same Captain. *Olympic*, now repaired, was at sea, eastbound out of New York. Apparently *Olympic* was in contact with her younger sister and some of the intercepted wireless messages suggested that the two ships were steering toward one another.

Preliminary passenger lists started to come in as reporters began knocking on doors and waking up sources. Even if *Titanic* was not seriously damaged, these would be a goldmine. Her passenger manifest read like the social register. She was full of the rich, famous, and influential.

The reputedly wealthiest man in the world, John Jacob Astor, was aboard. Astor was news not just because of his money, but because he had been the center of an enormous society scandal only the year before. Astor, a man of forty-eight, had divorced his wife and married a nineteen year old girl- who was now pregnant.

There were other notables on *Titanic*, like Charles Hays, President of the Canadian Grand Trunk Railway, Benjamin Guggenheim, the mining magnate, Isador Strauss, former congressman and the owner of Macy's, and Colonel Archie Butt, President Taft's military aid. There was even an influential, albeit somewhat eccentric, British journalist aboard- W.T. Stead. Stead was never at a loss for a comment or an opinion. When *Titanic's* passengers made landfall, his take on the accident would be a godsend.

A good number of the lesser lights of American and British social elite were also on the ship, such as Sir

Cosmo and Lady Duff Gordon. Although they were officially traveling under an assumed name- as Mr. and Mrs. "Morgan"- it hadn't fooled anybody. Those who cared knew they were aboard.

Sir Cosmo was a landowner with an inherited title- whose business was making fortified wines. He was reputed as having some skill as a fencer- but fencing was a sport like polo, something that the upper classes dabbled in- without much of a following. In short, he was somewhat boring.

In contrast, Lady Duff Gordon was much more exciting- and much better known. She, under the name "Lucille," worked as a fashion designer, creating and marketing ladies "unmentionables," some of it rather risqué for the time. Her whole family was unconventional- her sister wrote racy novels.

Margaret Brown, whose estranged husband had become wealthy after he had devised a method to mine precious metals from a difficult dig in Colorado, was also listed as a passenger. To "polite" society she was of no significance, interesting only because she had been on an extended trip through Europe and Egypt with the Astors.

Even a bona fide countess was reported to be aboard.

With the concrete news regarding the ship amounting- at the most- to a sentence or two, and eager readers demanding a story, the papers employed traditional ways of filling space.

They printed pictures, mostly of *Olympic*, misidentified as the stricken *Titanic*, and artist's renderings showing the liner- or *a* liner- plowing into an iceberg. These were accompanied by stories about the ship itself, the notable people known- or thought to be- aboard her[1], and interviews- mostly with those regarded as experts in nautical matters- each providing their own

---

[1] People like George Eastman, the founder of Kodak, and Luther Burbank (misspelled as "Borebank'), the horticulturist, were reported to be aboard *Titanic* and later- when their names failed to appear on the list of survivors- were presumed to be victims, which must have surprised both of them as neither sailed on the ship. There was also a report of the demise of a "Senator Allison". The only passenger aboard named Allison was from Montreal. Washington Roebling, the engineer who built the Brooklyn Bridge, was also reported lost aboard *Titanic*, but it was actually one of his nephews.

degree of speculation as to what might have caused the accident and the possible consequences.

Some of these authorities advanced the theory that the ship must have collided with the ice in an area of reduced visibility. Others stated the collision may have been with what was termed a “black” berg, which would have been practically invisible in the darkness.[2]

It was allowed that it was likely *Titanic* had sustained some damage, but all cited her extensive watertight subdivision, and therefore there was little to no possibility she or her passengers were in any actual danger. All it appeared to be was a matter of unfortunate inconvenience. The collision would likely cause little more than an arrival delay.

That was good news, not only for those who had relatives or friends aboard the big liner, but for the general public as well.

---

[2] If we wish to be totally correct in this matter, a ship striking any fixed object- like a rock or an iceberg- is actually called an “allision.” However, so as not to confuse the reader, we will continue to call it a collision.

Most of the newspapers decided to play the percentages and report that the ship, and her passengers, had survived.

A few hours later, when the sun rose in North America, there was more news about the incident- and it seemed to confirm what the authorities had concluded. The accounts were almost universally positive.

There were several versions of the story- they differed in details- but most of the newspapers agreed that while *Titanic* had been damaged, it was not serious. The ship was still afloat, and everyone aboard was safe, but her arrival time was now in doubt. Some reports stated that the ship was without power and therefore unable to maneuver.

The story also related that two smaller liners, *Virginian* and *Parisian* had intercepted *Titanic's* wireless distress call and were racing to assist her. At the most, it would only be a matter of a few hours before they would arrive at her side.

Later, stories were published that *Virginian* had arrived at the scene and had taken *Titanic* in tow. There was also a report that her passengers had been transferred to the two smaller ships where they were being well cared for.

Depending on the account, the three vessels were proceeding to either Boston or Halifax. The newspapers explained that the accommodations aboard the smaller liners would be more than adequate to handle *Titanic's* passengers.[3]

Later in the morning, landfall information became specific. *Titanic* was now reported to be slowly heading for Halifax and the White Star office in New York announced that they were dispatching chartered trains to retrieve her passengers and speed them on to New York.

Phillip Franklin, White Star's New York representative, was publicly nothing but the embodiment of composure and reassurance. He told the reporters

---

[3] The origin of this spurious story appears to have been a garbled- or mis-relayed wireless signal involving a ship called *Asian* towing a derelict tanker named *Deutschland* to Halifax. *Asian* played no part in the rescue. There were strong suspicions after the accident that irresponsible, careless, or even malicious operators- radio was unregulated at the time and many were amateurs- had helped to distort the message as it went through numerous relays.

besieging his office that he was certain *Titanic* could float indefinitely, so there was little to no risk to anyone aboard. However, privately, he was also frantically trying to contact the ship by wireless- "Anxiously await information and probable disposition of passengers."

Later in the day, the papers reported that White Star had decided to recall the trains and had instead diverted one of their smaller liners, *Baltic*, to retrieve *Titanic's* passengers. It was thought that the only problem they would have would be to undergo another transfer at sea between ships.

While almost all available wireless stations- both afloat and ashore- were busy relaying the news, *Titanic* herself had been oddly silent, although she possessed the most powerful, and modern, marine set available. During the night, her signals had slowly faded and sometime early in the morning, they had finally died away.

This was dismissed merely as problems in transmission- attributable to deteriorating atmospheric conditions or the reduction, or possible failure, of power aboard the liner. The fact that *Titanic* was reported to be under tow seemed to confirm this theory. The loss of power also seemed to explain why her passengers had been evacuated. However, whether the passengers and crew were still aboard or not, everyone was reassured that there was no cause for worry, the safety features incorporated into the design of *Titanic* made her unsinkable.

People shook their heads at the news of the accident. Some were even amused- the largest ship in existence being damaged on her maiden voyage. White Star had expected so much from their new flagship, and this was just more bad luck for the line. During the last few years, White Star had had more than its share of unfortunate incidents.

As previously mentioned, only the year before, *Titanic*'s older sister- *Olympic*- had been struck and seriously damaged by a Royal Navy cruiser as she left Southampton. Three years earlier, in 1909, White Star had lost *Republic* off the East Coast of the United

States. She too had been in a collision- with another passenger ship.

But not everyone agreed that this was simply an unfortunate setback for White Star.

One newspaper, the *New York Times*, dissented. The editors interpreted the absence of *Titanic's* wireless signals as evidence of her loss. Their headline was much darker- stating that the ship had foundered and an appalling number of people had gone down with her.

Because this headline contrasted so sharply from what the other papers were reporting, and everyone knew *Titanic* was incapable of sinking, most readers assumed it to be an obvious mistake- or dismissed it as a shameless tactic to sell more papers. Some of the other newspapers ridiculed their rival for alarming the public before making sure of the facts. But the headline caused only a minor stir, as in 1912 the *Times* was merely one of many New York newspapers scrambling for its share of readers. The story would surely be set right in later editions.

But the *Times* stuck with its version and as the day progressed the other papers reluctantly began to agree with it. Wireless contact had finally been established with both liners said to be involved in the rescue. The news was not comforting.

Neither *Parisian* nor *Virginian* reported having assisted *Titanic* in any way, and there were no survivors aboard either ship. In fact, the only vessel confirmed to have rescued *any* of those aboard *Titanic* was a small Cunard liner, *Carpathia*. It could not be immediately established who had been rescued because the wireless set aboard the small Cunarder lacked the range to contact any of Marconi's shore stations.

Nothing was mentioned about the fate of *Titanic*, and it was uncertain if she was still afloat.

Optimism began to turn to anxiety. Crowds of people, concerned about friends and family aboard, began to gather in front of White Star offices on both sides of the Atlantic, hoping for some definitive word. Late in the morning, confirmation came.

Titanic was gone.

And instead of being "all safe" as many papers had first reported, over a thousand of those who had sailed aboard her were gone too- including a number of the wealthy and prominent.

Phillip Franklin made the announcement. His source was unimpeachable; a wireless message that had originated on *Carpathia* and been relayed to New York by *Titanic's* sister, *Olympic*. It had been sent by J. Bruce Ismay, Chairman of the White Star Line. Ismay was in a position to know. He had been aboard the lost ship.[4]

As with most peacetime catastrophes, the sinking of *Titanic* was completely unexpected and occurred amid conditions of normality- which made her loss even more shocking. Less than a week earlier she had rested at White Star's new "Ocean dock" in Southampton, taking on stores and undergoing final

---

[4] Ismay also attempted to send a message directly to the White Star offices in New York, but it did not arrive for almost two days. There is evidence that it was intentionally delayed by the wireless operators on *Carpathia*- one of whom was Harold Bride who had been on *Titanic*- primarily because they wanted to sell exclusive news of *Titanic's* sinking to the newspapers.

preparation to begin her maiden voyage, scheduled for April 10.

Titanic's sinking was surreal to many, particularly those that believed a disaster of this magnitude had been rendered impossible by modern ship design and technology. This included most people, even those that should have known better.

The general public of 1912 believed *Titanic* to be an engineering marvel, primarily due to her size. She was much bigger than her contemporaries- almost 900 feet long and costing the unheard of sum of seven and a half million dollars- but *Titanic* had not been designed to impress engineers, and would not have.[5] To them, *Titanic* was merely the latest entry in the logical progression of shipbuilding technology- and actually, there was nothing new about her. She was a virtual duplicate of her older sister, *Olympic*, and there was

---

[5] To put this amount in perspective, Boston's Fenway Park, home of the Red Socks, was opened within a week of *Titanic's* demise in 1912. It cost $350,000.

nothing groundbreaking or radical about her design. Both sisters were just *big* ships.

But to the people she was intended to serve- the passenger trade of the North Atlantic- she was a beautiful vessel, with graceful lines, luxurious appointments, unmatched food and unsurpassed service- the last word in seagoing comfort and extravagance. Her design projected the image of grace and power, and she was also thought to be one of the safest ships ever to sail.

Contrary to popular belief, the maiden voyage of *Titanic* had not been a front page event, except in Southampton, where most of her crew had originated, Liverpool, where White Star was headquartered, and Belfast, where she had been built. In some papers, the only record of her departure was White Star's sailing notice. Many carried nothing about her at all.

Titanic's debut had been complicated by a coal strike that had gripped Britain for several months. As with many job actions, it was a dispute over wages. The strike was uncoordinated- the miners had walked off the job in different mines at different times, but by March 1912, most all had been idled and coal was in short supply. This put White Star in a serious bind. They had heavily advertised *Titanic's* first crossing and they were forced to scramble to protect it.

Her maiden voyage had already been postponed once, she had been originally scheduled to sail in March, but *Olympic's* accident had delayed *Titanic's* fitting out at the Harland and Wolff shipyard in Belfast.

As the coal strike began, so it ended. Some miners went back to work in early April, but not all of them. Many mines remained closed and the industry was still short of reaching full production. There were other customers, like the Royal Navy and Britain's powerful railroads, who took precedence when it came to the delivery of fuel.

Olympic- now back in service- had overfilled her bunkers in New York, and even used some unoccupied staterooms to store extra sacks of coal to help salvage her sibling's introduction. But this proved insufficient.

As a last resort, the departures of several smaller ships were cancelled and their coal was scavenged to supply *Titanic*.

Most of the passengers who were scheduled to sail aboard these vessels were rebooked aboard the new liner- she was not even near her capacity. Almost all were delighted with the change, because *Titanic* was reputed as being the last word in passenger luxury. Many were also pleased at the opportunity to participate in a maiden voyage- particularly of the largest and most prestigious ship in existence.

Even those passengers who were bumped from first class on the smaller ships to second on *Titanic* were not to be disappointed because second class aboard the new White Star ship was said to be better- much better- than first class on the ships they left behind. A few cancelled their passages, after all first class *is* first class, but they were not the norm.

Titanic's unparalleled luxury, coupled with the generally held idea that she was the safest ship afloat would make this the perfect voyage. *Titanic*, according to popular belief, went beyond merely being safe. She was one of a new generation of liners that were said to be invulnerable.

Her sailing drew its share of reporters and photographers, but there were only a few more than would attend the sailing of any large liner. Most of the press was there to cover those who were embarking. Interest in the ship herself was lukewarm at most. After all, *Titanic* was the second ship of what was intended to be a trio of almost identical liners.

Titanic's older sister, *Olympic- had* been a sensation- both in Britain and in America- when she made her debut in 1911, but her novelty had largely worn off. She too had been hailed as the "largest ship in the world" (and also tagged as unsinkable.) She had been in service for almost a year.

Technically, *Titanic* was larger than *Olympic*, but to the casual observer, the ships were indistinguishable, and her reign as the largest ship in existence would have been short, even had she survived her maiden voyage.[6]

White Star had a third huge liner on the ways in Belfast- and she would be slightly larger than *Titanic* after she was completed. Her name was to be *Gigantic*.

The competition was doing its best to keep up too. It was common knowledge in shipbuilding circles that the Germans were already building a ship bigger than *Titanic* and White Star's principal British rival, Cunard, had an even larger ship on the drawing board. It would be only a matter of time before all the other major players on the North Atlantic would too.

But *Titanic's* reign was briefer than anyone could imagine- only four days.

Her sinking placed her at the focus of one of the greatest peacetime sea disasters to date and she soon would become the most famous, or infamous, ocean liner of all time.

---

[6] Even today, many pictures of "*Titanic*," are actually *Olympic*.

Chapter Two- Writing History

One might think that composing ar

Titanic's demise would be a fairly simple t

so much is known about the disaster that befell her. All one would need to do is find several authoritative accounts, extract the relevant information within them, and begin writing.

However, it soon becomes apparent that, surprisingly, there are very few definitive accounts regarding *Titanic*. As noted in the previous chapter, newspaper accounts of the era are useless; they are rife with errors, omissions, and inventions. Scholarly essays about the disaster are few, and most of them concentrate on the obscure facets of the event, such as the quality of the steel of which the ship was built.

There are technical publications, passenger lists, and records of her sailing, plus a few photographs, but unfortunately, once *Titanic* left Queenstown, everything we know about her is based on memories of those who were involved, and personal recollections vary.

Some people misremember, some others recall more "details" after the passage of time, others incorporate the recollections of others into their accounts, and others lie.

Titanic has also been the centerpiece far more efforts of less import. She has been the theme of frivolity- a short-lived Broadway musical- and she has been the setting of countless works of fiction, and several major motion picture productions, all of varying value and authenticity. The disaster has even been the centerpiece of more than one computer game.

The very volume of information regarding the ship has become an impediment to discovering and accurately explaining the events of that dark April night in 1912.

And, unfortunately, many of these "facts" are erroneous, and all of them have done their share to change the story.

Regrettably any time an event enters popular history, truth undergoes distortion, supposition often becomes "fact" and the frequent result is something either completely at odds with reality- or bears little resemblance to it. This makes it difficult for a historian to separate fact from fiction. In the case of *Titanic*, it proves particularly complex.

Even authoritative sources about the ship disagree about many points.[7]

Let's use John Jacob Astor as an example. Was he really, as many accounts state, the "richest Man in the world" in 1912? It appears not. Astor's wealth is just one example of a detail that seems to have taken hold by constant repetition. Astor was believed to have been worth in the neighborhood of 135 million dollars in 1912, but John D. Rockefeller- today thought to have been the richest individual *ever*- was estimated to have been worth $900 million in 1912, the equivalent of $189.6 billion dollars in today's money. This is easily researched information, and yet almost no author has

---

[7] Then of course we have completely uninformed additions to the myth. Recently the author received a catalogue that featured nautical items. One of the products featured was a "*Titanic* officer's whistle", one of which was credited with saving "over seven hundred lives" on the night of the disaster. It must have been some whistle.

gone to the trouble of correcting it, perhaps because there is more irony in the fact that the richest man in the world would perish alongside those who were virtually penniless.

Many works state that Astor boarded *Titanic* in Southampton, yet others say that he came aboard in Cherbourg. Verifying Astor's embarkation point is not important to this discussion, but it shows that there may be a disparity between even facts that one would regard as elemental. Accept one fact over another and the entire course of the story may change.

Seemingly minor details remain in dispute. Today, there is even controversy about how *Titanic* was painted. We know that she was red below the waterline, her sides were painted black, and the upper works white, but the color of her funnels is unknown. Today, most believe that they were a dark yellow, but some works assert that they were a "salmon" color, which could be anywhere in a range between orange and pink.

Another enduring notion about the *Titanic* disaster is that it was the greatest maritime tragedy up to that time. However, a boiler explosion aboard a Mississippi riverboat, *SS Sultana*, in April 1865 near Memphis claimed almost a third more lives.

Many authors feel a duty to their reader to present the most accurate account of the subject, but others have a more liberal interpretation of their responsibility, and some apparently only wish to sell books. The latter feel free to extrapolate unknowns. They create conversations between people who failed to survive- and therefore nobody could possibly have any recollection of them- attribute actions to individuals that could only be surmised, and alter facts- either slightly or to a greater degree- to better suit the flow of their story. It may seem harmless, but again, it changes the history of the event, and often another author will take the original revision and further “improve” upon it.

Most accounts of the *Titanic* disaster have contented themselves with presenting a narrative of what happened that April night, and that appears to be as far as most authors have gone. They’ve concentrated on the compelling human drama of the event, and accepted- without question or serious examination- the conventional beliefs about what led to the catastrophe and contributed to the appalling loss of life.

It is an attractive option. The story of the *Titanic* disaster is a writer's dream. It features the innocent, the guilty, heroes, cowards, and villains. It is layered with irony and packed with drama. It is a great story.

But a lot of it's wrong.

Authors who merely rework the "conventional beliefs" are doing their reader a disservice. For an historical event to be properly presented, the facts must prevail, even if it destroys cherished ideas.

Over the years, the tragedy that occurred aboard on that April night has been morphed, stretched and finally neatly distilled into a few simple clichés- things that everyone knows to be true (or more significantly, *believes* to be true) about the sinking. And, at first glance, there seems to be some validity to them.

As traditionally presented, the story of *Titanic* seems to be simply the result of gross overconfidence.

Her Captain and officers- despite numerous warnings that all placed the ice danger squarely in her path- negligently sailed the ship into the area of risk at high speed- pressed by J. Bruce Ismay, the Chairman of White Star, who wanted to make a record passage.

They were content that their superior ship handling skills would allow them to deal with any danger, and if a collision did occur, the watertight integrity of *Titanic* would limit any damage- in fact, the ship was immune to damage serious enough to sink it.

The lookouts were hampered by unusual conditions on the night of the collision, profound darkness coupled with an abnormally calm sea. Because of a last minute shake-up in the ship's officers before *Titanic* sailed, the binoculars that were intended to supply the crow's nest were misplaced. They never found their way there.

After the collision, the evacuation of the ship was strictly governed by class- favoring first and leaving steerage passengers locked below decks to fend for themselves. Even if everyone had been afforded an equal opportunity to board the boats, the ship was seriously under-equipped with them- largely due to the willingness of the White Star Line and Chairman Ismay to exploit outdated regulations. The Chairman himself, however, was able to secure a place in a lifeboat, thus condemning an innocent passenger to death.

A frantic, and vain, effort was made during the night to attract the attention of a nearby ship- clearly visible to the north of *Titanic* - a ship that could have simply sailed to her aid and rescued everyone aboard.

This ship, *Californian*, made no response to any of the signals made by the sinking *Titanic* or any effort to investigate the rockets fired by her- which were obvious and unmistakable signs of a ship in distress. The Captain of the smaller ship- who was made aware of the rockets and dismissed them- was judged by history as incompetent, perhaps even evil.

Compounding this, *Californian* was equipped with wireless, but her operator had shut down his set around the time *Titanic* struck the iceberg. One of her deck officers had stopped by after his tour of duty to listen in on the airwaves for a few minutes before going to bed. Unfortunately, he did not know how to turn on the wireless set and never heard *Titanic's* urgent calls.

However, operators aboard other ships did intercept *Titanic's* distress signals and if it had not been for the heroic actions of *Titanic's* wireless operators- particularly her senior operator, Jack Phillips- who stayed at his post until almost the very end- the loss of life would have been much greater.

The actual story of the *Titanic* tragedy is an intricate weave of coincidence; vague, outdated, or ignored regulations; decisions that seemed insignificant at the time they were made; complacency; indifference; misunderstanding; heroism; cowardice; good and bad fortune; negligence; overconfidence; and above all- faith in a system that was inherently, and dangerously, flawed.

It is also, more significantly, the story of how a confluence of external factors, some that were set in motion years before *Titanic* sailed, came together with disastrous consequences.

It is also a story of an almost naïve faith in technology.

The chain of events that concluded on that night in April 1912 began before *Titanic* was built- even before anyone could conceive of creating a ship of her size. It started over a century ago, spawned by competition between several major trans-Atlantic passenger lines. Its main players were an American banker who wanted to monopolize the North Atlantic trade and the Governments of Britain and the United States, who both wanted to stop him.

It is the story of a ship; that- had she survived her maiden voyage and led a normal life- would have been forgotten- nothing more than an obscure footnote in the yellowed pages of the record of ships that plied the Atlantic- known today only to historians, a few ocean liner buffs, and those remaining few who traveled aboard her.

But instead of fading to obscurity- as have most of her contemporaries- *Titanic's* name has become synonymous with spectacular failure. Even today- a century after she plunged to the floor of the Atlantic, she remains a household word.

Titanic has become a symbol- debatably awarded more historical significance than perhaps she actually deserves- no longer simply a ship- or as Dr. Robert Ballard, who led the expedition that eventually found her, originally called her - "a big wreck in deep water." Instead of being real, she's become a legend, more myth than substance.

Historians have invested the disaster with all manner of import- eras ended- eras began- mankind was humbled and even punished by her sinking. She has been portrayed as a seagoing microcosm of Edwardian society- an icon of an outdated structure of class distinctions.

Her story has become the classic cautionary tale- an embodiment of the old adage about pride going before a fall.

She's also been seen as the great leveler- carrying the world's most privileged and celebrated men to their deaths as well as some of her most underprivileged and obscure.

It has been said that her fate was preordained. After the fact, people began to cite omens that indicated that she was cursed- a curse that began almost as soon as the first steel was placed on the building ways. It was said that even her name tempted fate. It has also been suggested that her sinking was a deliberate act- arranged before she sailed- the product of an immense insurance swindle perpetrated by her owners.

But in some cases, the story of *Titanic* is *less* than what has been usually presented over the years.

In the balance of this book, we will take a fresh look at the *Titanic* disaster, dissecting and discussing the elements that caused, and contributed to, the tragedy, plus also exploring some that *did not*.

This examination will reveal some interesting and, perhaps, startling faults in the accepted perceptions. Many factors that have always been portrayed as pivotal to the disaster, when examined carefully, assume far less importance than they have been given over the years. Some are actually reduced to irrelevancy.

What follows is not an exercise in revisionism, but is instead a dispassionate and objective examination of facts- facts that have been known since the time of the accident- and yet somehow, historians have never put together, or chosen not to.

I cannot guarantee that everything in this book is absolutely correct, the story has gone beyond that, and I admit to often having to employ Occam's Razor (the simplest explanation is usually the correct one) to decide if one set of "facts" should supersede another. However, I can state that the details are as accurate as anyone could make them.

In 1912, Archibald Gracie, a passenger who survived her maiden voyage, wrote a slim volume called *The Truth about the Titanic*.

What indeed is the "truth" about *Titanic*?

Chapter Three- The Early Twentieth Century

Most historians preface the main body of their work with section of exposition, or a portion of the book where they attempt to set the occurrence they are discussing in its historical context. In the case of the *Titanic* tragedy, this part of the work is essential in the reader's understanding of the event, and because of the complexity of the disaster, it is rather lengthy.

Therefore, I have done my best to limit this piece to events, circumstances, and information relevant to the accident. While it might be interesting to know what was playing on Broadway and who was starring, what books were popular, what fads were sweeping the nation, what musical works were in vogue, or other items of trivia- most of this would be extraneous to our discussion.

However, it will serve us to start with an examination of what the contemporary attitude was toward science and technology, as *Titanic* - and the environment in which she sailed- was a product of this.

1912 began as a year of unparalleled assurance. It was near the end of what Mark Twain had called the "Gilded Age," which most historians now refer to as the "Edwardian Era," and only two years before the first "Great" war, which was also naively labeled the "War to end all Wars."

It was a time of confidence in mankind and the works of man. The popular view was that the human race would shortly achieve victory over the forces of nature- and some believed we already had. Science was advancing on all fronts, and it would be only a matter of time before it triumphed over all the ills that had plagued earlier ages.

Only thirteen years before, in 1899, Charles H. Duel, Commissioner of the United States Patent office, had suggested it be closed because "everything that could be invented, had been."

It was the age of engineers- iron, steel, and steam- and most of that steam was generated in coal-fired boilers. Great Britain, Germany, and particularly the United States, had vast deposits of the mineral and it was being put to use, either generating power or, as coke, being used in Bessemer converters in Sheffield,

Essen, and Pittsburgh, to produce steel around the clock.

It seemed that almost anything that could be conceived could be built. Immense bridges spanned chasms that were once thought impassible and buildings rose into the sky. Telegraph cables under the oceans and railroad lines on the land laced the world together. On the sea, steam had largely supplanted sail and journeys that once consumed arduous months, now took weeks or days, and were achieved in relative comfort.

In 1903 the mystery of heavier-than-air flight had finally been solved, and the airplane was becoming less of a curiosity. In fact, only a little over two years previously, Louis Bleriot had flown the English Channel- and the day after *Titanic* went down, an American woman named Harriet Quimby would fly the same stretch of water, the first to do so.[8]

---

[88] Quimby was the first woman licensed to fly in the United States, and had earlier pursued a career as a journalist and screenwriter. Her life ended in July 1912 when she was tossed out of an airplane in which she was riding as a passenger. The airplane had not been equipped with seat belts.

To many it now seemed that much of what had always been viewed as impossible was now within reach. As an example, the Panama canal- once thought to be an enterprise for fools with deep pockets- was nearing completion. It would cut weeks off the voyage between the North American Coasts.

The men who designed the canal thought big, building it to accommodate the largest ships in the world at that time- ironically the *Olympic* class liners- none of which traversed- or even neared it. *Olympic*, in fact, was the only one of the three sisters ever to complete a voyage across the Atlantic, and she never ventured south of New York. However, today, one of the legacies of these liners is the "Panamax" ship, designed with dimensions to negotiate the canal. And since Canal Cruises are so popular, another irony of the *Olympic* class is how their proportions- and thus those of the canal- still influence the design of passenger ships.

It was also an age of remarkable contrasts- where these ships of immense size and power were riveted together by men wielding hammers and the materials were brought to the slipways in wagons drawn by teams of horses.

Paradoxically, and significantly, in this age where the average person believed that the human race was approaching the ability to "master the elements," there was little genuine knowledge of what we were actually up against.

As an instance, there was extensive debate as to what provided the source of illumination for the sun. For most, the age-old hypothesis continued to prevail. The sun was shining because of incandescent combustion of gases- put simply; it was on fire.

However, most scientists had rejected this assumption, instead believing that it might be related to the new field of atomic theory, possibly caused by the action of recently discovered elements such as radium, but nuclear science was in its infancy, and at the time it was concerned solely with fission- or the splitting of atoms. The idea that hydrogen atoms in the immense pressure and heat of the sun's interior could fuse and release enormous amounts of energy had yet to occur to anyone.

Although everyone knew that only the ignorant continued to believe that the sun revolved around the earth, astronomers had only shifted things slightly, thinking that the sun was at the center of the Milky Way and our galaxy *was* the Universe, but this theory too was beginning to crumble. Observers were puzzled by what were being termed “Spiral Nebulae,” that improved telescopes were now resolving in the night sky, and there was debate about what and where these objects were. Some felt that they were located outside the Milky Way. It would be several years before they would be found to be galaxies themselves, and they were much farther away, and more numerous, than anyone had imagined.

But for many, all of this was an obscure sideshow. The public was far more intrigued by the work of Percival Lowell, who had established an observatory in Flagstaff, Arizona for the sole purpose of charting Mars. Lowell’s research seemed to confirm the notion that there were canals on the red planet, and because of their apparently symmetrical structure, they seemed to be the work of intelligent beings. After other astronomers could not confirm any of Lowell's work, it was suggested that he may have been seeing the blood vessels inside his own eyes.

Even those sciences that were grounded more in the physical than hypothetical, such as archeology, were unsophisticated. British archeologists were soundly deceived in 1912 by the "discovery" of Piltdown man. It was hailed as a colossal discovery, the "missing link" between man and apes, and stunning proof that prehistoric man had lived in Britain- and more importantly for many- possibly predating Neanderthal man who had been previously discovered in Germany. In 1950, it was exposed as a colossal fraud.

The advances that had been made by medical science chiefly involved surgical practices. Because microbes were now known to cause disease, operations were conducted in sterile conditions- or as close to sterile as could be achieved- and the patient administered an anesthetic.

However, if an infection took hold, there was no effective way to fight it- other than relying on the body's natural defenses. Research into antibiotics had produced drugs as likely to kill the patient as the disease, and it would not be until 1928 before a safe one would be discovered.

Some pathogens could only be theorized, like the flu virus that would ravage the world in 1918.

Medical doctors often had rudimentary training, some went to medical schools, some apprenticed with established physicians, but some others received none. In many places a person could become a physician by simply declaring himself so. He could hang out his shingle and begin seeing patients immediately. Therefore, the efficacy of treatments, and cures, varied widely.

Because of this, most people had more confidence in home remedies and what were called "patent medicines," concoctions that were often advertised to cure any ailment, no matter how serious it might be.[9]

Some of these medicines were compounded by local drug stores, but often they were marketed nationally or regionally through advertisements in magazines or newspapers. There was little to no science behind their formulation- only trial and error- and their recipes were jealously guarded. Since regulations regarding their content were largely absent, these "tonics" or "elixirs" often contained dangerous drugs, such as cocaine, poisons in high concentrations, or powerful laxatives. However, just as often, these potions were perfectly safe. People were paying premium prices for nothing more than flavored colored water.[10]

Other disciplines were just as primitive.

In 1912, weather forecasting was more of an exercise in speculation than a science. Those who

---

[9] Early in the 19th Century, a self-styled physician named "Dr. Sibley" advertised a formula called "Solar Tincture" that was alleged to "restore life in the event of sudden death." It's not known if this was also the first use of the disclaimer "Results not typical."

[10] Many of our modern soft drinks started as patent medicines.

called themselves "meteorologists" were aware that high pressure usually meant fair weather, low pressure meant the opposite- and little more. Even the seemingly simple concept of weather fronts would not be advanced until 1919. Forecasters were aware of what they called "steering winds" or "squall lines" but they had yet to put it together.

Most people still found common maxims more reliable in foretelling the weather, such as "A ring around the moon means rain." For some people, Grandma's aching joints or the behavior of animals (the cat has the "wind in her tail") or insects, ("When bees stay close to the hive, rain is close by"), were the best indications of changes in the weather.

A copy of the *Farmer's Almanac* could be found in almost every rural home and people often found its predictions as accurate as anything issued by the government.

Attempts at using a scientific approach to forecasting consisted of simply plotting local conditions on maps. Cloud cover, temperature, pressure, wind speed and direction were the only data recorded, as no meteorologist had yet appreciated that there were factors in the upper regions of the atmosphere that could influence the weather. Even if they had, there was no practical way to gather any information from there.

The United States Weather Bureau relied on over two thousand observers scattered all over the county to record local conditions and wire this information daily to Washington D.C. where the master maps were compiled. Then, using a special code, the map information was retransmitted to local weather bureau offices around the country were it was laboriously drawn by hand on maps of the immediate area.

As it might be expected, the information derived from these efforts were hours old when they were distributed, and the “forecasts” were next to useless- particularly if the meteorologists were dealing with rapidly moving or developing storms. Even if a storm could be accurately predicted, which was rare, the Weather Bureau was careful to avoid alarming people.

In fact, they had stopped using the word "tornado" in 1894 because they felt it to be too frightening.[11]

At sea- a region of the earth where weather information would seem to be of paramount importance because of the obvious peril a storm could introduce into the lives of those who were present there- it was almost non-existent.

Nautical weather information was often inaccurate and incomplete- based totally on the observations and subjective reports of ship's masters. They often omitted data that today would be considered important, such as the direction and speed of the winds.

Reports were obviously limited to ships equipped with wireless, and normally these were larger vessels plying well-established routes. Because of this, storms that formed in less traveled areas of the ocean would frequently seem to suddenly spring from nowhere. Ships caught in them would often disappear without a trace.

---

[11] It was not reinstated until the mid 1950's.

As we will see later, when we examine the wireless messages sent by *Titanic* and the ships in contact with her, the information they exchanged regarding the weather was inexact and, because many of these messages were relayed several times- incurring serious delays- it was frequently stale and useless. There was no codified system of transmitting weather data.

There was no established system of relaying information about *any* hazard- including ice- and there was no requirement that this information had to be conveyed, although some ships did send such reports voluntarily to government entities, such as the United States Hydrographic department. Unfortunately, often nothing was done with the information once it was received to alert shipping to the dangers.[12]

As the ships became larger, it was found that many charts- some of which had not been revised since the Napoleonic wars- were incorrect regarding depths,

---

[12] The Hydrographic office did issue information about hazards and weather at sea, but only to those who requested it before sailing.

submerged obstructions, and the position of known navigational hazards. The location of many coastlines and islands were found to be seriously in error, and nobody knew how deep the seas were.

Sharp-eyed lookouts remained the only means of detecting hazards in the path of the ship. The only improvement made over the years was the telephone used to directly relay the sighting to the bridge. Radar was years in the future.

Even in the age of these fledgling "Superliners," methods of navigation had not changed significantly since mariners had first left the sight of land thousands of years earlier. There were no electronic navigational aids, like LORAN or GPS.

In fact, the only "modern" navigational aid was the chronometer- a clock used to determine longitude. Although considered state of the art at the time, today's cheapest quartz watch keeps more accurate time than the most carefully crafted and adjusted chronometer of 1912.

Chronometers of the era were key-wound, mechanical, and subject to inaccuracies caused by temperature and pressure changes- even the roll or pitch of the ship. It had not yet occurred to anyone that a chronometer at sea could be calibrated by a radio signal, and so a chronometer that lost or gained time would often lead to substantial navigational errors.

Latitude was determined by shooting the positions of stars or the sun with sextants. In the North Atlantic- where it is frequently overcast for days on end, making astronomical observations impossible- navigators frequently had to rely on a method called "dead reckoning" to determine their position.

This ominously named system (and nobody seems to be able to agree on exactly why it is so called) was simply an informed estimation of the navigator as to where the ship *should* be, based on her speed, heading, and an assessment of the effects the winds and currents had upon her.

Even the most skilled navigators could only determine their position within a few miles, unless they were within sight of land and able to take bearings on landmarks. Lookouts were often told to expect landfall within a range of several hours.

So, as we see, the modern and relatively swift *Titanic* used virtually identical methods of navigation as had the Viking ships that had traveled these same waters hundreds of years before.

One thing that *had* significantly changed since the time of the Vikings was that now the ships were immensely larger, significantly faster, and ironically, less maneuverable and harder to stop. While a Norse ship traveling- at most- at only a few knots, would likely have no difficulty evading an object sighted on a clear night- like an iceberg- a ship of the size and speed of *Titanic* might not.

Of course, it would be reasonable to expect the officers and crew that were charged with the safe operation of these large liners to take these factors into account, and take appropriate measures, such as reducing speed in areas where danger was expected, or of reduced visibility.

But in fact, unlike the days of the Norse seafarers, they now could be warned of hazards at sea and prepare for them- even as the danger evolved.

Chapter Four- The Wireless Revolution

In 1895 an invention swept the civilized world. Telegraphy, the only method of rapid long range communication, had gone “on the air” and could now be sent and received virtually anywhere on the planet.

It appeared to be just another manifestation of the supremacy of man over his realm. And, although it was science, it seemed like magic.

As to whom actually “invented” the device was, and remains, open to debate. Like a number of innovations, it was the product of what would be termed today as “parallel development,” with several inventors making identical discoveries and coming to similar conclusions at much the same time, but a persistent Italian inventor named Marconi, who devised his apparatus largely through painstaking trial and error, beat them all to the patent office.

“Wireless”, as it was called, proved largely redundant when it was introduced. Most cities were already connected to the telegraph network, and so there was little call for the invention. Early sets were very large and required enormous amounts of power.

However, when ships began carrying it to sea, wireless found its niche- proving itself to be particularly useful. Vessels were no longer out of touch with land or each other during voyages.

Shipping companies quickly recognized the benefits of having their vessels equipped with the new device. They could exercise much more control over their fleets- and their employees. Wireless spread rapidly over the globe.

However, it was an emerging technology, and the system was somewhat cumbersome and arcane. All wireless equipment, no matter who built it, used primitive "spark gap" transmission technology (somewhat like the interference produced on AM radio bands by thunderstorms or electric motors).[13] The signals covered a wide range of the electromagnetic spectrum, despite efforts at introducing tuning circuits.

---

[13] This is the reason that almost all radio operators were given the nickname "Sparks."

The "telephones," as the headsets were called, worn by the operators were as primitive as the radios and were uncomfortable- particularly when worn for hours on end. There was no method of regulating the volume in these units, and because of their unsophisticated design, they required that they be so firmly clamped to the operator's head that many of them developed cauliflower ears after years of service.

Anyone with a set could listen in on everyone else- and did. There was no voice transmission; it was all done by Morse Code- dots and dashes. The radio operators, to save time, had developed a sort of wireless shorthand to more rapidly communicate with one another- somewhat like the Internet jargon in use today.

And most all of it was done at a rapid-fire pace. Many operators became so adept at their craft that they could identify each other just in the way the messages were keyed into the air. The style of transmission possessed by each operator was called his "fist."

Wireless soon proved to be a significant advance in shipboard safety. Vessels could relay information about the weather and navigational hazards to one another. They could also summon help if it was required.

In 1909, a White Star ship had used wireless to do just this. *Republic* had collided off Nantucket with the Italian liner *Florida*. *Republic's* wireless operator, Jack Binns, sent out a distress call, or CQD, that was immediately answered by several nearby ships. Everyone on *Republic*, except for four people who had been killed in the collision, survived. Binns became a celebrity for a time, receiving a ticker tape parade in New York and even resigning his position with the Marconi Company to travel on the vaudeville circuit for a few months lecturing to audiences about his experience. He became known as "CQD" Jack Binns.[14]

---

[14] There are accounts stating that Binns had initially been selected to be the chief operator on *Titanic*. This is not true, but Binns did play a part in the disaster- at least its aftermath. He was hired by the Hearst newspapers to embark on a wireless-equipped tug that was to intercept *Carpathia* as she approached New York. The operators aboard *Carpathia* had been extremely reticent about revealing anything other than the names of the survivors aboard, even ignoring a telegram from President Taft. The idea was that they probably would talk to Binns. Eventually it came to nothing- a storm prevented the tug's sailing.

Wireless proved to be beneficial to passengers too. Businessmen, instead of literally being lost to the world for a period of several days during a voyage, could remain current with the trade ashore- and- in a limited fashion- still manage their affairs. There were several documented cases of people making large stock transactions- in which they made handsome profits- all via wireless. Passengers could revise their travel plans and notify those ashore of any changes in the time of their arrival.

Wireless had even assisted in the apprehension of an international fugitive who attempted an escape by sea.

In 1910 Dr. Harvey Crippen- a purveyor of patent medicines- had been arrested aboard the Canadian Pacific liner *Montrose* by a Scotland Yard detective who had boarded the ship as she took on her pilot in the St. Laurence River.

Crippen, an American who had immigrated to England, proved himself to be less than a criminal mastermind. He had poisoned his wife Belle with a toxin so powerful, and rarely used, that it had to be specially ordered- and then seemed to intentionally set about to make everyone suspicious of her disappearance and his complicity in it.[15] When Belle's friends became worried about her disappearance, Crippen concocted a series of stories to explain it- each of escalating implausibility.

Soon, Crippen was questioned by Scotland Yard Detectives.[16]

Although Crippen appeared calm to the policemen, the initiation of an investigation convinced him that flight was his only option. He and his mistress went to Belgium, where they boarded *Montrose*, a Canadian Pacific liner destined for Canada. Knowing that the authorities would be on the lookout for a man and woman, Crippen decided that his mistress would

---

[15] As one example of Crippen's cunning criminal brilliance, his mistress appeared in public within days of his wife's disappearance wearing several distinctive pieces of jewelry that had belonged to her. Additionally, he booked passage to a country where he could be arrested and extradited without delay. If he had instead sailed to the United States, where he was a citizen, it may have taken much longer.

[16] One of the people who expressed misgivings about the fate of Crippen's wife was Kate Roberts, a performer with the stage name "Vulcana," billed as a "strongwoman."

attempt to pass herself off as a young boy, and thus throw everyone off their trail. However, the plan backfired. *Montrose's* Captain, Henry Kendall, alerted by wireless, noticed them, primarily because of the odd, and inappropriate, way they held hands in public.[17] Evidence suggests that Crippen's mistress had not participated in the murder and was unaware of its occurrence. She simply saw the trip to Canada, and Crippen asking her to disguise herself, as an adventure. Captain Kendall sent a message to Scotland Yard shortly before the ship sailed out of wireless range of Great Britain to notify them of his suspicions.

Walter Dew, a detective who was working the Crippen case and had questioned the doctor, boarded another ship, White Star's *Laurentic*, which overtook *Montrose* at sea and beat her to Canada, allowing him to be waiting for Crippen.

---

[17] The Crippen case was also noted as one of the first where forensic pathology was used to identify a victim. A British doctor named Spilsbury identified Crippen's wife from a scar on her skin. The body had been completely de-boned and the head, hands and feet removed. Dr. Spilsbury was assisted in his investigation by another physician named Dr. Pepper.

The story created a sensation all over the world. The press eagerly followed each development, even publishing charts in the newspapers to show the relative positions of the two ships as the nautical chase progressed.

Aboard *Montrose*, Crippen- happily ignorant- perceived his voyage as a brilliantly successful escape, apparently being one of the few people in the world who was unaware that he had been discovered. He even made the remark to Captain Kendall that the wireless was a “wonderful” invention. Crippen was returned to England, convicted of murder, and hanged in a prison not far from where he had had lived with his wife.

All these publicized positives tended to obscure that there was also more than one downside to the wireless.

Although it was called a “service,” wireless was aboard most ships for one purpose- to make money for the wireless company. Although it initially went to sea to enhance safety, it soon became apparent that it could, through passenger telegrams, generate a significant profit.

Ships were staffed for the maximum and most efficient utilization of equipment and employees. Only a large ship with a large volume of message traffic- such as *Titanic*- merited a powerful long range set, and more than one operator.

Because there was money to be made, there were several companies at sea, all competing for their slice of the business- each working on a contract basis with the shipping lines. Marconi, Telefunken, United Wireless, and Lee DeForest[18] all vied for the business at one time or another.

---

[18] Marconi had, by far, the largest number of sets at sea- DeForest- which evolved into United- the fewest. In fact, the early DeForest companies were more con games than real concerns. Lee DeForest, the technical mind behind them, had a talent for falling in with shady speculators, who usually absconded with the receipts and left him holding the bag. DeForest was not entirely an innocent victim though- he was once quoted as calling his customers "suckers." DeForest "invented" a forerunner of the radio vacuum tube he called the "audion," which- when it worked- amplified signals. It was later proven that DeForest had discovered the device by accident and really did not know how it functioned. DeForest was a shameless self-promoter, and often attempted to take credit for, and patent, work done by others. To the end of his life, he called himself "The Father of Radio." Few others did.

Although the operators were technically under the orders of the ship's master, they were actually employed by the wireless company- not the shipping line. Most captains had almost no knowledge of how the wireless worked, or the procedures each company had established for its administration aboard, so the operators were generally immune from any direction from them.

It worked both ways. As the ship's officers knew little about the wireless, the wireless men knew little about the sea. They were not sailors, had no training on the ship or its procedures, and therefore often had no understanding of what information might be valuable to the crew. Sometimes a message that could be of benefit to the Captain or his officers went unreported because the wireless man did not appreciate its importance. Often, if a message was not specifically addressed to the ship, it went unread by anyone other than the operator who took it down or relayed it.

The wireless man would often know little more than a passenger, only aware of the ship's intended destination- but not of her current position, heading, or speed. In fact, many wireless operators did not understand the contents of the ship-to-ship messages they handled, the position reports and other information often being just an arrangement of meaningless numbers.

Even the set itself could cause problems with the ship. It was found that if the wireless apparatus was installed improperly- or too near the bridge- it could interfere with compasses. It was also exceptionally noisy- particularly on older ships that had not been designed with its installation in mind. And- significantly- because it was relatively new, and novel, many passengers regarded it as a toy.[19]

Although the cost of sending a ten-word wireless message was exorbitant- almost three dollars, which was a small fortune in 1912- it was a thrill to be able to

---

[19] The *Olympic* class liners had a seemingly odd feature aboard, a compass mounted on a raised platform located in between the second and third funnels. Obviously not used for navigation, this compass was in the area thought to be least affected by the wireless set and it was used to check the accuracy of the compasses on the bridge.

send "Marconigrams" to friends and family ashore- and to receive them too.[20]

Obviously, a good number of these messages were of little importance, except to those who sent or received them- and, as may be easily imagined, a great number were of no consequence at all- "wish you were here" and such- only significant to the senders and recipients because of the novel method in which they were transmitted.

The content of the communications made no difference to Marconi- or the other wireless companies- because passenger messages represented the backbone of their business- and sometimes, although it should not have, this traffic received priority. On the bigger ships, on which the majority of wealthy first class passengers sailed, the crushing number of these often frivolous private telegrams frequently swamped the operators.

---

[20] For example a good pair of shoes cost about $1.25.

The *Olympic* class ships had been designed after wireless had been invented and although some elements of the apparatus and its installation appear to be carefully considered- particularly when it came to the generation of revenue- others seem to have been somewhat of an afterthought.

A passenger who wished to send a Marconigram would find it relatively simple, tendering it to the purser's office. After charges were collected, it would be dispatched, via pneumatic tube, to the wireless room. Inbound messages addressed to passengers would be sent to the purser's office via return tube, and bellboys would be dispatched to locate the recipients and deliver them.

However, messages that involved the safety of the ship were handled in a completely different manner. There was no tube between the wireless room and the bridge- there was not even a telephone- so the message had to be physically carried to the officers on duty or the Captain. There was no bellboy either, so the operator would have to either stop transmitting or receiving and deliver the message himself, or wait until the other radioman became available to complete the task. If he was very busy, the delivery of the message might be delayed for a significant period of time.

Ironically, the ships that generated the most volume were often also obliged to relay messages that originated on smaller ships. Because they possessed larger and more powerful sets- with greater range- ships like *Titanic* (with a daytime wireless range of over 400 miles and a 2000 mile plus range at night) could frequently contact shore stations when a smaller ship could not.[21]

Relaying a message was time-consuming and far from simple. The operator on the intermediate ship did not simply press a button to pass on the message- nor was it done automatically. The incoming telegram had to be taken down and then laboriously re-transmitted. Obviously, many operators on the busier

---

[21] During *Titanic's* trials, her wireless was able to make contact with a station in Port Said, Egypt- three thousand miles from Belfast.

ships would allow these messages to accumulate and send them later when it was more convenient.

Nature was frequently unkind to wireless operations too. Electrical storms- even at great distances from the station- would often introduce so much interference into the radio bands that it was either impossible to receive any messages- or they had to be repeated several times for the entire message to get through.

Sometimes even the sun would play havoc with transmission. Solar flare activity would disturb the ionosphere, which reflected signals, and destroy long-range communications. The physics of radio were still somewhat a mystery at the time, so these disruptions were called "atmospherics." When conditions were good there was an understood urgency to transmit and receive as much as possible before the state of airwaves deteriorated.[22]

---

[22] At the time that wireless was introduced, nobody- including Marconi himself- really understood how it worked. Several scientists postulated that there was an invisible and previously unknown medium, which they called the "ether," which carried the signals.

So even with messages being sent "at the speed of light," there was no guarantee that the communication would arrive rapidly. There might be a gap of several hours between when the message was presented for transmission, when it was eventually keyed into the air, and- depending on the number of relays it had to make- when it was finally delivered.

Obviously the larger ships would give priority to anything tendered to the operators aboard. Messages from other ships would be relayed only when the time- or the inclination- was available. It sometimes took several days before a wireless message finally made it to who it was addressed.

Radio operators assigned to the larger ships found their berth to be somewhat of a mixed blessing. While they occupied positions of some prestige, they were worked mercilessly- sometimes not being able to emerge from their radio rooms for the entire voyage- even having to take their meals while working.

The transmission and reception of messages was not their only duty either.

One task was maintaining what were called the "accounts." Records were kept detailing the number of Marconigrams sold and the money collected for each. On *Titanic*, this job had largely been assumed by the staff of the purser's office.

Another requirement was to listen in on a nightly news broadcast transmitted from Marconi's powerful trans-Atlantic station in Poldhu, on the southwestern tip of Britain, and take down several pages of text to be included in a newspaper called the *Atlantic Daily Bulletin*, which was sold to passengers aboard. Most of the newspaper was printed ashore- with only the news being added at sea.

Most travelers who could afford the cost of the newspaper- nothing Marconi featured was inexpensive- believed it to be an excellent value- and it was a novelty to be able to remain current with events on shore.

Of course, the wireless operation had an implied pecking order too. Operators on smaller vessels were expected to stay off the air until the larger ships were finished working their traffic.

Smaller ships often only had one operator- the volume of traffic would make any more unprofitable- so the service they received varied. They were off the air while the operator ate, slept, was out of his cabin, or simply disinclined to work. Operators on smaller ships often "called around" to nearby ships after a period off the air to ascertain if there were any pending messages for them. Responding ships would relay what they had, so it was not difficult for a lone operator to keep up- unless something unforeseen occurred.

Marconi operators were expected to stay on hand at their sets during the time they were awake, but because they were unsupervised the hours they worked- or when the set was idle- was left to them. As may be expected from this arrangement, the quality of the service was somewhat inconsistent.

The Marconi Company had recognized that this peculiar set of circumstances might be detrimental to safety, so they specified that their operators remain on duty during "periods of danger." However, the company issued no guidelines about what conditions or circumstances would constitute such periods or to who the "danger" might apply.

So, some operators would keep bankers hours, others would transmit during the late evening or early morning because during hours of darkness the ionosphere was more stable and the sets had greater range. Even then they had to be careful not to interfere with the larger ships that also used the nighttime hours to "work off" the bulk of the passenger traffic.

There were human factors that affected wireless too. Some operators were more industrious, or ambitious, than others. Many were like today's computer nerd- with an intense- almost fanlike- interest in radio, constantly tweaking their sets for better performance and seeking to discover and implement improvements. However, to some operators working in the wireless room was just a job- and a rather mind-numbing one at that- particularly on the smaller ships where there was not much traffic. Operators often fell asleep while on duty.

For an operator on a small vessel, life could quickly become routine. Since Cyril Evans, the operator aboard *Californian* played such a prominent part in this story, let's examine what would be a typical day for him.[23]

On most mornings he would arise around 0700. He would switch on his set, electronically announce his presence, determine what ships were within range of his transmitter, and then listen in for a few minutes to take down any messages for the ship or ensure that there was nothing pressing waiting for him. He would then wash, shave and have breakfast.

At about 08:00 he would return to his set, transmitting and receiving as required- and because *Californian* usually carried no more than a handful of passengers at most- and many of them traveled in her plainly appointed cabins because they did not have a ready surplus of cash- there were probably very few

---

[23] *Californian* was the ship observed north of *Titanic* on the night of the disaster. Her role will be discussed in much greater detail later.

outbound messages. Around noon he would break for lunch, returning to his cabin between 1245 and 1300.

Between 1430 and 1700, it was Evans' habit to take an afternoon break- usually by taking a nap. *Californian's* captain stated that he never received any wireless messages at that time, so he assumed his operator was off duty.

Evans would go to dinner around 1800 and by 1900 would be back in his cabin. As night fell, he would be able to hear more and more ships over his apparatus. Between 2230 and 2300, depending on the activity on the airwaves, he would switch his set off and turn in.

So, instead of being driven to the point of exhaustion as his counterparts aboard *Titanic* frequently were, Evans' existence was one of relative inactivity.

Wireless was not a homogenous system either. Because of the competition between the differing wireless companies, it was common practice for them to forbid their operators to communicate with ships using different systems- except in cases of emergency- and frequently it was left up to individual operators to determine what constituted such. However, this rule was somewhat hollow because there was no way to prevent ships using other systems from overhearing transmissions.

Communication between wireless stations was sometimes hampered by other problems too, as there were at least three different forms of Morse code in use at the time.

The Marconi Company used what was called "Continental" Morse, but there were also "American" and "German" versions too. The differences in the codes concerned call signs, and code groups that were used to designate common functions, like the "CQ" signal.

While it was permissible to communicate with a ship using a competing system if it were sending a distress signal (all companies officially specified that their operators respond), an ice report or storm warning might not be relayed. The business had not yet grown to the point of regulation, so it was not beneath the operators of rival companies to intentionally jam a competitor's signals- and many bored wireless men delighted in doing so.

Jamming could be unintentional too. A ship transmitting in close proximity to another would often create a startling, uncomfortable, and frequently angering, detonation of noise in the headset on the receiving ship. It sometimes led to important messages being missed.

Conversely, radio signals, even under optimum conditions- and without jamming- were very difficult to detect at long range- and almost all communication at sea was of this nature. Ship to ship messages comprised only a small percentage of wireless traffic. Most of the communication in the North Atlantic was with the coastal stations located at Poldhu or at Cape Race, Newfoundland. Amplification circuits had yet to be devised and operators were obliged to listen carefully. One author accurately described the dots and dashes as "whispers," although some sets, like the one installed on *Titanic*, were able to provide its listener with an audible tone.

After the *Titanic* disaster, Marconi was honored throughout the world because of the lives wireless saved, but as we will see later, the invention also may have contributed to its cause.

Marconi himself- later in his life- questioned the value of his invention- asking, “Have I done the world good, or have I added a menace?”

To *Titanic*, it would prove to be both.

Chapter Five- The Evolution of Travel in the North Atlantic

Olympic, *Titanic*, and their third sister- originally to be christened *Gigantic*- and later, after it was suggested that the very names of these enormous new liners had somehow tempted fate, was named *Britannic*- were just the latest entries in a series of successively larger vessels designed to carry passengers on the most heavily traveled- and incidentally the most dangerous- sea route in the world- the North Atlantic.

Ever since the "discovery" of the New World in the 15th century, people had their reasons for braving the perils of the Atlantic- an ocean so violent and fraught with hazards, storms, heavy seas, and ice; that the immense ocean to the west of the North American continent would be called the "Pacific" because of its perceived docility.[24]

---

[24] Although at the higher latitudes, the weather in the Pacific is almost identical- if not actually worse.

As previously mentioned, the first people known to have successfully embarked on this particularly treacherous stretch of water were Norse explorers. They even established a settlement for a time on the northern tip of Newfoundland- long before the voyages of Columbus.

Once colonization of the North American mainland began, people began to make the journey for economic gain, political or religious freedom, or simply to answer the call of adventure that settling any new territory inspired in them.

Early voyages were made in sailing ships, in primitive accommodations, and were almost invariably miserable. Vessels were cold, damp, and cramped. The food was appalling, infested with insects, covered with mold, and often rotten. On many ships, passengers were an afterthought. The only space available for them- the majority of the vessel being dedicated to cargo holds- was at the stern, near the cables that moved the rudder. Because of this, passengers who were accommodated here were said to be traveling in the "steerage" spaces.

Often, a traveler would be required to wait for a considerable period of time before he or she was able to find a ship going their way, and voyages aboard these early sailing vessels, that were totally at the mercy of the wind and weather, sometimes consumed months, and many were never completed. Vessels sailed and simply disappeared- with all hands presumed to be lost.[25]

Samuel Johnson summed up the prevalent attitude toward sailing at the time, "Going to sea is going to prison, with a chance of drowning besides."

In the early 1800's the invention of the steam engine, and its incorporation into vessels, shortened voyages and added a measure of control over the ship previously unknown, but the primitive nature of these power plants frequently only added to the misery of the passage.

---

[25] It was estimated that as late as 1860, one out of every six ships that sailed failed to reach its destination.

Early marine steam engines were often modified railway designs, sometimes nothing more than simply placing a locomotive within the ship and connecting its driving mechanism to paddlewheels or a propeller shaft. Unreliable and inefficient, they consumed enormous amounts of fuel- initially wood and then later coal- which produced thick clouds of smoke.[26] And, until the closed loop system was introduced, where steam exhausted from the cylinders was captured, conducted through condensers, and sent back to the boiler as feed water, they used vast quantities of fresh water- which was always at a premium at sea, or they used sea water which severely limited the time they could operate. Many times, the engine was used only as a last resort, when the ship was becalmed or the Captain desired additional speed.

The presence of engines aboard ships also introduced their own unique hazards. Sparks from the funnel or firebox frequently set the ship ablaze, and if the

---

[26] It was not until the early 1920's that a liner first used oil to fire her boilers- *Olympic*.

water level was allowed to fall too low in the boiler or there was a problem with the safety valve- it would explode, often taking the ship with it.

People continued to travel only when conditions or events made it imperative.

But soon things began to change. By the middle of the 19th Century, ships began to evolve, and the first were built that placed more emphasis on the carriage of passengers and less on the transport of cargo. These ships were still not the "liners" that would eventually dominate the North Atlantic, but instead started as "paquebots" or mail ships.

The French designation was soon changed by the English speaking world into "packet boats," and then simply to "packets." Originally sailing ships, these vessels were designed to make swifter passages to allow the mail- which was becoming more and more essential for commerce- to be delivered more rapidly.

Passengers began to show their preference, and willingness to pay more, for the shorter voyages afforded by these ships and soon vessels began to appear with more and more cabins available for what was proving to be a lucrative trade.

The steam plants also evolved and became more reliable, and it could be predicted when these ships would arrive and depart. Routes were established between larger ports and ships soon became subject to schedules.

Passengers reacted favorably to this innovation, and soon began to expect it. More and more people traveled, and because the same vessel would often be employed in regular sailings between two or more predetermined ports, people began to refer to these ships as "liners."

Ships soon appeared with the primary purpose of transporting passengers, their hold space sharply reduced and dedicated to the carriage of baggage, mail, and if space permitted- small amounts of cargo. But even so, an ocean voyage could still be an adventure.

One of the most famous of these early trans-Atlantic passengers was a British author who crossed in 1842 on Cunard's *Britannia*, Charles Dickens. As you might expect, Dickens wrote about his journey between Liverpool and Halifax, and it becomes quickly apparent that he was not employed in Cunard's public relations department.

Britannia was Cunard's first liner. Constructed of wood, she was a hybrid of sailing vessel and steamer. She had two masts that carried sails and one smoky funnel planted slightly aft of amidships. Her propulsion was equally crude- large side-mounted paddlewheels, somewhat like a riverboat.[27]

Dickens, who lamented that he had been somewhat deceived by the effusive advertising featuring the ship and her amenities at the counting house where he purchased his ticket , quickly summed *Britannia* up as "not unlike a giant hearse with windows in the sides."

Her accommodations did not impress him either. Dickens found his cabin to be "an utterly impractical, thoroughly preposterous box," and his bunk- "nothing

---

[27] Samuel Cunard, who had founded the line, was a notoriously frugal Nova Scotian, and resisted equipping his ships with propellers, even after they had been proven to be a superior form of propulsion, because he perceived the paddle wheel system to be less expensive.

smaller for sleeping was ever made except coffins." Dickens dark descriptions reveal that he may have had some serious reservations about surviving the voyage. But at least he *had* a cabin; some passengers did not- having to sleep in berths rigged in the public rooms- which incidentally were also much smaller than the advertising had led everyone to believe.

It was not to be an easy crossing. The Atlantic behaved itself for a couple of days, but then *Brittania* encountered a storm. She pitched and rolled deeply, enough to let the sea come aboard, and Dickens was highly dismayed to find the deck of his cabin under a few inches of water. Even if he had not been deathly seasick, this would probably have not contributed to his peace of mind.

Brittania creaked and groaned as she fought her way through the seas- she must have been a literal symphony of noises. After a while, most of these sounds became routine and even unnoticed, but there was a different sound one day- a large crash. Undoubtedly fearing the worst, Dickens quickly went on deck to investigate. He found that the heavy seas had smashed one of the lifeboats.

If this was not bad enough- it was not all. The starboard paddle box (the enclosure for the wheel) had carried away- leaving the paddle wheel exposed and able to throw water over the ship.

The entire voyage took fifteen uncomfortable and frequently frightening days. To top it all off, *Brittania* ran aground for a while outside the entrance to Halifax harbor- despite the fact that Cunard had boarded the Halifax pilot in Liverpool prior to the sailing.[28]

Unfortunately for the passengers of this era, Dickens' voyage was nothing out of the ordinary.

But by 1912, conditions at sea had changed appreciably.

Ocean travel had vastly improved and in many respects had become almost routine. Voyages could still be miserable, depending on the weather or the size

---

[28] Today, Cunard cites, in various media, Dickens as being one of their first "celebrity" passengers, but they somehow fail to mention his low opinion of the voyage.

or design of the ship. Even on the larger ships, this could apply. As an example of the latter, Cunard's big liners, *Mauritania* and *Lusitania*, were known as "wet" ships because the design of their bow tended to throw a great deal of spray into the air- and over the ship, particularly when they were driven at speed. Passengers who chose to "take a turn" around their open decks often found themselves drenched when they completed their walk.

But instead of being possibly life threatening, this was merely an inconvenience- a price a passenger paid for a swift passage. Modern ships were powerful, crewed by experienced and skilled professionals, and they were safe- at least that was the common perception.

And the most modern ships were larger than ever before. Around the turn of the twentieth century, progress in shipbuilding had been rapid and dramatic.

In the ten years prior to the launching of *Olympic*, liners had more than doubled in size.

Ships had grown so big that they seemed invulnerable. To many, it was simply inconceivable that something of their scale could be fatally endangered. These ships could ride out storms- sometimes even outrun them- and they were designed that in the event that their hulls were breached, they would remain afloat.

It was not just the naïve or uninformed that believed this either. Even experienced mariners had embraced the idea. Edward J. Smith, a senior White Star Line Captain who was later to become Commodore of the fleet, had remarked several years earlier about one of his charges, "I cannot conceive of any vital disaster occurring to this vessel- modern shipbuilding has gone beyond that."

Smith's last command would be the maiden voyage of *Titanic*.

Chapter Six- The North Atlantic racetrack

As mentioned in the previous chapter, most accounts of the *Titanic* disaster cite a shipbuilding "revolution" that commenced at the beginning of the 20th century. Vessels began to grow almost exponentially, doubling in size in less than ten years.

Most also assume that this event was due to advances in technology- improved engines, building techniques, and materials.

However, if we place *Olympic* or *Titanic* next to *Oceanic*- the last White Star liner to be built before the turn of the century- it is difficult to see any real differences, other than the obvious disparity in size.

Oceanic entered service in 1899, and because of her magnificent appointments was instantly christened the "Millionaires yacht." Compared to *Olympic* and *Titanic*, she was small, only 17,272 gross tons. She sported two funnels amidships, and was the first White Star liner to be built without the capability to carry sails on her masts.

Powered by two triple-expansion reciprocating engines, her hull was traditionally built, composed of a structure of frames and stringers attached to a central keel, with a skin of three quarter inch steel plate riveted overall.

Aside from the presence of a low pressure turbine within the *Olympic/Titanic*, that drove a third propeller, the ships were very similar to *Oceanic*, including the thickness of their hulls.[29] The only significant difference in their construction was the employment of a newly designed hydraulic riveting machine.

There was no "shipbuilding" revolution at the beginning of the 20th century- the revolution was in the *funding* of these giant vessels.

In 1912, if you crossed an ocean, there was no option other than to travel by ship. And although we

---

[29] The exterior plating on *Olympic/Titanic* was thicker in the middle of their structure, but only a by a quarter of an inch. At the bow and the stern, the plating was the same thickness as *Oceanic's*. A thinner hull cost less to build, produced less drag in the water, and weighed less- thus increasing the fuel efficiency of the ship.

today tend to view the early 20th century as a more leisurely-paced era where people were content to while away time, lolling in their deck chairs sipping hot tea and munching scones as they cruised to their destinations, speed was as important to them as it is to us today.

Passengers did not book aboard ships to relax or engage in pointless visits to Caribbean shopping centers. Most sailed to conduct business or to start new lives and they all desired one thing- a *rapid* and comfortable voyage to their destination.

Pleasure trips in those days were virtually unknown- except to a handful of the privileged classes- and their excursions could be more accurately termed as seasonal migrations. It was common for the affluent American social elite to spend the winter in the more temperate climate of southern Europe and return home in the spring.

Many of the wealthier first class passengers aboard *Titanic* were concluding winter stays abroad. For instance, as mentioned, John Jacob Astor accompanied by his young wife and Margaret Brown was on his way home after touring Egypt.[30]

Even those fortunate to be able to travel for pleasure did not regard the ship as anything other than a means of getting to where they were going.

The North Atlantic run was, by far, the busiest route on the planet- connecting the primary political and economic centers of the early 20th century. Because there was no way- other than by ship- to get between them, the route had become a maritime speedway. Vessels of many different lines served it, and because the rewards could be so great, competition was intense.

The two largest British passenger lines were Cunard and White Star. But oddly, White Star was not actually British- at least not anymore. Although White

---

[30] All three had made the eastbound trip in January aboard *Olympic*. Astor normally would have shunned someone such as Margaret Brown. She was somewhat accurately perceived by the American Social elite as being rather unrefined and the product of "new money." But if Astor wanted to socialize with anyone he really had no choice. He had been ostracized by his former friends for divorcing his wife and marrying a younger woman. Divorce was the social and moral kiss of death in the early 20th Century. Even the minister who married Astor and his new wife was eventually forced to resign. After Astor died aboard *Titanic*, there were more than a few who attributed his death to Devine retribution.

Star ships were registered in Great Britain, crewed by British subjects, and flew the British flag- an American firm- the colossal International Mercantile Marine Company- owned them.[31] The IMM was more of a cartel than a company.

IMM was controlled by American bankers- most notably J. Pierpont Morgan. Morgan was a notorious builder of "trusts" or monopolies, and he wanted to rule the shipping business on the North Atlantic- if not the entire world. Morgan did not simply want to reduce competition at sea; he wanted to eliminate it.

Through IMM, he was well on his way- having embroiled his company in a series of brutal rate wars- and in the process engulfing several shipping lines on both sides of the Atlantic.[32]

---

[31] Actually, the Oceanic Steam Navigation Company, White Star's official name, went through about four progressions of holding companies before it could be traced to IMM ownership.

[32] The most devastating of these rate wars concluded in 1908, and led to the establishment of the Atlantic Conference, which was an association of the lines serving the North Atlantic. Its function was to set standard rates for passage.

The White Star Line had been IMM's biggest- and most prestigious- acquisition. White Star's Chairman, J. Bruce Ismay, was installed as IMM's chairman. But Morgan was not yet satisfied. In his view, *any* competition was too much. He envisioned IMM absorbing Cunard too.

Germany was in the fray as well with the Hamburg-America and North German Lloyd lines, but because of their route structure, they were not in direct competition with IMM. The German companies did not serve Great Britain, and IMM had an agreement with them to feed passengers into each other's routes.

North America had two major shipping companies. United States Lines operated several ships in trans-Atlantic service, as did the Canadian Pacific Railway.[33]

---

[33] United States Lines was never really a contender in the North Atlantic, even when they operated the world's fasted liner, *S.S. United States*. The service aboard the European liners was always regarded as superior to the American, and prohibition, when American ships were not allowed to carry any type of alcoholic beverage, further took its toll. United States Lines continually needed government subsidies and after making a series of questionable decisions about their fleet, went out of business in 1989. Canadian Pacific decided to concentrate on its railroad business and divest itself of its hotels, ships, and airline

France's entry was the Compagnie Generale Transatlantique- "The French Line," and there were other, lesser, competing corporations.

While each of these lines had its own ideas about service, they all sought to lure one type of passenger- and not the one you might expect. While it might be a windfall for a company to have the newspapers report that society luminaries patronized their liners, it was not the millionaire trade the lines were really in search of, but instead- it was the immigrants who were flocking in record numbers from the old world to the new.[34]

---

in the late 1970's. They sold their maritime operations to a small line headquartered in the United States called Carnival, which has now become almost the modern day equivalent of IMM, having taken over Holland America, Princess, P&O, Costa and - Cunard.

[34] In the early 20th century people followed the activities of the wealthy and socially prominent much in the same way that people follow the doings of celebrities today. Movies and recorded music were in their infancy and therefore the culture of Hollywood had not yet invaded the press. Most large newspapers had society pages, with their own reporters and editors, and the major wire services made sure that their subscribers in the smaller towns and cities were supplied with timely information too. One of the last photographs taken of John Jacob Astor was a press photo snapped as he prepared to board the boat train.

It would be inaccurate to state that *all* the people immigrating to North America traveled in steerage, but the majority of them did.

The average immigrant in "third class" was almost invisible aboard ship. It was fortunate that they required little, because that's what they received. Although they represented the largest number of people embarked, they occupied the smallest areas aboard.[35] The staff devoted to steerage was equally minute. While each first class stateroom might have two stewards assigned to it- or even more, depending on the level of service, steerage might have one steward assigned to an entire passageway.

The deck space allocated to first and second class was equally disproportionate to the number aboard, and it was in the most desirable area on the ship- the top. Here, the shipboard elite were provided with comfortable deck chairs and blankets to shield them

---

[35] For instance, the space allocated aboard *Titanic* to the first class dining room- or "saloon" as it was called- was approximately 10,000 square feet. The *entire* area allocated to steerage was about 24,000 square feet.

from the cold. Stewards hovered at a respectful distance ready to bring hot drinks- or something stronger- if desired.

Steerage was allowed access to light and air either at the bow or the very stern, decks that were cluttered with hatches, cranes, capstans, and other machinery used in either loading or mooring the ship. Instead of deck chairs, steerage made do with fixed benches.

First and second classes could avail themselves of deck games, and if the weather was foul- or it just suited them- there were other amenities, such as concerts or dramatic readings. If they desired a quiet hour or two, there was a well-stocked library. They also had spacious, comfortably-appointed, public rooms in which to play bridge or whist and seek refuge if the weather was disagreeable.

Third class areas were devoid of diversions of this type. Steerage passengers were largely responsible for their own entertainment. If they were lucky, the line might provide them with a piano in a tiny public space that often did double duty as their dining room.[36]

However, aboard *Titanic*, steerage, which was usually the most Spartan of accommodation, was excellent by the standards of the time- exceeding average by a wide margin- almost rivaling second class on some lesser liners. On smaller ships steerage passengers were often housed in what was called a "dormitory" arrangement- where public rooms were converted to sleeping areas at night. The big White Star liners did have some common berthing- for unmarried males located forward- but they also featured numerous separate cabins equipped with bunk beds. Some even had washstands.

To her steerage passengers, *Titanic* must have seemed lavish beyond anything they had previously experienced. It was clean, well lit, (and for some immigrants it would be the first time they had been

---

[36] *Olympic* and *Titanic* did provide separate public rooms for third class, but they were tiny and we must assume that they were often quite crowded. The steerage "dining room" was smaller than a similar first class space intended for the use of their maids and valets.

exposed to the innovation of electric light) and the food, although simple, was plentiful and satisfying. It was also more than a novelty for many of the women to have someone else do the cooking and cleaning, and they experienced a first in their lives- idle time.

While the common perception is that the majority of these immigrants were Irish, this was often not the case. The Emerald Isle had no monopoly on them- immigrants were streaming to the United States and Canada from all over Europe- even India, the Middle East, Africa, and Asia.

Immigrants were the backbone of the business, far steadier than shuttling the well-to-do. Although the latter group added some measure of glamour to a voyage, and spent small fortunes for their passage, their business was largely seasonal. For the shipping lines, their trade was merely icing on the cake.

But the immigrant traffic also had its share of problems. Since most lines had jumped on the bandwagon, there was a problem with overcapacity- more berths than customers. Additionally, the volume was beginning to drop off, and as one might expect, it was largely one-way. Steerage quarters were almost deserted on eastbound voyages- the only passengers being the handful of people who wished to return to the old country or those who had been refused entry into North America, either due to poor health or their political views. To make things worse for the shipping lines, the United States was beginning to tighten its immigration laws.[37]

Because of competition, the price of passage dropped significantly. The average one-way steerage fare aboard was around $36.00 (seemingly nothing today but in 1912 it was still a considerable sum- equivalent to almost a year's income for many.)

---

[37] Although the impression is often given that the United States was a haven for people who had been oppressed in the country of their birth, accepting anyone who applied for admission, there were numerous restrictions and conditions applied to those who wished to enter the country. The government had imposed quotas limiting the number of people who could emigrate from specific regions or countries, for instance there was a strict limit on the number of Chinese who could enter in any given year. People thought to be anarchists were also turned away- in no small part because President McKinley had been assassinated in 1903 by a man who proclaimed himself to be one. In 1924, partially as a result of a "Red Scare" that followed the war, the United States decided to close the doors, enacting legislation that virtually ended the immigrant trade.

What made things even worse for companies like White Star and Cunard, a number of the foreign lines were being subsidized by their respective governments-so the revenue produced by fares was less important to them.

For instance, the German companies received healthy payments from the Kaiser, in part so they could keep the Imperial German flag flying on international routes, and partially to assuage his pronounced inferiority complex when it came to his cousins across the English Channel.[38]

Of course, the British Government, through the award of mail contracts, was essentially doing the same with their lines. In fact, the letter prefix, "RMS" meant "Royal Mail Ship, or Royal Mail Steamer."[39]

---

[38] The German and British Royal families were essentially the same, which led to a number of odd juxtapositions. For instance, the Kaiser was an Admiral in the British Royal Navy and also a Field Marshall in the British Army. Two German princes even attended the British Inquiry into the *Titanic* disaster. They were given preferential seating-in front of the bench, just in front of the lawyers representing both sides.

[39] J. Bruce Ismay, testifying before the Senate Investigation into *Titanic's* demise, stated that the contract to carry the mail aboard the ship represented over $100,000 yearly to White Star.

Some companies were "flag carriers"- owned by the countries from which they operated, and therefore making a profit was a secondary consideration- and in some cases- of no importance at all. However, some of these same governments were becoming concerned about the number of their citizens- particularly skilled tradesmen and their youth- who were fleeing their countries for North America, and so therefore some of the fares featured on these lines were actually higher than they were on the competition.

This somewhat uneven, and inconsistent, playing field had far-reaching consequences. It was a cutthroat business with everyone looking for any kind of edge.

Unsurprisingly, passenger desires drove most of the competition. As previously mentioned, although we today tend to view the early 20th as a more unhurried time, when people were less concerned about the pace of their progress- this perception is incorrect. Then, as now, speed was considered a prime commodity. To the majority, time spent traveling was viewed as time wasted.

Passengers continually demanded newer, more comfortable, and above all- *faster*- ships. Unfortunately, new liners cost immense sums of money- money that the companies often did not have- and many could not borrow. Paradoxically, the same passengers who favored these ships were unwilling to pay the higher fares their construction and operation would require.

Around the turn of the 20th century, many shipping lines found themselves compelled to make some extremely difficult decisions about the conduct of their business. Some decided to abandon the North Atlantic run and concentrate on different markets. Those who remained would soon be nearing a point of no return. They either built bigger, flashier, and faster or they were destined for oblivion.

White Star reached this juncture in 1902. J. Bruce Ismay, Chairman of White Star, after weighing his options, decided it was fruitless to try to compete with IMM and accepted a buy-out from them.

Cunard was nearing its own crossroads, but the chairman of Cunard, Lord Inverclyde, continued to resist selling out to IMM. Inverclyde, realizing that there was another option available to him, approached the British Government with his hat in his hand, but also with an ace up his sleeve.

He explained that his fleet was unremarkable and being swiftly outpaced by foreign liners. For emphasis, he reminded everyone that the Blue Riband- the record for the fastest crossing of the Atlantic- which had almost always been a British possession- was now in the hands of the Germans.

He then detailed his vision- a duo of magnificent turbine-driven speed queens, designed to put the British back where they belonged in the shipping world- the forefront- and send the competition reeling.

There was one minor snag- the ships would be extraordinarily expensive- requiring resources far beyond what would be available to Cunard through normal means. They were going to need a few quid.

Otherwise, alas, the line would have to seek "alternative financing" (the greedy Americans.)

Surely Great Britain, a country steeped in the traditions and ways of the sea, would not want to see both its major passenger lines controlled by foreign interests. [40]

As might be expected, the initial reaction of the British government was mixed. Some officials were cool to the idea; seeing it as unfair to single out one company for support. Others favored it, making the strong case that Cunard was a national asset, and their ships were vital to the survival of the Kingdom- particularly if there were a war. The threat of a European conflict was looming ever larger and the United States appeared to have a decided interest in staying out of it. There was always the possibility that if the United States declared itself neutral, White Star ships, and the vessels of other British companies that had been consumed by IMM,

---

[40] What is not generally known is that both White Star and Cunard also operated a large number of cargo ships in addition to their liners.

might become unavailable to support the realm as troopers or hospital ships.

At least one of the Empire's premier shipping companies had to remain in British hands. Not only was Cunard given the money- but laws were passed that restricted possession of Cunard stock to British subjects.[41]

A deal was finally struck- benefiting both the government and Cunard. Cunard would get the money for their liners, loan guarantees, and even some subsidies, but the Royal Navy would have a hand in the design of the new ships. Additionally, in the event of a war- everyone knew the Kaiser was furiously building a navy to rival Britain's- these two ships could

---

[41] It was only a matter of time though. As mentioned, Cunard now belongs to American owned Carnival Cruise lines. To add insult to injury, Cunard's current flagship, *Queen Mary 2*, was built in France- by the same shipyard that built the majority of the French line ships. *Queen Victoria*- the replacement for the aging *Queen Elizabeth 2* was built in Italy, as was the third modern Cunard Queen- *Queen Elizabeth*. To be fair, Cunard did look for a shipyard in the UK to build *QM2*, but the few that remain lacked the capability to build such a large vessel. Harland and Wolfe was in the running for a while until it was found that they intended to subcontract much of the construction. Although many within the UK have professed to have disowned Cunard, the author took a Christmas cruise in 2007 aboard *Queen Mary 2* that sailed from New York, and the majority of those aboard were British.

be requisitioned by the Admiralty to support the war effort, transporting troops to the war zone, acting as floating hospitals, or even escorting other ships as auxiliary cruisers. Their design incorporated features that would allow their rapid conversion to any of these configurations.

The two new liners would be christened *Mauritania* and *Lusitania*- after the Cunard fashion of ending all their ship names with "ia."[42]

Because the government was fronting most of the money for the construction of these mammoth liners it was decided that two shipyards, in different parts of the country, would be awarded contracts. *Mauritania*, which was to be launched first, would be built by Swan Hunter in Newcastle and *Lusitania* by John Brown in Scotland.[43]

---

[42] White Star ended all theirs with "ic." This practice led to some rather odd names (like White Star's *Nomadic*, *Ceramic*, *Medic*, *Traffic* - a tender- and even one ship called *Magnetic*) assigned to ships in both companies. It continued until the Cunard and White Star lines merged in 1934. The first new ship placed into service by the merged company was the original *Queen Mary*.

[43] John Brown built all three original "Queens," the Royal Yacht, and *HMS Hood*. The company was amalgamated into Upper Clyde Shipbuilding in the 1970's, was sold off and ended its life building oil

Everyone in Britain, except Cunard's competition, was happy and excited about the new additions to the merchant fleet.

White Star saw things differently from Cunard. While the new *Lusitania* and *Mauritania* were hailed as technological achievements, they actually were somewhat uncomfortable- despite the amenities Cunard had built into them. Both vessels were essentially powerful marine power plants with passenger ships wrapped around them. Their design favored the achievement of speed above all else. As mentioned above, they were considered "wet" ships because their bows threw spray over them at high speeds.

In the early 20th Century, fluid dynamics was an almost unknown science. Instead of attempting to design a more efficient hull- one that would cut through the water with greater efficiency, the practice was to build a traditional hull and simply pile on more and more horsepower to achieve greater speeds. The slab-sided

---

platforms. Swan Hunter built *HMS King George V* and *Carpathia*. As of this writing, they are being dissolved.

bows of most liners- up to and including the original *Queen Mary* and *Queen Elizabeth*- literally blasted water into the air which was carried back over the ship.[44]

The designers of *Lusitania* and *Mauritania* had anticipated this- so each was built with a slight outboard slope to their boat decks to help shed this water. There were also some other design compromises. To permit the ships to reach their intended speed, they were given slender hulls. This enabled them to slice through the water with greater efficiency, but at the sacrifice of some stability. Therefore, they rolled more readily, and deeply, than some other ships, and the vibration caused by their turbines, reduction gearing, and propeller shafts was severe in some areas aboard- particularly when the ships were being driven at full speed.

Generating the power required to propel these ships demanded extraordinary amounts of steam- and

---

[44] In fact, until the launch of *Normandie* in the mid 1930's, apparently nobody wanted to take the risk on a significantly new hull design. *Normandie* proved herself to be not only swift, and after a problem with her propellers was resolved, considerably more fuel efficient as well. Today almost all ships incorporate design elements pioneered in *Normadie's* hull, particularly her bulbous bow.

coal- so both ships spewed immense clouds of grimy black smoke from their four funnels, and depending on wind speed and direction, this often covered the open decks, and any passengers who braved them, with a coating of oily soot.[45] The grime also presented challenges in keeping the interiors of the ship spotless, and despite earnest cleaning efforts, it eventually worked its way into crevices and nooks, giving each ship a faint "industrial" odor. The roaring furnaces below the boilers also demanded an enormous volume of air, and so the upper decks of both ships were literally a forest of ventilators.

Nevertheless, when the two new Cunarders entered service, they proved popular and their presence instantly began to take a toll on the competition.

---

[45] Both *Lusitania* and *Mauritania* were requisitioned by the British Government after the start of World War One to be auxiliary cruisers, but their coal requirements were too much for even the Royal navy who soon returned them to Cunard. The Navy later re-requisitioned *Mauritania* as a hospital ship, but dictated that she sail at much slower speeds than she had been designed to achieve. During the war, when the Royal Navy was consuming most of the coal that was being produced in Britain, Cunard was forced to mandate slower speeds for *Lusitania* too. It made her an easy target for *U-20*.

White Star weighed its options and resolved to compete in a different way. To use a current catch phrase, they had a different "business model" than Cunard. White Star knew that a fast passage in an uncomfortable ship could seem much lengthier than a slightly longer trip on a well-appointed one. To them, there was a great difference in the words "journey" and "voyage."

Instead of spending the bulk of their money on propulsion- with the achievement of only a few knots speed advantage (and the attendant higher operating costs) which would be inevitably eclipsed by the new construction of competitors- they would instead invest in solidity, magnificence, and- above all- comfort. The *Olympic* Class liners would be the largest, steadiest, and most luxurious ships the world had ever known.

But this idea, as practical as it appears, put White Star at a serious disadvantage.

Ships of all lines *had* to make their arrival and departure times as advertised, lest the complex schedule of connecting ships and trains collapse.

Because of their deeper draft, the larger liners had to closely observe the tides too. In New York harbor, for instance, ships had to wait for what is called “slack water” when the force of the incoming tide is balanced against the flow of the rivers.[46]

If they arrived too late, favorable tide conditions would be lost and they might have to wait as long as twelve hours for another chance to enter the harbor. The cycle of tides would also affect their departures. If a ship was significantly delayed, she might even find her intended mooring occupied by another ship when she arrived.

Additionally, a late arrival would often cause a “cascade” effect, making the ship late for her next arrival and sailing- requiring that schedules, and printed advertising be amended.

For a faster ship, a schedule could be designed that allowed her to sail a knot or two below maximum

---

[46] For this reason, many passenger ships serving New York have begun to use the Brooklyn ship terminal, where the tides are much less pronounced, allowing more flexibility in sailing and arrival times.

speed- still outdoing the competition- but affording the opportunity to make up time if she had to temporarily slacken speed to avoid hazards or deal with storms.

Unfortunately, a slower ship would be deprived of this luxury. Although comfort might be an important lure to a passenger, a significantly longer voyage would often not be tolerated. Therefore a slower liner often had to be driven at full speed throughout the voyage to maintain schedule, and any time lost was irretrievable. This need to arrive and depart on time put a great deal of pressure on White Star captains.

What, in 1912, what was considered proper and prudent action on the part of a White Star Master- or one of any line on the North Atlantic?

As previously noted, any European country with a deep-water port had one or more shipping companies, all operating what were called "express" liners- ships that were expected to arrive and depart on time- exactly like trains. Masters had twin responsibilities- passenger safety and maintaining schedule. It was a juggling act- balancing calculated risk and duty to the company.

None of the lines serving the North Atlantic officially sanctioned this devotion to maintaining schedule, and most had one or more regulations that expressly prohibited the practice.

As an example, a White Star directive stated: "No thought of making competitive passages must be entertained, and time must be sacrificed or any other temporary inconvenience suffered rather than the slightest risk should be incurred."

However, like many large companies, White Star preached one gospel and practiced another. Therefore, this instruction was regularly ignored.

Officers who obeyed the letter of the regulation cost the company money and earned the disfavor of management. Missed arrivals, particularly on the North Atlantic route, increased costs and led to lost passenger and cargo bookings.

Captains who consistently placed safety above schedule soon found that they never advanced above commanding smaller ships on less coveted routes. Those who proved to be sticklers often found themselves assigned to ships where it made little difference- freighters or tankers. Some were even demoted or dismissed from their positions- always- officially- for other reasons.

And, of course, it was also a matter of personal pride. A Captain who managed to maintain schedule- even under adverse conditions- was looked upon as a superior mariner, not an "old woman," as a more cautious master might be regarded.

For the most part, passengers were blissfully unaware of the dangers to which they were being exposed. However, in a tacit way, they were accepting them too. Lines that had a reputation for keeping schedule garnered the most business. Attitudes toward accidents were the same as they are now- they were rare and only happened to other people.

Those aboard the liners were not the only ones in peril. Commercial fisherman quickly learned to steer clear of areas where these ships operated, lest they be run down and left to the sea.[47]

Simply put, an ocean liner sailing in the early twentieth century rarely slackened speed for anything. As hard as it may be to believe today, it was actually the accepted practice for liners of that era to maintain speed in areas of risk so as to clear them as rapidly as possible- at least that's what was said to justify the custom. Passenger ships would continue, without slowing, through any type of hazard- fog, ice, storms, with the Captain hoping that the odds would favor him.[48] Luckily for the passengers and crew aboard most of these ships, they did.

---

[47] It was a custom in the early 20th Century to illustrate the size of liners by placing smaller craft, usually one-masted sailboats, in pictures of the ship. It always appeared as if there was little margin for error in the navigation of either vessel as the liner was invariably making good speed.

[48] For a period- a short period- after *Titanic* sank, ships slowed in fog and other areas of peril, but soon returned to the old practice. When radar was introduced after the Second World War, the rule was disregarded entirely. In fact, Commodore Harry Manning of *SS United States* was criticized for maintaining a speed of almost forty knots in an area of dense fog on her maiden voyage. *Queen Mary 2*, under Commodore Ronald Warwick, also maintained a speed of over thirty knots in fog on her maiden voyage. Both had radar.

Unfortunately, for those aboard *Titanic*, over the years this practice of literally gambling with the safety of the ship had somehow been transformed from being a reckless and somewhat foolhardy means of navigation into an acceptable- even prudent- method of operation. It was somewhat akin to playing Russian roulette and each time the revolver fails to fire, interpreting it as being increasingly safe to continue.[49]

White Star was further hampered by its choice of port. They had recently relocated the majority of their trans-Atlantic operations from Liverpool- on the west coast of Britain, to Southampton- on the southeast coast. Although the three *Olympic* class liners would show Liverpool as their home ports, they would rarely call there.[50]

---

[49] The accident that claimed the space shuttle *Challenger* proves that this kind of thinking still prevails. After the first few launches, NASA realized that the design of the field joints in the solid rocket boosters was deficient and the fault was exacerbated by low temperatures. However, as the flights continued, and nothing serious- other than some burn-throughs in the boosters- happened, it appeared that the practice of launching with the faulty design was an acceptable risk.

[50] *Titanic*, in fact, would never go to Liverpool. She had originally been scheduled to sail there, where White Star's headquarters were located, before going on to Southampton. There she was to be "thrown open"

Southampton was farther away from New York, almost a half days steaming, but it had several positives. Southampton was closer to London- just a relatively short train ride away- and it was also much closer to France, enabling the White Star ships to tap into the growing European market by calling on Cherbourg. They would then sail on to Queenstown (now Cobh) on the southern coast of Ireland before embarking upon the Atlantic.

White Star's plan was to construct three of the huge liners, enabling weekly service- in each direction- across the Atlantic. The ships would be opulently appointed, rivaling or exceeding the standards of the finest European hotels. Only the best of everything would be incorporated, and the staff unsurpassed.

No cost would be spared. In fact, Harland and Wolff, in Belfast, who built all of White Star's ships,

---

as allowing the public to come aboard and inspect the ship was then called. The line would collect a small fee from each visitor which would be donated to local hospitals. However, delays at the shipyard postponed her delivery to White Star until just days before she was to depart on her maiden voyage, so the Liverpool visit was cancelled.

worked on a "cost plus" basis with them- receiving a fixed amount of four percent over and above the actual construction cost of the ship.[51]

There was no reason to cut corners and Harland and Wolff did not.[52] They had a reputation for building solid, reliable vessels and only the finest of everything went into *Olympic* and *Titanic*. In fact, people who had been aboard both ships confirmed that *Titanic's* appointments and interiors were even better than her older sister's. For instance, in many places where *Olympic* had linoleum flooring- *Titanic* was carpeted.

---

[51] This arrangement between White Star and her builder eventually proved ruinous for the line. It could take years of operation for a ship the size of *Olympic* to pay off the cost of her construction. IMM was hit particularly hard by the loss of *Titanic*, as the company was largely self-insured. After *Titanic* went down, *Olympic* was almost completely rebuilt- with the installation of higher watertight bulkheads that rose forty feet above the waterline, watertight decks, and an inner skin. This not only cost White Star the equivalent of half of *Olympic's* original construction costs, but it also took the ship out of service for several months. *Britannic*, which was building at the time, also had to be retrofitted with these modifications, significantly increasing her cost and delaying her delivery.

[52] Well almost. Until the wreck of *Titanic* was found, many believed that her outside decks had been made of traditional teak. It was found that her builders had used cheaper pine, and possibly billed White Star for the higher priced wood.

Almost everyone agreed that *Titanic* was *Olympic* perfected.[53]

The superlatives would not stop there. The *Olympic* class would be almost one hundred feet longer than *Mauritania* or *Lusitania*, and wider as well. They would have lavish furnishings, spacious public rooms and features never before seen aboard a ship, like a swimming pool, Turkish bath, gymnasium, and squash court.

They were to be the last word in everything-except lifesaving equipment.

---

[53] Even this is not completely true. Had *Titanic* survived, there were plans to reduce the size of her "reading and writing" room. This space was intended to be a place where the first class ladies could retire after dinner, which in 1912, they were proving less and less willing to do.

Chapter Seven- *Titanic*

Now having finished examining the environment in which she sailed, we need to look at *Titanic* herself. We particularly need to discuss- and dispel- some popular myths and assumptions people have made about her over the years.

Since the sea closed over her stern in 1912, the tale of *Titanic* has grown- and with it the attendant legends and misconceptions. As mentioned previously, several of these have been the result of careless research- misunderstanding- or simple invention.

A good example of the above is the idea that *Titanic* was called the "*Ship of Dreams*," as alleged in the James Cameron motion picture.[54]

Titanic, undoubtedly because of her short life, was never bestowed with a memorable nickname.[55]

---

[54] The author has also seen the name "Ship of Dreams" applied to the airship *Hindenburg*.

[55] *Titanic's* sister, *Olympic*, was given the name "Old Reliable" by her crew. This is probably because she was the only one of the three White Star giants that survived. During the First World War *Olympic*, because of her consistency in transporting troops from Canada to Britain, was also called "The Ferry Boat."

White Star advertising referred to her as "The Queen of the Ocean," (a year earlier it had featured *Olympic* with a variant of this name "Queen of the Seas") and she also had several other informal names- all coined by the press- "Ship of Luxuries", "Wonder Ship," and probably the least imaginative, the "Largest Ship in the World."

Titanic was not called the "Ship of Dreams," until Cameron decided to label her as such. It probably would not have suited the plot of his movie to have the "poor little rich girl" character of Rose embark on a ship called (another press invention) the "Millionaires Special."[56]

Another prevailing myth about *Titanic* is that she was the largest ocean liner *ever* built, with attendant amenities. The ship was said to have had a small herd

---

[56] A related issue is the occasional erroneous reference to the "*H.M.S. Titanic*." The H.M.S. prefix denotes a ship of the Royal Navy. *Titanic* is also often referred to as a "Cruise Ship." *Titanic* was a liner. There is a difference between the two types of ships. A cruise ship is generally employed in sailing to different resort destinations and her itinerary may vary throughout the season. The passengers generally return to the port of embarkation. A liner regularly serves the same ports and passengers embark and leave the ship at each destination.

of dairy cattle aboard to supply her passengers with fresh milk. Feeding these cows apparently presented no problem, because one of the diversions supposedly featured aboard *Titanic* was a regulation golf course, which amply furnished them with freshly mown grass.

One of White Star's Directors, Harold Sanderson, made light of how large people believed the new ships to be when *Olympic* went into service, as he spoke at dinner in her honor.

"Some of those present who had read the descriptions of the vessel in the papers might have been disappointed at not finding a motor racing track, the skating rink, and the botanical gardens and the zoological gardens, but they would be so disappointed as the motorists, the professional skaters, the head gardeners and the lion tamers who had applied to the White Star Line for appointments which they had not been able to give them."[57]

---

[57] When the script of James Cameron's *Titanic* called for the character of Jack Dawson to dine in the first class dining room- requiring him to have a dinner jacket, Cameron thought that Jack could obtain one from the ship's tailor shop, as one was featured in the 1953 *Titanic* motion

Titanic was large, but today her size would be unremarkable, about average- if even that big. In fact, if *Titanic* and *Queen Mary 2* were moored alongside one another, a person standing on the foredeck of *QM2* (deck seven) would be above the boat deck of *Titanic*, and someone on *QM2's* top deck (the private one reserved for the high dollar passengers aft of the stack) could look down into *Titanic's* funnels.

Even at the time she entered service, her status as the "largest ship in the world" was actually predicated only on the arcane way ship sizes are determined.

There are two types of "tonnages" that have to be considered when the size of a ship is determined. One is "displacement tonnage," or roughly how much water the ship pushes aside to float. The other is "gross tonnage"- figured by the amount of enclosed space she has aboard. As a simple example, if you have two identical open boats, they would be classified as being

---

picture. Unfortunately, research revealed that the real *Titanic* did not have such a shop. The 1957 movie *A Night to Remember*, features a children's rocking horse seen first in a playroom aboard the ship, and then later floating in the sea. The real ship did not have a playroom.

the same size, but if you build a deck on one of them- because it now has enclosed space- it would be considered to have the larger "gross tonnage." Both ships had the same dimensions, the same displacement tonnage, and except for a few small differences, they were identical. In fact, many of the photographs allegedly featuring "*Titanic*" are actually of *Olympic*.

The most visible difference between the two was the enclosure of the forward portion of *Titanic's* promenade deck on each side of the ship. The promenade deck was the covered deck directly below the open boat deck (where the lifeboats sat).

When a new ship is planned, her designers usually attempt to incorporate the sum of knowledge and experience derived from the vessels that preceded her. However, after she enters service, things are invariably discovered that do not work as intended, are not as popular with the passengers as anticipated, or require improvement. Despite the planning, research, and care taken by White Star and Harland and Wolff to make *Olympic* as perfect as possible- she was no different.

Soon after she began her career, it was discovered that the new pride of White Star had a major problem with her forward promenade deck. The area had been intended to be a sheltered place where her first class passengers could take a leisurely stroll or sit in deck chairs and enjoy the view. It instead proved to be windy, cold, damp, uninviting and- when the ship was at sea- deserted.[58]

Therefore, White Star decided that on *Titanic*, this area would be screened off by large windows and incorporated into the adjacent first class cabins- giving each an enclosed, heated, and- above all- private promenade.

---

[58] This was not the only problem with *Olympic*. Because nobody had anticipated the amount of heat that would be generated by her extensive electric lighting- there was concern about her ventilation, and she had to be supplied with extra fans. The ship was also found to be significantly short of chairs, particularly in her Ala' Carte restaurant and Parisian Café. There was also a problem with the swimming "bath." Apparently someone decided that it might be a good idea to remove the diving board on a pool that was less than six feet deep. Ismay, who had been aboard the maiden voyage, also had modifications made to the first class beds, saying that the mattresses were "too springy."

These private promenades also allowed *Titanic* to feature two spacious "millionaires" suites, intended to command thousands of dollars per voyage. However, because very few people could afford the price of these accommodations, and it would be expensive to leave them vacant, each could be split into as many as four smaller first class cabins by employing movable partitions.[59]

On *Titanic's* maiden voyage, one of these suites was to be occupied by J. P. Morgan, but his health had been failing and his doctors advised against it.[60] It was then reserved by a paying passenger, but the booking was cancelled just before *Titanic* sailed.

---

[59] Many books about *Titanic* quote the number of passengers that could be accommodated in each class aboard her. However, the numbers could vary- significantly- from voyage to voyage. The *Olympic* class liners were designed to allow the capacity of each class to be adjusted based on bookings. Some first class cabins could become second class, second class could become third, and some third class areas could actually be converted into cargo space. Of course, all this could be accomplished in reverse too.

[60] Lord Pirrie, the chairman of Harland and Wolff- *Titanic's* builders- was also supposed to make the voyage. He also missed the trip because of ill health. However, there is some dispute as to whether Morgan was actually too ill to make the trip or had other reasons for failing to sail.

This was a bit of luck for the Chairman of IMM and White Star, J. Bruce Ismay, who was slated to occupy less a less opulent cabin on the same trip. In the absence of a paying customer, he happily installed himself in Morgan's accommodations.

There were other minor differences between the two sisters. *Titanic* had a dissimilar window arrangement on B deck, her bridge was squared off- as opposed to the rounded front of the bridge of *Olympic*, her bridge wings extended farther out from the ship- and the dead giveaway- *Titanic* was four inches longer than *Olympic*.[61] However, the enclosed promenade officially made her the larger ship.

---

[61] This discrepancy in length between the two sisters was probably the result of *Titanic* being measured on a warmer day than the one when *Olympic* was measured. Ships are measured using surveying instruments and their length determined mathematically. After *Titanic* went down, *Olympic* was almost rebuilt, and several of the features that had been incorporated into *Titanic* were worked into her, including the changes to her bridge. However, she was never fitted with the enclosed forward promenade as had *Titanic* and eventually *Britannic*. Two theories have emerged- both of equal merit. The first is that White Star felt it unwise to modify *Olympic* to so closely resemble her lost sister. The other is that after *Olympic* was fitted with additional lifeboats, her boat deck had such a limited view of the sea that most passengers would avoid it. When *Britannic* was built, Wellin davits were not installed; instead she received "gantry" type davits, which-

Another established myth about *Titanic* is that she was built to be an ocean greyhound and was being pushed on her maiden voyage to set a speed record.[62] In truth, she, like most liners, was designed to be faster than the average ship of her day, but her design focused on comfort and luxury- speed was subordinated to appointments.

As we've discussed, White Star's principal rival, the Cunard Line, had much faster ships, *Mauritania* and *Lusitania*, which held the "blue riband" for the fastest crossing of the Atlantic.[63] Both ships were smaller than

---

while they were exceedingly ugly- did not block the view of the ocean from the boat deck.

[62] Some accounts state that the *Olympic* class ships were capable of thirty knots- untrue. *Olympic*, later in her career, was able to occasionally work up to twenty-five knots. It appeared that her engines functioned better as they got older, and the improvements made in boiler technology and oil-firing had a hand in it too.

[63] The "Blue Riband" was not an official honorarium. In fact, the lines never publicly acknowledged that there was any competition between their ships, although it did not prevent them from making sure the public knew whose ships were swiftest. For instance, when *Normandie* broke the record, she arrived in New York with an immense blue ribbon flying from her foremast. However, when a trophy was commissioned to "officially" recognize the blue riband holder, Cunard, who had the fastest ship at the time, refused to accept it. The award, christened the "Hales Trophy" finally was accepted by United States Lines when *S.S. United States* demolished the speed record in the

the *Olympic* class liners and had turbine engines of greater horsepower. Turbines were the coming thing in shipboard power plants. They occupied far less space aboard ship and because they had less revolving weight, they converted more steam to power. However, because their design had yet to be perfected, early turbines had problems with fuel consumption and reliability. Turbines also ran much faster than the propellers- thousands of revolutions per minute as opposed to hundreds of revolutions per minute or less- and therefore had to have a complex array of reduction gears to transfer their power to them.

Titanic's design was old school and conservative. She had been equipped with reciprocating engines, which used cylinders, pistons, connecting rods and crankshafts. Each of her two engines produced fifteen thousand horsepower at an operating steam pressure of 215 lbs. per square inch. Unlike the turbines, these engines were immense, standing three

---

1950s. It now resides in the U.S. Merchant Marine Academy's museum in Kings Point, New York.

decks tall, and using the steam four times before it was exhausted, hence the name "triple expansion." They were probably the most sophisticated obsolete engines ever installed on a liner.

Other than being proven, the only real advantages a reciprocating engine had over a turbine was that it could be coupled directly to the propeller shaft and it could also be reversed- and full power could be applied astern if need be. Turbine equipped ships had to be have separate "astern" turbines (generally of much lesser power) to reverse the direction of the propellers. The main turbines could not be reversed.

There was one drawback to reversing reciprocating engines- particularly enormous ones like those installed aboard - the inertia of the revolving weight of the engine itself had to be overcome before it could be stopped and sent astern.[64] From "full ahead" to "full astern", it might take as long as forty seconds- or more- before the engine was producing usable astern

---

[64] For example, just the *crankshaft* of each reciprocating engine aboard *Titanic* weighed one hundred eighteen tons.

power. Reciprocating engines also required a break-in period to allow their large number of moving parts to wear properly. The builders would suggest that a reciprocating engine be given a voyage or two to "run in" before it would be driven at full speed. However, it appears that White Star had no general policy for breaking in the engines on new ships, and most of their Captains gave the matter little thought.

Titanic's only nod to evolving propulsion technology was a low-pressure turbine that drove her center propeller. After the steam was used in the main engines- each of which drove an outboard, or "wing" propeller- it was routed to the turbine at a pressure of eight pounds per square inch. The turbine managed to produce eighteen thousand horsepower from this seemingly insignificant amount of steam (and showing how efficient these engines could be.)

The steam was then routed to the condensers- where it was cooled by seawater pumped in from outside the ship- returning it to the liquid state to be sent back to the boilers. Unfortunately, as mentioned above, the turbine could not be reversed, so when the other engines went astern, the center propeller ceased to revolve and therefore was useless in trying to stop the ship- other than creating a large amount of drag in the water.

Titanic actually had very little power by today's standards, possessing slightly more than the equivalent horsepower of *one* Rolls-Royce MT30 gas turbine, of which *Queen Mary 2* has two, in addition to her diesel engines. The MT30 is the marine equivalent of the *Trent* engine that powers the Boeing 777.

But *Titanic's* propulsion was not what excited the public- it was the idea that she was unsinkable.

Chapter Eight- The "Unsinkable" legend

The most unfortunate fiction surrounding *Olympic* and *Titanic* - prior to the disaster- is that they were endowed with an inability to founder. The perception of the general public was that the new class of White Star ships had been designed to be the last word in everything- including safety. It was accepted without question that they would be "unsinkable" although, surprisingly, neither Harland and Wolff, nor the White Star line, ever referred to them as such- in *any* formal context.[65]

Had the reader approached any responsible marine engineer, such as Thomas Andrews, the builder of *Titanic*, and asked him if she or *Olympic* were actually "unsinkable," the answer would be no. Andrews might explain that the ships were soundly constructed, and were quite well protected, but no matter how extensive a ship's watertight subdivision is, damage that exceeds a

---

[65] There was a single promotional flyer issued by White Star in 1911 that stated "as far it is possible to make them, the *Olympic* and *Titanic* will be unsinkable." Again we must note that the statement was tempered.

certain threshold will sink her- unless she is made of an inherently buoyant material. The "unsinkable" ship is as unattainable as the "uncrashable" airplane.

Then how did this enduring myth originate- and then take hold? Apparently, it was unintentional- a creation of an unknown copywriter who worked for a magazine that very few people were aware of- and even fewer read. It was an obscure technical publication called the *Shipbuilder and Marine Engine Builder*, a British journal written for the maritime trade.

The *Shipbuilder* had established a tradition of sorts by publishing a "souvenir" copy each time that a new class of liner was launched. It had published one such edition in 1907 when *Mauritania* and *Lusitania* were put into service. The offering had been popular- selling out quickly- and so in 1911, another was published featuring *Olympic* and *Titanic*.

The magazine is a wealth of information about the ships, complete with detailed drawings and photographs, weighted more to the side of structure, construction, and details such as layouts of the engine rooms, the telephone apparatus on the bridge, and information about arcane details- such as the total grating area of each firebox. It was an early 20th century techies dream.

Virtually everything about the new liners was covered- like the fact that the fourth funnel was a fake- added to balance the look of the ship and used to ventilate the kitchens and engine rooms[66]. The magazine even went to the point of detailing a system that utilized submerged bells mounted near the approaches to harbors to allow ships to determine their positions in fog or reduced visibility by ranging on the underwater sounds.

Of course, the watertight subdivision of the *Olympic* class liners is not overlooked. The magazine talks about how each ship will be equipped with a "cellular double bottom," which meant that each had a second interior skin located above the outside hull, with

---

[66] So, if you ever see a rendition of any of the three *Olympic* class liners with smoke issuing from the fourth funnel- somebody either made a mistake or something was seriously wrong.

the area in between subdivided into tanks, used to store fresh water or trim the ship with ballast. It was readily apparent that a ship with the draft of *Olympic* could conceivably come into contact with some uncharted underwater obstruction, so the second skin was just good sense. Unfortunately, the double bottom only extended, at its maximum depth, seven feet- to the curve of the bilge- not all the way up to- and above- the ship's water line. A deeper double bottom would introduce complication into the design, limit interior space on the lower decks, add weight to the ship and additional cost to construction. The Marine architects who designed the ships thought that the shallower double bottom would be more than adequate.

But what provision had been made to deal with other kinds of collisions? What if the ship ran into something- or something hit it? The designers believed that they had this covered as well.

The plans provided for safe flooding of any two adjacent compartments- the most that anyone expected could be opened by a collision with any ship- all of which were smaller than *Olympic* or *Titanic*.[67] Even if somehow the two big White Star liners managed to collide with one another, they would survive.

The design also accounted for head on collisions. The first four compartments could be flooded and the ships would survive. The watertight bulkheads located in the bow and the stern of the ships extended farther up into the ship than those in the middle, so they could deal with some settling of the liner at either end.

Of course, it was expected that the officers of these ships- obviously the cream of the White Star Line and debatably the British Empire- would take care with their charges, slowing down as they approached harbors and carefully steering around obstructions and other vessels, so there would be little chance of this kind of damage occurring.

The *Shipbuilder* details how the *Olympic* class ships would be subdivided into sixteen watertight

---

[67] Even the warships of this age were much smaller than the *Olympic* class liners. For instance, *USS Texas*, the only surviving World War I battleship, launched less than a month after *Titanic* sank, displaces 27,000 tons and is 573 feet long.

compartments by fifteen transverse bulkheads (literally steel walls that spanned the width of the ship and extended at least ten feet above the waterline). Obviously, these bulkheads would serve as a serious impediment to anyone wishing to travel between compartments during normal operation, so several were equipped with watertight doors.[68]

The *Shipbuilder* was excited about the latter feature. The magazine spends a few sentences discussing the mechanism of the doors, describing how each was held open by a "suitable friction clutch that can be instantly released by means of a powerful electro-magnet controlled from the captain's bridge, so that in the event of accident, or at any time when it may be considered advisable, the captain can, by simply moving an electric switch, instantly close the doors throughout and make the vessel practically unsinkable."[69]

---

[68] The plans of the *Olympic* class liners indicate that the first three compartments did not have doors, probably because there was little reason for anyone to have to travel between them on the lower decks, as they would farther aft.

[69] The same publication used less than a half page to detail *Olympic's* lifeboat accommodation- and most of this section concerned the

And thus the legend was born.

It's important to note the use of the word "practically" in the sentence above. There is no record of any informed publication ever making a positive and unconditional statement that the ships *were* unsinkable. It was always coupled with the words "almost," or "virtually," or other words of similar meaning.

However, most people, including many in the popular press of the time, ignored the qualifiers and the myth took root. And as we have already discussed, although it appears that White Star never referred to the ships in this fashion, they apparently never did anything to correct the misconception either. The business could only benefit if the public insisted in believing your ships were invulnerable.

Because of this, a large number of people were led to have unfounded confidence in the safety of the liners. It's been often repeated that a woman by the name of Mrs. Albert Caldwell asked one of the crewmen

---

revolutionary Wellin davits- serving to illustrate that there was little interest in this subject.

in Southampton- as he was in the process of loading her baggage- “Is this really a non-sinkable ship?” He reassured her by remarking, “God himself could not sink this ship.”[70]

As an aside, the *Shipbuilder* seemed to have a knack for making “famous last words” type statements about its subjects. In 1935 a souvenir edition of the magazine was devoted to the French Liner *Normandie*. The magazine was taken with the fact that the ship had been designed with extensive fire detection, fire proofing and fire fighting systems, concluding with the statement, “The Compagnie Generale Transatlantique have never lost a liner by fire and it can scarcely be visualized that their latest liner for the North Atlantic Service will mar this fine record.”

Normandie was destroyed by fire less than ten years later while undergoing conversion to a troop ship in New York Harbor. To be totally fair, we must note that

---

[70] This was later cited by some as another example of “tempting fate,” and leading to the loss of the liner. It’s comforting to know that God would allow, or even cause, the death of over a thousand people because of a comment uttered by an uninformed longshoreman.

her fire systems were not functioning at the time the fire started (they had been turned off), the conversion crew aboard at the time of the blaze had not been trained to operate them, and several of her massive fire doors- designed to be closed in the event of a fire in order to contain it- had been blocked by equipment and construction materials. The fire, originally thought to be the work of German saboteurs, was found to have been caused by lax fire prevention. A welder was using a cutting torch to remove a steel stanchion near a pile of highly inflammable kapok life preservers. A stray spark did the rest.[71]

An odd, and apparently little known, fact about the *Olympic* class is that they were no safer than a number of ships that had preceded them, and in some respects, they were *not* as safe. But if you read some of the literature about them, you might be persuaded to believe that they were the *first* ships ever equipped with watertight bulkheads and doors, and this was a striking

---

[71] To add insult to injury, the French Line lost *Paris* to fire in 1939- even before *Normandie* sailed.

and dramatic advance in shipboard safety. From a historian's standpoint, it would have been a godsend if true, because it would heap even more irony on the *Titanic* disaster.

However, almost every ship built as a contemporary to *Titanic* had some form of watertight subdivision and in many countries it was required by law.

The idea wasn't even new.

A forerunner of the system had first come into use over sixty years earlier- in 1858, with the launching of *Great Eastern*, a ship that *was* a genuine revolution in shipbuilding technology.

The product of the fertile mind of Scottish engineer Isambard Kingdom Brunel, *Great Eastern* was innovative, way ahead of her time and, when introduced, an absolute failure.[72] She was simply too large. Her power plant was inadequate, and her draft prevented her from entering most harbors. Cargo handling technology and coaling facilities had yet to catch up to a ship of her

---

[72] In fact, for many years in engineering circles, any overambitious or seemingly ill-considered project was called a "Great Eastern."

size, so loading, unloading, and fueling her could consume days. Even launching a ship of her size presented serious problems.[73]

Despite her drawbacks, *Great Eastern* was an unparalleled advance in safety. Brunel realized that if he placed watertight barriers in strategic places throughout her hull, *Great Eastern* would be far less likely to sink because of a simple puncture in her outer skin. Instead of the whole ship flooding, only a small portion of her would. So, the ship was equipped with an inside skin- essentially a double hull- and watertight bulkheads rising three decks, thirty feet, above the waterline- none compromised by openings of any kind. The crew was compelled to use ladders to travel between compartments.[74]

---

[73] *Great Eastern* had been built almost three hundred yards from the river. It took three months, and several lives- before the ship was safely afloat. Brunel himself died shortly afterward.

[74] *Great Eastern* survived an accident similar to the one that would later claim *Titanic*. A large and lengthy gash was opened in her hull by a submerged rock as she was approaching New York. Her double skin saved her and she was able to complete the voyage under her own power.

Great Eastern eventually found employment as a cable laying ship. She laid the first successful trans-Atlantic telegraph cable in the late 19th century. She was the only ship that could carry the entire 3,000 plus tons of cable in her hold. She remained the largest ship ever built until White Star built the *Oceanic*, in 1899.

Today, Brunel is recognized as one of the early geniuses of engineering. His hallmark was over-design- building better and stronger than was required- and so a good deal of his work (mostly in the form of bridges) survives today.[75]

But his method worked against him here. As ships continued to evolve, many of the safety features Brunel pioneered in *Great Eastern* were viewed as excessive. Some were abandoned entirely, or they were modified to allow more economy in building and/or operating the ship.

---

[75] Most of the engineers of Brunel's day were of the "cut and try" type. The strength of construction materials was inconsistent, particularly steel produced by the Bessemer process, so the tendency was to assure durability by overbuilding. Also, they obviously did not have access to the detailed computer models that engineers employ today.

For instance, if the watertight bulkheads on the *Olympic* class ships had extended thirty feet above the waterline- they would have intruded into the passenger areas and the required watertight doors would have spoiled the look and feel of the public rooms and passageways.

That would hardly do- the desired effect was to persuade passengers they were not aboard a ship, but instead in a luxurious seagoing hotel. So, the *Olympic* class ships- oddly enough- were *not* as safe as some of the other liners in service at the same time, despite the perception of their safety.

The Cunard liners, *Lusitania* and *Mauritania*, were actually better protected from collision than their younger White Star rivals. If one considers only the matter of watertight subdivision, they could- at least in theory- have easily survived the collision that claimed *Titanic*.[76]

---

[76] A fact that Cunard- after the disaster- and in the unquestionably understated British fashion- made sure the general public was more than aware. They also stressed that they had never lost a passenger.

Both Cunard ships, at the insistence of the British Admiralty, had been equipped with longitudinal bulkheads that ran fore and aft just inboard of the outside hull along the boiler rooms, essentially furnishing each ship with a second skin in those areas.

Whether either of these two ships *actually* could have survived the collision has been a matter of debate for years. Both used the spaces between the outer and inner hull for storage of coal.[77] The bulkheads were outfitted with large hatches to allow it to be moved from the bunkers to the boiler rooms. The watertight doors that were to seal these openings were designed to slide closed horizontally on tracks. These tracks were soon caked with coal dust, packed rock solid by the passage of years- and an obvious impediment to rapidly closing the doors. The sills also may have leaked from the damage produced by years of rolling metal-tired

---

White Star, even before the *Titanic* disaster, could not make the same claim.

[77] At the time the large Cunard liners were built, the general belief was that coal stored in bunkers beneath the exterior skin of a vessel would absorb, and thus protect a ship from, shellfire. Unfortunately, *Lusitania* was struck by a weapon of which little was known- a torpedo.

wheelbarrows, used to transfer the coal, across them. However, had the circumstances been the same as the one of *Titanic*- on a maiden voyage- with everything being relatively clean and new- the doors probably could have been easily closed and the ship saved.

Ironically, had *Titanic* been torpedoed, *she* may have survived. There was a secondary explosion aboard the Cunard ship after the torpedo struck, which was originally thought to have been a second torpedo impact. However, German records made available after the war revealed that *U*-20 had fired only one- her last.

Today most historians believe that a coal dust detonation in one of *Lusitania's* bunkers caused the second explosion. *Titanic's* bunkers were located in a different area- transversely fore and aft of the watertight bulkheads in each boiler room- and unless the torpedo struck one directly, the explosion may have only led to some localized flooding aboard the White Star Ship. So, had the roles been reversed, with *Lusitania* striking the iceberg and *Titanic* being torpedoed, both liners may have lived to tell their tales.[78]

But on the *Olympic* class liners- being built with private money- the idea of equipping the ships with a double hull was rejected as an expensive and seemingly unnecessary extravagance, adding weight to the ship and thus decreasing her fuel economy, reducing her cargo space and complicating her design.

So why were these ships thought to be so safe, as opposed to some of their better protected contemporaries?

Even with the advent of increased watertight subdivision in more modern ships, they continued to sink, sometimes because of poor seamanship, fires, and violent storms, but often the loss of a ship was

---

[78] While submarines have sunk many passenger ships, there is only one recorded incident of a *liner* sinking a *submarine*. During World War One, a requisitioned British liner being used as a troopship rammed the *U103* and sent her to the bottom- *Olympic*.

After the war, *Olympic* underwent a thorough refit before she was returned to passenger service. A large crack was found in her hull, below the waterline, roughly amidships. It was theorized that the source of this crack had been the impact of a torpedo that had failed to explode.

attributable to nothing more than the crew failing to close the watertight doors before flooding reached critical levels.

On most ships, watertight doors had to be closed manually, and since ships of this era did not have public address systems or hand-held radio technology available, the word to close the doors would have to be passed through the ship by telephone or runners. This would obviously take time, and door closure could not be verified unless someone was dispatched to physically check the status of each and report back. In the event of catastrophic flooding, the doors might become submerged before they could be closed. Often the doors had seen so little prior use that they were jammed in place by corrosion or they were blocked. Sometimes the doors could not be sealed because the inflow of water opposed closing.

On the *Olympic* class liners, it was felt that these problems had been eliminated. The doors were designed to close vertically, not horizontally, and therefore there was a smaller chance that they could be blocked. In addition, they incorporated what would later be called a “fail safe” feature. As the *Shipbuilder* noted, each door was held open by an electromagnetic clutch that would release the door if the power failed. Each door was also equipped with a float mechanism that would trip a switch if water entered the compartment and close the door automatically.

There was a third feature too. Both *Olympic* and *Titanic* featured a master door control station located on the bridge. From this station, all the doors could be closed simultaneously with a single switch, or they could be shut individually. Lights on the board, either illuminated or extinguished, showed the ordered position of each door.

So, in effect, with the flip of a lever, the Captain could instantly isolate each flooding compartment and render his vessel, as the *Shipbuilder* stated, “practically unsinkable.”

But the door control system was not as sophisticated as the magazine led many to believe. The control panel lights on the bridge indicated only whether the door was *supposed* to be open or closed, not its actual position. A door could be reopened manually after the bridge commanded it closed, and not only would the position light on the bridge still indicate it was closed, but the door would remain open until someone chose to physically close it again.

Chief engineer Bell, following the maiden voyage of *Olympic*, suggested that the door control panel be equipped with "telltales" to eliminate these problems, but *Titanic* was never fitted with them, and it was not until after the First World War that these issues were resolved on *Olympic*.

There were other unforeseen problems with the new liners.

One that the *Shipbuilder*- or any of the other contemporary, pre-disaster, literature failed to address regarding the *Olympic* class was their lack of maneuverability.

Each ship had a sizable rudder- it weighed fifty-three tons.[79] However, a great deal of its function was ornamental. The *Olympic* class was designed with a "clipper" stern, which meant, depending on her draft, between one fourth and one third of her rudder was above the waterline and therefore useless. Moreover, the rudder was far less effective if the turbine-driven center propeller was stopped- as it would be when the engines were put astern.

After *Olympic* was completed, she spent two days in Belfast Loch testing her engines and maneuvering. Data was gathered on how rapidly the ship could be brought to a stop from full speed, what her turning radius was at various velocities, how rapidly she would answer her rudder, etc.

This should have given the company a basic idea of how the ship would behave under various conditions, but at the time of the trials the ship was not

---

[79] Even this is in dispute. The *Shipbuilder* states this figure as the weight of the rudder, a book called *RMS Olympic- Titanic's Sister*, lists the weight of the rudder as over 100 tons. Either way, everything on these ships was very heavy.

carrying cargo, stores, passengers, or even a full load of coal.[80] Even so, the results showed that these ships were going to require skillful handling. They were slow to stop and their helm response was sluggish.

It appears that even Captain Smith was uncertain of how *Titanic would* respond to her rudder, it being reported that he took her through a series of lazy "S" turns after the ship departed Cherbourg. Earlier, aboard *Olympic*, he had remarked to one of his junior officers that after commanded her on several voyages, he was finally beginning to be able to predict how she would react.

But of course, the ship would never be called on to make any radical maneuvers at high speed.

---

[80] Photographs of *Titanic* leaving Belfast to undergo trials reveal that there was a considerable amount of her red-painted bottom exposed, which confirms that she was lightly loaded. If one examines photos taken on the day she embarked on her maiden voyage, she is riding much lower in the water.

Chapter Nine-The Boats

Another "truth" about the *Titanic* disaster- perhaps the primary- is that she sailed with an insufficient number of lifeboats. The idea, as seen in the crystal clarity of hindsight, is that if her owners had taken the elementary and seemingly obvious precaution of furnishing her with enough lifeboat space to accommodate all her passengers and crew, the loss of life would have been minimal. It has even been stated- many times- that there may have even been no lives lost at all. But any study of history- particularly any dealing with maritime matters- will tend to undermine this contention.

In 1912, as it remains today, a boat was the refuge of last resort if your ship was sinking.

Early vessels did not have boats because they were little more than boats themselves- small enough to be beached ashore. However, as small craft evolved into ships, it became necessary to ferry people or cargo to and from landings where the larger ship could not approach because of her draft, or could not be moored.

It was quickly found that these boats could also be used to evacuate at least some of those aboard if the ship went down. However, ships did not begin to carry designated "lifeboats" until ships were built with the primary task of transporting passengers.

Most seasoned mariners looked upon the lifeboat as a dubious addition to their ships at best- and perhaps a source of false comfort to people uninitiated in the ways of the sea. Some still do.

Wooden "lifeboats", which had no duty other than to be launched in a time of emergency, would frequently become an afterthought on most vessels, receiving only a moderate amount of maintenance- or often none. Therefore when called to service, they often proved inadequate, their rotten wood allowing the boat to quickly break up and sink. Even if the boat proved to be sound, the falls- the cables or ropes used to lower it down the side- often would have decayed to the point where they were unusable. Preserved foodstuffs and water casks provisioned aboard the boats to sustain the survivors frequently disappeared over time- or were so old they were useless.

It seemed to matter little anyway. Often there were external factors that limited or even prohibited the launching of lifeboats. Most shipping catastrophes occurred when ships were overwhelmed by storms- and a lifeboat in those conditions would be of no value. Even if it could be launched, it would be almost instantly swamped and lost.[81]

In those cases where a ship was threatened by other hazards, there usually was little to no time to launch boats before the ship foundered. Often, in desperation, the falls would be cut and the boat allowed to plunge from the side of the ship into the sea. However, unless both were severed simultaneously- which was almost impossible- the boat would often drop

---

[81] Today's lifeboats- as mandated by SOLAS, the international convention for the Safety Of Life At Sea- have to be covered, both for this reason and also to protect their occupants from exposure. However, launching even a modern lifeboat in a raging storm would likely still be a difficult- if not impossible- task.

one end first, rapidly fill with water, and sink. If people were aboard, they would be spilled into the sea.

In the event of a fire aboard, the lifeboat would burn as readily as the ship- sometimes more. In fact, lifeboats were occasionally the source of shipboard fires as unthinking passengers would set alight the boats' canvas covers as they attempted to toss cigar butts overboard.

Even securing a seat in a lifeboat was not a guarantee of survival.

If the boat did not clear the ship in time, there was a real threat of it being sucked into, and destroyed by, the ship's propellers.

If none of these factors came into play, the boat was sound, able to be safely launched and made it away from the ship, the people aboard could still be lost.

Before wireless was invented, ships would vanish and not be missed until weeks- or even months- later when they became overdue at their destinations, and that was only if someone were expecting them. Rescue depended entirely on the chance that another ship would sail near enough- in conditions of good visibility- to spot the lifeboats, or the wreckage of the sinking, before the occupants succumbed to thirst, starvation, or exposure.[82]

During the 19th century, there were a number of inventions- many rather harebrained- patented to reduce the loss of life at sea. Most of these took into account the problems with loading and launching lifeboats and therefore concentrated on personal flotation devices.

One such apparatus was essentially a hollow buoy that would float vertically in the water, holding a single survivor. It would be equipped with a large flag marked "lost."

Few of these contraptions ever found use- mostly because supplying a ship with them would require an immense amount of space and be prohibitively expensive.

---

[82] Charles Lightoller, who had one of the most eventful lives of any of the *Titanic* survivors, had been shipwrecked twice before. He was even cast away on a deserted island for a period with other members of his crew. The island was far away from the normal shipping lanes. They were eventually rescued by a ship whose Captain had radically altered course because he had a *feeling* that there were people who needed rescue in that direction.

What was needed was something practical- meaning something cheap and easy to store- that allowed a measure of security to the passenger. The solution was a canvas garment donned somewhat like a sleeveless coat over the clothing- featuring spaces inside that could be filled with a suitable buoyant material.

But wearing the "lifejacket," as it was to be called, did not guarantee survival. Often it would only allow a person cast into the water the luxury of not being troubled with drowning as they froze to death, or in warmer waters permitting them to float until they were located by sharks or other predators.

Even if neither of these hazards proved to be a threat, a lifejacket could still prove to be a detriment to a survivor.

For instance, in the 1890's The United States Lifesaving service- which was one of the forerunners of the U.S. Coast Guard- had established standards for lifejackets. However, the law was written imprecisely, only specifying how much each life jacket should weigh to conform to the regulations. The intent was that the mass of the jacket would largely result from the lightweight buoyant substances inside.

Unfortunately, these materials were expensive. Both cork and kapok, the most commonly used, were derived from plants that are not native to the United States- and there were other- cheaper- ways to meet the weight regulations- such as partially filling the lifejacket with lead shot.

In 1904, an American excursion steamer named *General Slocum*, which had been provisioned with lead ballasted lifejackets, caught fire and foundered in New York Harbor.[83] Many people who donned the heavy jackets were pulled under and drowned by them. Obviously, had the jackets been properly filled; many of the people who were lost may have been able to save themselves.

---

[83] It was also discovered that the crewmen aboard *General Slocum* had never been trained in the fighting of shipboard fires and never participated in a fire drill. It would have made little difference if they had- the fire hoses- years old and rotten- burst when water pressure was applied.

The law was re-written.

Of course, the issue of lifejackets has no bearing on the sinking of *Titanic*, as she was provisioned with far more than were required.[84] But the matter of imprecise regulation does.

As shipwrecks go, *Titanic's* demise was rather out of the ordinary.

The collision with the iceberg produced no casualties, not even minor injuries. The brush with the berg was so gentle that it hardly disturbed the ship. *Titanic* did not sink in the midst of a raging storm- the sea was abnormally calm and the weather, though cold, was perfect.

There was no fire, no explosion- not even any obvious damage. The ship did not capsize or list appreciably, and she did not plunge to her death quickly,

---

[84] During the filming of *A Night to Remember*, the producers strove to replicate everything aboard *Titanic* as closely as they could. However, they found out that the cork-filled lifejackets that had been provisioned aboard her were dangerous. A person who jumped into the water from the deck while wearing one ran a real risk of breaking his neck. Identical lifejackets- filled with kapok- were substituted. This also indirectly solved the mystery of why so many bodies recovered from the sea after *Titanic* sank had broken necks.

as did Lusitania or *Empress of Ireland,*[85] both of which sank in less than twenty minutes, leaving hundreds stranded aboard.

And, instead of being marked by chaos, as many ship disasters are, the evacuation of *Titanic* was relatively calm. And until just before the end, when the people who remained aboard finally began to grasp the seriousness of their situation, there was no appreciable panic.

Titanic lived for two hours and fifty minutes- plenty of time; it would seem, to get everyone organized, safely into a lifeboat, and away from the ship.

There was not even a problem launching the boats, the gear was new and worked perfectly.[86] *Titanic* met or exceeded all the regulations set for lifesaving appliances for her. She even had power and lights until just moments before she left the surface. If one wanted

---

[85] *Empress of Ireland* was commanded by the same Captain Kendall who had identified Dr. Crippen aboard *Montrose*.

[86] One of the problems in launching the boats on *Lusitania* was that the winches and davits had received so many coats of paint over the years that they had become jammed with it.

"textbook" conditions for the abandonment of a liner, *Titanic* surely supplied them.

So it seems that given these almost ideal conditions for an evacuation, insufficient lifeboats had to be the primary cause of the loss of life aboard *Titanic*. It's the most commonly held assumption about the disaster, shared by both the relatively uninformed and a number of historians. It neatly sums up the catastrophe, assigning the reason for the appalling loss of life to a clearly foreseeable, easily rectified, and ironic cause.

But nothing in a disaster of this magnitude could be that simple, and the matter of lifeboats is much more complex that it appears on the surface.

Like the erroneous idea that *Titanic* was the first ship to sail with watertight subdivision, there is an almost identical myth that she was the only ship of that era that failed to carry sufficient lifeboats.

However, most large liners of that era, including *Lusitania* and *Mauritania*, were underequipped when it came to survival craft for all aboard.

Perhaps the first item we should examine about *Titanic* was why she sailed with fewer lifeboats than she required. The bottom line- and this is not just a lame cliché in this case- is that equipping the ship with additional boats would cost money.

White Star's management- not because of malevolence, negligence, or stupidity- decided for simple business reasons that the ship need only sail with the number of boats that were required by law.

While everyone- if pressed- would have admitted that the laws were outdated, the view was that contemporary marine design had actually rendered the lifeboat obsolete. It was almost as if Amtrak trains today were still required to carry a locker full of firearms to repel Indian attacks.

If the ship really was as safe as she had been designed to be- and few doubted that she was- there would be little to no need for more lifeboats than those specified by law.

They would never see use unless the ship broke down and the passengers were required transfer to other ships. Lifeboats also might be employed in the rescue of passengers aboard another ship in distress.

There were other practical considerations. The deck would be cluttered by these “extra” lifeboats, and the expense required in equipping the ship and maintaining the boats could be put to better use providing more luxuries. After all, lifesaving equipment did not sell tickets. The public did not care about lifejackets and lifeboats. Passengers wanted Ala’ Carte restaurants, opulent cabins, carved woodwork, thick carpets, and swimming pools.

It’s much the same today. No cruise line features pictures of lifeboats and fire extinguishers in their brochures or on their websites. They make no mention of how quickly the ship may be evacuated, or how well the crew is trained to deal with disasters. Instead, we see opulent cabins, fine dining, cozy bars, and plenty of young bikini-clad women lounging around the pools. We rarely give safety features a thought, and if so we assume that the government agencies tasked with our protection are implementing and enforcing requirements to ensure it.

Today, safety at sea is determined by international agreement, but in 1912, regulation regarding lifesaving equipment was left to the country in which the ship was registered, and it appears that the British government, under whose regulations *Titanic* sailed, had failed to do this.

In 1912, for ships flying the Union Flag, laws concerning lifeboat accommodation were entrusted to The Board of Trade.[87] Most popular histories of the *Titanic* disaster mention, and vilify, their lifeboat regulations, which failed to specify boats for all.

But how did these infamous regulations come about, and what was the reasoning behind them?

Around the middle of the 19th century, people began to desert Europe for the promise of a better life in

---

[87] The Board of Trade's official name was, and still is- "Lords of the Committee of Privy Council appointed for the consideration of all matters relating to Trade and Foreign Plantations."

North America. The trickle of immigrants turned into a steady stream that eventually became a torrent.

Unfortunately, the sea has always attracted more than its share of unscrupulous people who are willing to exploit the lack of regulation and enforcement that operating upon the high seas affords them. Many ship owners wishing to profit from the trade employed vessels of questionable seaworthiness and safety.

As early as 1886, concerns were being voiced that the rules dealing with the provisioning of lifesaving equipment aboard "immigrant ships" crossing the Atlantic were hopelessly out of date, and that many of the vessels employed in this service were carrying next to nothing to save the lives of those aboard. It was stated that it had been fortunate that none of these ships had been involved in an accident involving a great loss of life.

To deal with this problem, the British Parliament convened a Select Committee of the House of Commons and appointed Lord Charles Beresford chairman. Their task was to investigate the question of safety on the seas and make recommendations.

The report seemed to confirm what everyone had thought for years, stating:

"That many passenger ships could not, without great inconvenience, carry so many of the ordinary wooden boats as would suffice to carry the whole of the passengers and crew with safety in bad weather. Under such circumstances the crew would not be sufficient to man so many boats; nor could they all be got into the water in sufficient time in the event of very rapid foundering. Having regard, however, to the fact that accidents occur probably as often in moderate weather as in bad, and having regard also to the fact that the very cause the accident frequently incapacitates many of the boats, and to the further fact that in insufficiency of boats undoubtedly tends to cause panic, we are the opinion that all sea-going passenger ships should be compelled by law to carry such boats, and other life-saving apparatus, as would in the aggregate best provide for the safety of all on board in moderate weather."

So, in other words, the report said that it would be impractical for a ship to carry enough boats for everyone aboard. There would an insufficient number of crewmen to launch them in a timely fashion- or man them, many of the boats would probably be damaged in the accident, and if the weather did not cooperate, it would be extremely difficult, if not impossible, to fill them and get them away from the ship.

However, the report then backed off a bit, stating that it would be a good idea to equip the ship with enough boats to save the maximum number of passengers in an accident that did not involve a major storm.

The result was the Merchant Shipping, or Life Saving Appliances, Act of 1888. This is the law that first established the requirement of a specific amount of "cubic feet" of lifeboat capacity as opposed to a number of lifeboat seats. This law scaled the requirements based on the size of the ship.

Many authors have seized on the seemingly odd way this law was written as an example of how useless and shortsighted the regulations were, and at the same time, by implication, cast doubt on the intelligence of the people who drafted them. However, they are missing one vital point.

The original impetus for the regulations was, as stated above, that many ship owners were sailing with minimal lifesaving equipment- demonstrating that they were less than concerned with the safety of their passengers.

It would be of paramount importance that the law was written with airtight specificity, allowing no loopholes that an owner could sail his under-equipped ship though.

If the law was vague, stating that there had to be "boats for all aboard," or "boats sufficient to carry one hundred people," the owner could simply claim that a boat that formerly held only a few people was now capable of carrying many more. By specifying the lifeboat requirements in cubic feet, the BOT could ensure that there would be adequate space in the boats to carry the number of passengers desired.

It was one way of preventing an unscrupulous ship owner from doing the same thing with his lifeboats as the owners of *General Slocum* had done with their lifejackets.

In 1894, the regulations were revised. Tables now specified how much space a ship had to carry, based on her size, but the regulations also allowed fewer lifeboats to be carried by ships that had been built with watertight subdivision.[88]

However, and most significantly, the scale ended with ships of 10,000 tons. At the time, the largest ship afloat was Cunard's *Lucania*- of about 13,000, and because of the expense of building large ships, many believed that she would retain her title for many years.

The rapid advance in the size of ships that occurred at the turn of the 20th century outstripped the

---

[88] There was an additional provision to the Board of Trade regulations, specifying that "rafts" be provisioned aboard ships to supplement the lifeboats. However, these were not actually rafts, but what we would recognize today as life rings.

regulations and at the time *Titanic* sailed- a ship four times larger than for which they were written- they remained unrevised.

The obvious inference is that the British Government was content that the regulations were sufficient. But, the truth is that the Board of Trade had recognized that the laws regarding lifesaving appliances were again hopelessly outdated and it had been announced that they were to be reviewed and new regulations were going to be published.

However- in typically official fashion- the Board of Trade gave no other details- even avoiding fixing a date when these new regulations might be expected.[89]

There seemed to be no real urgency in issuing new rules. A significant sea disaster had not occurred in years, and it was thought that the likelihood of one was

---

[89] Although most books about the *Titanic* disaster give the reader the impression that the Board of Trade dealt exclusively with maritime matters, that was only a very small part of its jurisdiction and responsibility, which may furnish a reason why updating the lifeboat regulations was not given priority. In addition to overseeing the British Shipping industry, the BOT was also charged with assignment of patents, trade marks, administration of labor and factories, even farming. They were roughly analogous to three departments- Commerce, Agriculture, and Labor- in the United States.

swiftly receding. New ships appeared to be virtually immune to serious accidents, and the employment of wireless during the sinking of White Star's *Republic* seemed to show that the new device had created, in effect, a "lifeboat pool" between ships in any given area.

Almost all passenger liners were now equipped with wireless, so it would be a simple matter of an endangered ship calling for help and waiting for nearby vessels to appear with their lifeboats which would be used to supplement those aboard the stricken liner.

Today it's unknown if the Board was merely planning to update the lifeboat to tonnage ratio, or they were going to require boats for all aboard. Evidence may be found pointing in both directions, and there were a number of people external to the board advocating either position. In fact, there was even a third option being discussed. Some thought the revised regulations should be written to require *fewer* boats than before. Perhaps the members of the board were themselves unsure of what their strategy would be.

Harland and Wolff apparently decided to plan for the "worst case" in lifeboat accommodation for the new liners- a regulation that would require lifeboats for all aboard. In 1909, the shipbuilder recommended to White Star that the *Olympic* Class ships be equipped with a newly designed davit, the Wellin "Quadrant Double Acting Davit."[90]

The conventional davit of this period could lift a boat and swing it outboard for lowering- possibly two if one boat was nested inside the other. The Wellin davit was designed to not only swing outboard, but also could pivot inboard so a second set of boats could be attached. Because of this feature, each set of davits could accommodate as many as four boats beneath it, giving the ship a total capacity, if she was fitted with the sixteen davits she sailed with, of sixty four boats- providing her with space for 4352 people. White Star, also anticipating the change in regulations, decided it

---

[90] This decision may have been based less on a concern for safety and more on increasing the profit derived from construction of the ships. Each lifeboat would have been built by the shipyard and charged to White Star on the "cost plus" basis mentioned above.

would be cheaper to fit the new davits during construction, rather than retrofit them, so the davits were ordered and included in the planning for the trio of new liners.

Evidence indicates that Harland and Wolff intended to equip the massive new liners with sixty-four boats each, even going as far as to notify the Board of Trade of this decision.

However, the customer- White Star- differed. Ismay and Harold Sanderson decided that the number was excessive.[91] Their view was that equipping the *Olympic* class ships with sixty-four boats would be unnecessary- after all they would never see use aboard an unsinkable ship. Not only would they represent a needless expense- the money could be put to better use elsewhere- but they would clutter the boat deck- even if they were nested inside one another.

---

[91] Sanderson was a rather odd piece of work himself. He stated, *after* the *Titanic* disaster, that he still failed to see the reason for equipping a ship with enough lifeboats for all aboard!

Properly built, sturdy lifeboats were also heavy, and at the time they were invariably stowed on the topmost decks, where their weight would have the most effect on the trim of the ship. A number of boats would often alter what was called the ship's "metacentric height"- or her longitudinal center of gravity- making her roll more readily, deeply, and take her longer to recover.[92]

There was an aesthetic component too- a large number of boats would spoil the first class passengers' view of the sea and interfere with their enjoyment of the voyage.

As stated above, the decision to supply *Titanic* with twenty lifeboats would have been simple- based on business reasons, prompted by Ismay's desire to provide his passengers with something that they

---

[92] The change in the lifeboat regulations after the *Titanic* disaster led directly to the loss of another ship several years later. A Great Lakes passenger ship, *Eastland*, capsized with great loss of life because of the combined weight of passengers and mandated lifeboats on her upper deck. *Eastland* had always been known as a "tender" ship- somewhat unstable- even at the time she had been built. The weight of additional lifeboats on her upper deck made this problem worse.

preferred- something that might influence them to book with White Star instead of the competition.

Even in the early part of the 20th Century, companies were engaging in a primitive form of market research. Frequently, this was nothing more than listening to passengers voicing their desires and disappointments.[93]

White Star's information had revealed that many of Cunard's passengers- traveling aboard *Lusitania* or *Mauritania*- had been dissatisfied with their obstructed boat decks.

If someone wanted to take a walk along the deck of either ship, they had to thread their way around railings, ventilators, rigging and lifeboats. White Star decided that they would do whatever they could to make the boat decks of *Olympic* and *Titanic* as free of obstacles as possible. The open boat deck was

[93] Of course, none of the lines were above directly spying on the completion. It was not uncommon to find employees of competing companies booked aboard, notebooks in hand- particularly when a new class of ship was embarking on her first trip. When *Olympic* sailed on her maiden voyage, Chief Engineer Bell discovered a couple of representatives of the French line trying to sneak into his engine room- he bid them a firm adieu.

particularly important aboard - even more than on *Olympic*, since the millionaires' suites blocked her forward promenade deck.

During meetings and through correspondence White Star had with Harland and Wolff management, the number of lifeboats was reduced to thirty two- or two under each davit. The Board of Trade was notified of this change on March 16, 1910.

Even this smaller complement of boats would allow the rescue of 2176 people- just about the number of people who were aboard *Titanic* the night of April 15, 1912. If she had been fitted with four additional collapsible boats, as she actually was, there would have been room in the boats for everyone.

The number of boats briefly ratcheted up to forty-eight- which again would have provided space for everyone aboard on the night of the disaster (3264 people) - but soon White Star again reduced the number to thirty-two.

Harland and Wolff pressed the Board of Trade to require the new liners to sail with at least forty-eight boats, but the BOT, undoubtedly unwilling to set the precedent of determining lifeboat capacity on a ship to ship basis, decided to defer judgment on the number until the new lifeboat rule was considered.

While there is no hard evidence, it appears that someone within White Star may have received unofficial word from within the Board of Trade that the whole matter of lifeboat rule revision had been tabled, because they changed their minds yet again.

Harland and Wolff was notified in 1910, by White Star, that *Olympic*, *Titanic* and *Gigantic* would only require one lifeboat under each davit plus four additional collapsible boats that would bring the total number to twenty.

It would seem that the logical place to position these collapsible boats would be to nest them on the boat deck underneath the regular boats, enabling their rapid launch, but it was decided instead to stow them on the roof of the officer's quarters, just abaft the bridge and one level above the boat deck. This location offered only one advantage- it kept the collapsibles out of the way. The view was that they would never be needed and therefore almost no provision had been made for launching them. A small network of lightweight cabling had been installed over them to assist getting them down to the boat deck, but a large number of men would be required to fit them to the davits afterward.

So, no matter what had happened prior to the departure of *Titanic*, she sailed woefully short of boats. If only she had enough for everyone, we think, her sinking would not have been a disaster, but just a curiosity, again buried in the footnotes of history books.

But, as we have seen already, nothing involving the sinking of *Titanic* is that straightforward. The shortage of boats was a large component of the loss of life aboard her, but it is only part of the whole story.

A major factor affecting the number of people saved had to do with the orders that were issued regarding the use of these boats. Therefore, we need to know more about those who issued them- the Officers of *Titanic*.

Chapter Ten- Captain Smith

There is an old saying that states "Victory has a thousand fathers, but defeat is an orphan." This applies equally to sea disasters, but in the case of the latter, there has always been one man- or woman- aboard who shoulders the blame if something should go wrong- the Captain.

Ever since watercraft became large enough to carry more than one person, logic, common sense, and eventually the law, demanded that a single individual be responsible for navigation, speed, and discipline aboard- a final authority. The quarterdeck or bridge is not the place to engage in prolonged debate between interested parties, particularly when the ship is standing into danger.

In the early days, a Captain might be selected for command simply because he owned the ship or had a significant financial interest in her. Often the "Captain" knew little more about sailing the ship than the cabin boy and left the operation of the vessel to his subordinates.

But by the time *Titanic* put to sea, being a mariner had evolved into a licensed profession. Officers aboard ships were required to acquire official certificates stating that they possessed the knowledge and experience to be entrusted with the lives and property of others.

Popular accounts of the *Titanic* disaster seem to be polarized regarding Captain Smith- either portraying him as a hero or as a grossly negligent- almost criminal- incompetent. The truth lies somewhere in between, but undoubtedly- because of his position of authority aboard the ship- he was the chief architect of the disaster- the father of the "orphan."

Very little is known about Smith's early life- except some statistics- and these vary from account to account- sometimes significantly. The most widely accepted date given for his birth is January 27, 1850 in Hanley, Stoke-on-Trent in Staffordshire. He spent his youth in Litchfield and married on January 13, 1887. The union produced one child- a daughter.

Edward John, or "E. J.", as most knew him, went to sea at the age of thirteen as an apprentice on the clipper *Senator Weber*.[94] He then went to work for Gibson and Co. - a line based in Liverpool. As was the practice in those days, he worked his way up through the ranks aboard several ships, learning his trade in both sail and steam. Through experience and study he was able to secure the licenses he would require to command. Eventually he rose to command a ship named *Lucy Fennel*.

But Smith was apparently not content with commanding small ships on backwater routes. He wanted to work the crack Atlantic liners, and so he joined White Star in 1880, serving aboard *Celtic* as fourth officer.

---

[94] The 1953 movie version of *Titanic* indicates that Smith served originally aboard a ship called the *Star of Madagascar*, but this is an invention of the screenwriter. In the movie, just before *Titanic* departs Southampton, Smith receives a parcel containing a tattered flag that supposedly flew aboard this mythical ship years earlier. Instead of placing it safely in his cabin, as a treasured keepsake- Smith has it hoisted on the foremast! Somehow it survives intact and is still there when the ship sinks.

Smith made a favorable impression on the management and less than seven years later, in 1887; he took command of White Star's *Republic*.[95]

During the Boer War, *Republic* was used by the Royal Navy as a troopship, under Smith's command. For his service, E.J. was awarded the British Transport Medal and given an honorary commission in the Royal Navy Reserve as a Commander, which allowed him to fly a flag called the "blue ensign" from the jackstaff of his commands.[96]

By 1912, he had advanced to the summit of the maritime world- Commodore of White Star and the highest paid sailor on earth- making about 1500 pounds yearly- approximately 75,000 dollars in today's money.[97] He was popular with the passengers and the management of his company. Most of his subordinates

---

[95] White Star frequently recycled names. Smith's *Republic* was not the same one that sank in 1909.

[96] The predominately red flag of the British Merchant Marine is called the "Red Duster."

[97] This was before either the United States or Britain decided to impose income taxes so Smith's salary had much more purchasing power.

had a great fondness for him too, not because he was a soft touch, but because he appeared to exude authority, confidence and competence.

Smith was stocky, white-haired with a full beard to match, and of average height. He was said to have a pleasingly deep voice and a love of children. He was a cigar smoker and almost always had one in his hand or nearby.

On April 10, 1912, Smith was sixty-two years old and he had been with White Star thirty-two of them. He was nearing the end of his career, and many accounts state that he was making his final round trip of the Atlantic- taking *Titanic* on her maiden voyage before he retired.

In this age, when ships were the only way to get from Europe to America, knowledge of a popular Captain commanding a certain ship would often persuade travelers to book aboard her, sometimes even significantly changing plans to sail with someone they trusted and liked. E.J. was such a Captain. He spent a good deal of his time mingling with his passengers and through this had earned a loyal and devoted following. Masters such as Smith were coveted and valued by their companies.

E. J. was not just popular with the customers. White Star management liked him too. He had a reputation for meeting schedule, and successfully bringing his ship through just about anything, earning him the affectionate title "The Storm King."[98] There is documentation that he commanded several consecutive trans-Atlantic voyages that differed only in minutes from each other, and Lightoller, serving under Smith aboard another ship, made admiring comments about the way Smith would enter New York harbor, "smartly judging the distances" and making the required turns- all at high speed.

However, despite his elevated position with White Star, Smith's career was not without blemishes:

---

[98] Smith once told a reporter that bad weather no longer concerned him, as ships were now so large and well constructed that they could ride out the largest storms. What concerned him, however, was fog.

On January 29, 1889, Smith ran *Republic* aground off Sandy Hook, New Jersey. The ship was stranded for several hours, and later after entering port, one of her furnace flues cracked, killing three of her crewmen and injuring several more.

Later In 1889, *Germanic*, under Smith's command, partially capsized at her berth in New York under the weight of ice that been allowed to accumulate in her rigging and along her topsides.

In 1890, Smith ran *Coptic* aground at Rio de Janeiro.

In 1901, *Majestic* caught fire as she was making her approach to New York. The fire was thought to have been caused by a short in wiring and crewmen fought it for five hours, finally requiring a hole to being cut through the deck above and water directed into the area. The fire appeared to have been extinguished, but it flared up again later, accompanied by thick smoke. Flooding the area with steam finally put it out.

Smith later stated that he had not been informed of the fire and was unaware of it until the incident was over. One has to wonder what he had been doing during the period the crew battled the flames to have been oblivious to the danger to his ship- and why nobody had thought to bring the matter to his attention.

However, Smith's experiences as a Captain were apparently the norm for the era. White Star had the one of the worst safety records of any shipping line in the North Atlantic; they had even resorted to offering their captains an annual two hundred pound bonus (about $10,000) if they managed to avoid damaging their ships.

Smith failed to collect the benefit during his tenure on *Olympic*. The most celebrated of Smith's mishaps- prior to the *Titanic* disaster- was the collision of *HMS Hawke* with *Titanic's* older sister.

Soon after she entered service, it was discovered that when *Olympic's* propellers were turning; they created a large, and unexpected, area of suction aft. This phenomenon was first observed on her maiden voyage where, as Olympic was docking in New York, she drew a tug- *O.L. Halenbeck*- under her stern. The tug was heavily damaged and narrowly avoided sinking.[99]

While *Halenbeck* was almost lost, *Olympic* came out virtually unscathed, her only damage being some scratched paint and a couple of small dents to her hull. She would not be so fortunate the next time this event was observed.

Olympic was outbound from Southampton on her fifth voyage, on September 20, 1911. Still in Southampton water, she was under the direction of Trinity House pilot George Bowyer (affectionately called "Uncle George" and incidentally the same pilot who later brought out *Titanic*.)

If the reader is unfamiliar with the role of pilot, he or she is a master (captain) who is knowledgeable about the idiosyncrasies of the port- the currents, obstructions, and depths- and therefore asked to guide the ship until she either reaches the open sea or is safely moored-

---

[99] One of the newspapers in New York recorded the collision as *Halenbeck* giving *Olympic* a "playful touch" at her stern. *Halenbeck's* owners were not as playful. They sued White Star- and lost.

clearly depending on whether the ship is inbound or outbound. A pilot never officially takes command of the ship, but it is understood that his or her orders will be followed unless the Captain becomes aware of something obviously amiss and decides to override the commands given by them.

Olympic was nearing the Isle of Wight, where a decision had to be made. There were two courses to the sea, and it was up to the Captain to choose which course he preferred. Smith invariably chose the shortest, and trickier, of the two.

This course was made difficult because it required some complex maneuvering- what amounted to a reverse "S" curve- around an obstacle called Bramble bank, or simply the "Bramble." Neither Bowyer nor Smith was particularly concerned about the route. They had taken *Olympic* this way before without incident.

As the ship neared the Bramble, Bowyer ordered a speed reduction from seventeen to twelve knots. He then reduced speed to eleven knots, as the helm was put over one way and then the other- in concert with a series of engine commands- to safely move *Olympic* around the obstruction. *Olympic's* whistle sounded to notify surrounding vessels of her course changes.

Around this same time, another ship was observed on *Olympic's* starboard bow- at the most, four miles away. It was *HMS Hawke*, a 7,530 ton, 360 foot long vessel of the Royal Navy. *Hawke* had just undergone a refit and was in the area testing her engines.

Hawke was a "protected cruiser." Her design- and the ship- was hopelessly obsolete. Instead of being armored overall, *Hawke's* shielding was installed only in areas where it protected her engines and boilers. She was equipped with a few small guns and had a ram-type bow designed, as an offensive option of last resort, to puncture the hull of an enemy. She was only being retained on the Royal navy's roster because of increasing tension with Germany.

After *Olympic* completed her maneuvers, speed was again increased. *Hawke's* velocity was nearly identical and she shortly drew abeam (beside) of *Olympic* on a roughly parallel course. Accounts later stated that she closed to within 650 feet of the liner.

Olympic continued to pick up speed, and she began to slowly leave *Hawke* behind.

Then something happened- and nobody knew, or wanted to admit later, what.

Hawke suddenly- and radically- altered course, turning into *Olympic's* side, the cruiser's reinforced bow opening a massive V-shaped puncture in the liner's starboard quarter. *Hawke* sustained serious damage to her bow- and lost her ram (which was later extracted from *Olympic* in Belfast.) *Hawke's* crew stated that they had attempted to avoid the liner, but found her helm jammed. According to them, they were powerless to avoid the collision.

While Bowyer had been supervising the maneuvering of *Olympic*, Captain Smith had moved to the starboard bridge wing to observe *Hawke*. He had seen the cruiser begin her turn, and thought she was attempting to steer behind the liner, but it soon became apparent that she was on a collision course. He quickly warned Bowyer and *Olympic's* helm was put over, but it made little difference. If she had turned at all, it was only a degree or two before the impact.

Olympic was rocked by the collision.

The watertight doors were immediately closed; the engines were briefly brought astern and then stopped after the ship came to a halt. An inspection was made. It appeared that most of the damage was above the waterline- but two compartments aft- containing empty second-class cabins- flooded.[100] Because of her watertight subdivision, *Olympic* was in no danger of sinking; she just settled a few feet at her stern- just as she had been designed.

The opening of two compartments to the sea without endangering the ship seemed to confirm the myth of unsinkability regarding the *Olympic* class liners. In fact, the size of the hole in *Olympic*- in square

---

[100] Fortunately, the collision occurred around noon and all the passengers who normally would have been in the cabins were at lunch.

footage- was several times larger than the one that would sink her sister less than a year later, but the majority of damage was located above the waterline and it was not elongated for a third of her length.

Seriously damaged, *Hawke* almost sank, but her crew was able to able sail her to the nearby Portsmouth naval base. *Olympic*, because of her draft, was required to anchor in the channel and wait for favorable tides on the twenty-first to return to Southampton. It was obvious that she would not be able to continue her voyage. *Olympic* was towed back to port the next morning and brought alongside the pier to allow her passengers to disembark.

Further inspection revealed that White Star's flagship had been badly wounded. Not only had a good number of her steel plates been destroyed, but many of her frames had been twisted and broken. Her starboard reciprocating engine was inoperative; having sustained substantial damage to the crankshaft and propeller shaft and the starboard propeller had also been heavily damaged and would have to be replaced.

This presented a dilemma to White Star because there was no place on the southern coast of Britain able to accommodate the mammoth liner for repairs.

The nearest facility with a dry dock large enough to house *Olympic* was in Ireland, at Harland and Wolff. At this moment though, the space was occupied by *Titanic*, finishing her fitting out.

Nevertheless, there was no other option than to sail *Olympic* to Ireland. It took ten days to construct and fit an immense wooden patch to her, watertight enough to allow her to be pumped out and make the two-day trip.

The ship hobbled back to her birthplace on one engine.

When *Olympic* arrived in Belfast, there was no way to repair her without moving *Titanic*. The younger ship's fitting out took a back seat to returning *Olympic* to service.

Because many of the components required to restore *Olympic* to service took weeks to manufacture, and it was paramount that she be repaired as soon as possible, *Titanic* was compelled to donate several large parts to her older sister, such as her starboard propeller shaft. Even so, *Olympic* was out of service for almost two months undergoing repair. *Titanic's* maiden voyage- originally scheduled for March- was postponed.[101]

Almost immediately after the collision, accusations began to fly and the lawyers got busy filing suits. White Star asserted that *Hawke's* Captain, Commander William F. Blunt, had misjudged his turn, his speed was excessive, and he had no business being as close to *Olympic* as he had been.[102] The theory was advanced that perhaps Blunt had closed on *Olympic* to permit his crew to look over the new liner, and also had allowed himself the liberty of a bit of "showboating" by attempting to sharply turn behind her.

---

[101] If one is so inclined, the *Titanic* disaster could be attributed to a small labor dispute that delayed *Olympic's* sailing on the morning of the collision with *Hawke*. If the ship had sailed on time there would have been no collision; *Titanic* would not have been delayed on her maiden voyage, etc. etc. etc.

[102] White Star, by statute, was prohibited from suing the Royal Navy, so they named Blunt as the defendant. One wonders, had White Star prevailed, how Blunt would have managed to pay the damages.

The Royal Navy's version, as we may imagine, was somewhat different. White Star's account was indignantly dismissed as an absurd fantasy. The *very thought* of an officer of the Royal Navy engaging in any such practice! According to them, the *Hawke* was observing the rules of the road. Blunt was behaving responsibly and it was the suction of *Olympic's* giant propellers, exaggerated by the confined and shallow channel, which irrevocably drew the smaller vessel into her side. Despite their valiant efforts, the crew of *Hawke* was powerless to prevent the collision.

After a period of extensive debate involving nautical minutia, involving who the "overtaking" and who the "crossing" ship was, the court found in favor of the Royal Navy. It agreed with the suction theory- attributing *Hawke's* loss of helm control to the phenomenon- and found White Star responsible for the collision.[103]

---

[103] This was not the only legal matter involved in the collision. The crew of *Olympic* was demanding that they be paid for entire round trip voyage instead of only the three days they were actually paid. White Star was able to circumvent the claim by declaring *Olympic* a "wreck." It was much the same with *Titanic*. Her surviving crew ceased to be paid the moment she left the surface.

The line pursued numerous appeals- including a final attempt at reversing the decision in the House of Lords- but it was all in vain. The whole affair cost White Star thousands of pounds in legal costs, repairs, and lost business- both by having *Olympic* out of service and delay in the completion of *Titanic*. By the time the last appeal had been exhausted, *Hawke* herself was gone- having fallen victim to a U-boat.[104]

Smith had one last bit of bad luck with *Olympic* before he went to his final voyage on *Titanic*. In February 1912, she was eastbound, about 300 miles off Newfoundland, when she lost a propeller blade- again on the starboard side. She completed the voyage at reduced speed on one engine and after dropping her passengers in Southampton, was again forced to return to Belfast for repair.

---

[104] An odd irony of *Titanic* disaster is that most of the ships involved in it still exist as wrecks. The *Carpathia* lies off the coast of England, *Californian* off the coast of Greece, and *Titanic's* younger sister, *Britannic*, lies on the floor of the Mediterranean. All three were casualties of war.

It was suggested that somehow *Olympic* had struck a submerged wreck and this had loosened the blade.[105] The propeller blades were bolted to the hubs- so it may have just worked loose and fell off- it could even have been the final artifact of the collision with *Hawke*.

Olympic's starboard propeller shaft had noticeably more vibration than the port shaft after the accident- it would have been next to impossible to align it perfectly when the ship was repaired. Nevertheless, whatever happened, it was not Smith's fault. He turned *Olympic* over to another master at that time and went on to his next and last command, *Titanic*.[106]

---

[105] It seems odd that the ship could have struck a wreck in an area where the water is miles deep- but in the early 20th century, large wooden ships were still somewhat common. Sometimes when such a vessel would founder, it would not immediately descend to the ocean floor, but instead would linger just beneath the surface for a period of time. This is undoubtedly the type of wreck that *Olympic* may have encountered.

[106] It may surprise the reader to know that Smith was the *second* captain to command *Titanic*. Captain Herbert J. Haddock brought her to Southampton from Belfast, and then took command of *Olympic*.

Smith, despite the problems he had with *Olympic*, seemed to be more than optimistic about his new command, *Titanic*. He had been asked about his career and had replied, "When anyone asks me how I can best describe my experiences of nearly forty years at sea, I merely say 'uneventful'. I have never been in an accident of any sort worth speaking about. I never saw a wreck and have never been wrecked, nor was I ever in any predicament that threatened to end in disaster of any sort."

Smith was also reported to have made specific statements about the safety of *Olympic* after the *Hawke* collision, but they originated in a newspaper account, and therefore may be apocryphal. However, if Smith actually made these comments, it serves to illustrate the confidence he had in his large charges.

"…The *Olympic* is unsinkable, and the *Titanic* will be the same when she is put into commission. Why, either of these vessels could be cut in halves and each half would remain afloat almost indefinitely. The non-sinkable vessel has been reached in these two wonderful craft.

"I venture to add that even if the engines and boilers of these vessels were to fall through their bottoms, the vessels would remain afloat."

Smith must have had strong confidence indeed, but it also serves to illustrate how misinformed he was about these new liners. Maybe he was exaggerating, but if the boilers and engines of either ship had fallen through her bottom they would have been swiftly joined on the ocean floor by the rest of the ship.[107]

Of course, when Smith made these remarks, he had no intention of having to make a practical determination of the safety of his ship, but it was nice to know that she had a large margin of protection in the event of an unexpected occurrence.

---

[107] Smith may have had no idea of how his ship was protected. During the New York hearings, following the disaster, 2nd officer Lightoller testified that he believed *Titanic* had "forty or fifty" watertight compartments. He may however, been including those that made up the double bottom of the ship.

However, his job- a task shared by his officers- was to make sure that nothing unforeseen was allowed to happen- that every eventuality was anticipated and dealt with.

Chapter Eleven- *Titanic*'s Officers

Captain Smith was assisted by a staff of seven junior officers. All had master's certificates, meaning that they had been licensed to command their own vessels, and most held what were called "extra" master's tickets, meaning they could legally take command of any ship at sea. All had their specific duties and their share of responsibility.

All *Titanic's* officers stood two four-hour watches in a twenty-four hour period. The three senior officers would be responsible for the safe navigation of the ship during their time on duty; and would be assisted by at least one junior officer- sometimes two.

Bridge duty entailed more than simply maintaining ordered course and speed, but also seeing to other matters, such as avoiding other ships, noting changes in the weather, ensuring that the Captain was informed of any safety matters, and supervising the seamen and quartermasters.

The watch schedule of the senior officers was fixed, but the junior officers rotated watches daily, so they would serve with each senior officer in turn, and occasionally would work consecutive watches.

Captain Smith, of course, did not stand a formal watch, but technically he was always on duty. He was expected to make frequent appearances on the bridge throughout the day to consult with his subordinates, to issue or amend orders, or simply to observe the efficiency and skill of his crew. He was also expected to make a daily tour of the ship, and he was often accompanied by one or more of his senior officers.

Assisting Smith was his second in command, Chief Officer Henry T. Wilde, a thirty-eight year old Englishman. After serving an apprenticeship at sea that included service aboard both sailing ships and steamers, Wilde joined White Star in 1897.

Wilde had served aboard several White Star ships, eventually rising to the position of Chief Officer of *Olympic*, sailing under Smith. When Smith left *Olympic*, Wilde had stayed behind, and was scheduled to depart with Captain Haddock for New York on April 3rd.

However, just before *Olympic* sailed, word came down that Wilde was being reassigned to *Titanic*- but only for her maiden voyage. He would assume the duties of her Chief Officer, which would require the temporary demotion of William Murdoch and Charles Lightoller to first and second officer. *Titanic's* original second officer, David Blair, was detached from the ship.

It is unknown why this shakeup in the senior staff occurred. The commonly accepted theory is that Smith requested Wilde's assignment, and even if the idea was not his, he must have approved the change.

There are a number of theories regarding Wilde's change in orders, each of roughly the same validity and logic, ranging from Smith's simple preference for his former Chief Officer to a personality conflict between the Captain and Murdoch. It may have just been a matter of the Captain deciding to go with someone known to him- and who would be familiar with the ship- particularly on a voyage that would potentially see several company bigwigs aboard.[108]

Whatever the reason, it caused a disruption on the ship, and it probably did not sit well with Murdoch to be reduced in rank. Aside from the fact that he had done the lion's share of work preparing *Titanic* for her debut, there was also the obvious suggestion that he was somehow unfit for the job on her maiden voyage. He also undoubtedly did not appreciate being evicted at the last moment from the Chief Officer's larger cabin.

Wilde, probably realizing this, had absented himself from *Titanic*, visiting his family and not reporting aboard the ship until only a few hours before sailing time- 06:00 on the morning of April 10. He kept a low profile throughout the voyage. After assisting with her undocking, Wilde- in effect- vanished, being the least remembered of her senior officers by those who were rescued. He was not on duty at the time of the accident,

---

[108] There is another theory about Wilde's assignment. It states that Wilde was sent to *Titanic* because *Olympic* was being repaired. However *Olympic* was operational at this time, and was at sea when *Titanic* struck the berg, so we may discount this.

appeared here and there during the sinking, and did not survive.

Wilde may have not played a major part in the disaster, but his appearance on board did, because it placed William Murdoch on duty at the time the ice was sighted and the collision occurred.

Undoubtedly Murdoch is one of the major players in the story, and again, unfortunately, very little is known of him or his life. He was thrust onto the stage less than three hours before he died. Before that he was just another nameless officer serving on a North Atlantic liner. He was a thirty-nine year old Scot, born on February 28, 1873 in Dalbeattie.

The most widely reproduced image of him is later in his life. It's an unflattering three-quarter view, with his mouth partially open and the tail of his buttoned coat flapping in the breeze. This picture has been cropped from a larger photograph- usually billed as "the officers of the *Olympic*" that includes Captain Smith, and the way the officers are spaced, it appears that Murdoch may have walked up as it was snapped and was not originally intended to be in it. The effect it conveys is of a humorless, dour individual.

Fortunately, there are other photographs of Murdoch and we know that as a youth, he cut a rather dashing figure- sporting a handlebar moustache and a broad smile.

The Murdoch family had been seafarers for generations- and there is a source that states that the family name was derived from an old Norse word meaning "sea warrior."

Murdoch's father, his grandfather, and four of his great uncles had been Captains. Like many officers of the time, he had begun his career in sail. Murdoch first went to sea as an apprentice on a sailing ship named *Charles Cosworth*.

He qualified for his master's certificate by the age of 23, and served as chief officer under his father in a steel rigged ship named *Iquique*.[109] Ironically, it was while sailing on this ship that he met another sailor- an

---

[109] The name was derived from the port city of the same name in Chile.

apprentice named Stanley Lord, who was serving on another ship named *Naiad*. Lord would be in command of *Californian* on the night *Titanic* sank.

Both Murdoch's and Lord's ships had called on the same port and the crews visited each other.[110] Murdoch presented such a youthful appearance that Lord mistook him to be an apprentice as well.

Murdoch's career with White Star had begun in the line's Australian service- on *Medic* and *Runic*, later transferring to the North Atlantic where he had been assigned to *Arabic*. Later, after a brief posting to *Olympic*, he was awarded the post of Chief Officer on *Oceanic*.

Murdoch was known to be a good officer and his assignment to *Titanic* was regarded as a logical step to his eventual assumption of a White Star command.

We know little of Murdoch's character, which is unfortunate. The only sources that address this subject

---

[110] Some accounts state that Murdoch and Lord both served aboard *Iquique*- and that Lord was unaware of Murdoch's rank aboard the ship- which is somewhat preposterous. There is no evidence at all that the two men ever served together.

are as polarized as those that characterize Captain Smith. As we have seen before, neither end of this spectrum would be a logical or reasonable image of him.

There are some assumptions- based on facts- we can make about him. His record appears to have been unblemished by any accident or event prior to his posting to *Titanic*, so we must assume that he was a capable and responsible officer.

We do know that he was reputed to have had excellent ship handling skills, complimented by sound judgment and coolness in difficult situations. There is one documented case of him, serving on White Star's *Arabic*, overriding the commands of a senior officer in a potential collision situation, and when he felt the helmsman was not reacting quickly enough, pushed the man out of the way and spun the wheel to its stops himself- holding course until the accident was avoided.[111]

---

[111] Here, again, the accounts disagree. Some state that Murdoch ordered an evasive maneuver belayed and thus spared the ship from collision.

Although only temporary, the demotion to first officer from Chief was a serious setback for him. If Murdoch had an ego- and he would be odd if he didn't- it would have been a substantial blow to his pride, no matter what the circumstances were. We do not know if he and Captain Smith ever discussed the personnel change and whether Murdoch was satisfied with the reasons if they did.

Maybe Murdoch understood why the change was made and took it in stride, but perhaps he was one to brood over the shuffle in officers. He may have taken it as an insult. Obviously, we will never know with certainty.

It seems strange that Captain Smith, if he was concerned about the ship's approach to the ice field would have failed to appear on the bridge at the time of the watch change to consult with his first officer himself- instead of having Lightoller merely pass on his concerns. It may indicate that the Captain preferred not to have personal contact with Murdoch because of the friction generated by the shuffle of officers or it merely may be that he felt the ice threat was a routine hazard and it did not warrant anything more than Lightoller relaying his message.

However, the other side of the coin may be that Smith had such confidence in his first officer that he felt that a reminder would be unnecessary.

We may only speculate.

Titanic's Second Officer was Charles H. Lightoller. Lightoller was the only senior officer to survive the sinking of *Titanic*, and instead of sketchy information about his life, we have a wealth of detail.

The most common image we have of Lightoller at around the time of the *Titanic* sinking is one of a young man- neatly dressed in his uniform, complete with celluloid collar, a uniform cap set squarely on his head. He seems to have a rather stern expression on his face, fitting with his reputation as being somewhat of a "hard case."

Lightoller was born in England in 1874 to a family who owned a cotton mill. Lightoller's mother died when he was less than a year old and his father deserted the family before Charles was thirteen. Not wanting to be trapped working in a factory the rest of his life, Lightoller went to sea for four years as an apprentice aboard *Primrose Hill* and *Holt Hill*. During this time, he survived a South American revolution, being shipwrecked and castaway, a major shipboard fire, a smallpox epidemic, and malaria.

In 1898, he caught another disease- gold fever- and decided, along with a few of his friends, to abandon the sea and travel to the Yukon to seek his fortune.

The first step was to get to Alaska. There were several ways to do this- none very attractive. One was to sail around the southern tip of South America to San Francisco, and eventually the Yukon. A shorter route involved sailing to Panama, crossing the isthmus, embarking aboard another ship, then continuing north up the coast. You could also take the train across the continent, but all of these options could be expensive, and the objective was to get to the goldfields with enough money to spend some time prospecting.

Lightoller and his companions chose another way- overland through Canada. Not only did it allow them to buy the bulk of their equipment before they left at reasonable prices- it also appeared to be the shortest route too. However it wasn't long before Lightoller's band realized why they were virtually alone on their expedition. They had badly underestimated the difficulty of the journey, and they never made it to Alaska. Later, Lightoller's companions credited him as being the primary reason that they had survived.

Out of money, Lightoller took a job as a cowboy in Western Canada, hopped trains to get back to the east coast and eventually returned to England aboard a cattle boat as a wrangler.

In 1900, he accepted employment with White Star on the Australian run, assigned to *Medic*. It was a good position with an excellent future.

Despite this, Lightoller then proceeded to place his situation with White Star in serious jeopardy. The Boer war was in full swing at the time and everyone was edgy about it, which, it seemed to Lightoller, were the perfect conditions to play a colossal practical joke on the people of Sydney. Lightoller and some of his mates aboard *Medic* decided to make it appear as if Fort Denison, which had been built to protect the harbor, had been captured by a Boer raiding party. Under the cover of darkness, they launched a boat from *Medic* and rowed to the fort. There, they hoisted a makeshift Boer flag and filled a cannon with blasting powder. They lit the fuse (which was several feet long) and made haste back to the ship in order to watch the effects of their effort.

It was more than they could have hoped for. The resounding blast broke windows in the neighboring area and woke up people for miles. When the flag was spotted over the fort, it set off a general panic in Sydney that did not subside for several hours.

Lightoller and his friends thought that their little prank was hilarious until some passengers aboard *Medic* turned them in.

White Star was ordered to pay for the damages and Lightoller found himself in some serious hot water. The line issued him a formal reprimand which delayed an advance in rank. He only kept his position because *Medic's* Captain admired him for shouldering the blame for the prank and refusing to name his accomplices. The Captain also thought that Lightoller's practical joke was amusing, although he probably kept that to himself- at least until *Medic* was safely at sea.

Lightoller then began to behave, and soon proved to be a capable officer. He later joined *Majestic*, under Smith, and then served on *Oceanic* before coming to *Titanic*.

After the *Titanic* disaster, Lightoller remained with White Star. When the First World War erupted, he entered the Royal navy as a lieutenant. Eventually he was given command of a destroyer and twice won the Distinguished Service Cross. He left the Navy with the rank of commander.

Lightoller returned to duty with White Star, but soon realized that his association with *Titanic* would prevent him from ever being awarded his own command and so he resigned. He took up inn keeping for a time, tried chicken farming, and eventually found some success as a real estate speculator.

In the mid 1930's he wrote an autobiographical book called *Titanic and Other ships*. The book was a success, but had to be withdrawn from publication because of a threatened lawsuit involving the Marconi Company. Apparently *Titanic's* former second officer had some harsh words about their operators.

Lightoller participated in the evacuation of Dunkirk, taking his own yacht, *Sundowner*, to the French coast several times. After the war he managed a small boatyard. He lived until 1952.

Titanic's third officer, the most senior of her junior staff, was Herbert Pitman. Pitman had come from a post as second officer on *Oceanic*. Pitman was in bed at the time of the accident and later described the sound of the ship striking the berg as like "the chain running out over the windlass," or dropping anchor. Murdoch ordered him to take command of one of the lifeboats, so he survived the accident.

Afterward, Pitman remained with White Star for several years, but failing vision eventually disqualified him from retaining a post as a deck officer, and so he finished his career as a purser.

Titanic's fourth officer was Joseph Boxhall, a twenty-eight year old Yorkshireman. He had come from a post in White Star's *Arabic*, and had joined *Titanic* in Belfast. Boxhall was reputed to be the best navigator aboard the ship and Smith had assigned him to maintain the ship's charts.

Like Pitman, Boxhall was ordered to take charge of a lifeboat and also survived the accident.

He joined the navy during the First World War and returned to White Star, eventually rising to the rank of second in command of Cunard-White Star's *Aquitania*, but as all surviving officers of *Titanic*, he was never given his own command. He retired from the sea in 1940. In 1958 he served as technical advisor for the motion picture *A Night to Remember.*[112]

---

[112] In the late thirties, Boxhall was featured in a Cunard- White Star print advertisement that bore the headline "ON WATCH." One might

Of all the junior officers aboard *Titanic*, perhaps the most colorful was Harold Lowe, her fifth officer. Lowe was a Welshman, and had served at sea since he was fourteen. He had experience with almost every type of ship from clippers to coastal boats, and he was reputed as perhaps being the best practical sailor among the officers.

He had come to *Titanic* from White Star's *Tropic*. At time of the collision, Lowe was asleep in his cabin, slept through it, and had to be summoned by one of the other officers. He later explained that sleep was precious aboard any ship and "when we sleep, we die."

Lowe's experiences in evacuating the ship were somewhat dramatic. He quickly began to assist in the loading and launching of the lifeboats, and while so occupied, had a heated exchange with a person he presumed to be a passenger who was exhorting him to lower one more quickly. He finally called to the man "If

---

question why an officer who served aboard a ship involved in perhaps the most notorious collision in maritime history would be employed in this fashion.

you will get the hell out of this then I shall be able to do something! Do you want me to lower away quickly? You will have me drown the whole lot of them!"

The man Lowe took to be a meddlesome passenger was J. Bruce Ismay. Ismay, abashed, left Lowe alone. Some of the crew who were nearby felt that Ismay would have the last word in New York, but there is no evidence that he did.

Lowe stayed with the ship until near the end, and at one point fired his pistol into the air to prevent a rush on a boat he was filling.[113] He took command of it and also survived the accident. Lowe took the initiative to distribute the passengers in his boat into several others and took boat number fourteen back to the area where many passengers were in the water. It was largely in vain. His crew picked up only four survivors, one who later died.

---

[113] In the motion picture *A Night to Remember*, the argument with Ismay and the pistol shots were attributed to Lightoller. Apparently it would have complicated the plot of the movie to develop another character.

In the morning, when a light wind sprang up, Lowe hoisted a sail in his boat and steered it to *Carpathia*.

Lowe, like the others, entered the Navy during the war, but did not return to White Star afterward.

The last officer aboard *Titanic* that night was James Moody. Little is known about him; except he was a twenty-four year old Englishman and that he had also come from *Oceanic*, where he had served with Lightoller.

Moody was standing watch on the bridge at the time the ice was sighted. He answered the call from the crow's nest and relayed the warning to First Officer Murdoch.

After the collision, Moody assisted in the evacuation of the ship, and is known to have refused assignment to a lifeboat, stating that he would find one later.

There was no other boat. He did not survive.

To a man, all the officers of *Titanic* were later hailed as heroes of the disaster.

However, there was another man who exerted more than a little influence aboard *Titanic*. After the disaster, there was disagreement about whether he should be treated as a member of the crew, or a passenger, but there was no debate about one other matter. Almost everyone agreed that he was not a hero.

Chapter Twelve- the Chairman

One of the first lessons covered in any creative writing course is that for a story to be successful, it requires a strong protagonist- a hero- and an almost equally strong antagonist- one who puts up a good fight but is ultimately defeated- and a plot that sets these two powerful people in motion against each other. The story may be enhanced by concealing the identity of the evil character for a time- to build suspense.

The story of *Titanic* has more than its share of heroes, but after the accident there seemed to be little debate as to the identity of its principal villain- J. Bruce Ismay. Unfortunately for our little drama- and all the literary devices we might wish to employ to heighten our reader's enjoyment- he appears to have been vanquished even before he fully appeared in the narrative.

To many, the Chairman of White Star personified the perception that his corporation was willing to risk the lives of its passengers rather than compromise the profits derived from them.

Ismay arrived on the scene almost after the fact. Prior to the sinking of *Titanic*, he was almost unknown to the general public. However, when his name appeared on the list of survivors posted outside White Star offices, the newspapers, particularly those owned by William Randolph Hearst, instantly recognized that they had a sensational angle that begged exploitation.

The issue seemed to be cut and dried. *Titanic's* "owner" had been aboard the doomed vessel and had deserted it in a lifeboat, leaving innocent passengers- *innocent women and children-* behind to perish in the icy darkness. It seemed as simple as that. The public- who were demanding a scapegoat for the disaster- were going to be fed one.

And, as we have seen, it was not that simple.

Many accounts concerning aftermath of the *Titanic* disaster portray Ismay as an emotional wreck after the ship was lost. He had to be sedated with narcotics while aboard *Carpathia*. Shortly after he boarded the rescue ship, he secreted himself in the doctor's cabin- not to emerge until the ship reached New York. If true, we may easily sympathize with him.

He had been- if you will pardon the allusion- "King of the World" the day before- the chairman of the most powerful shipping concern on earth- enjoying a voyage aboard the largest and most luxurious vessel on the planet- on which he occupied the most opulent suite, benefiting from service and privileges that few men would ever experience- and because he was chairman of the company- it was probably superior to what even his famous and well-to-do customers received.

Now he had spent a miserable, cold, and undoubtedly frightening night in a small boat, brought face to face with the primal fear of imminent death, and having narrowly escaped that, realizing that his greatest achievement had sunk beneath him as he heard the cries of people not as fortunate as he fade in the darkness.[114]

The image we form of White Star's chairman is one of a shivering, cowering, psychologically ruined man- a bit of human wreckage- sitting alone in the dark and talking to himself. This may be an accurate assessment, as Ismay had a lot to answer for, and there were a number of people who were eager to begin pressing him with questions.[115]

Second Officer Lightoller testified that Ismay, aboard *Carpathia*, continually stated that he should have gone down with *Titanic*, because there were women and children left aboard- a fact that he said he was unaware of until he reached the rescue ship. This account may

---

[114] Ismay was asked at one of the inquiries if he had watched *Titanic* sink. He stated that he had turned his back to her, not being able to bear the sight of her going down. He was one of the few exceptions.

[115] This included most of his surviving shipmates from *Titanic*. Ismay's presence aboard *Carpathia* became known to them shortly after they were rescued. *Carpathia* was designed as a "dormitory" type ship, devoted primarily to steerage class. She had very few private cabins. It became a sore point to many surviving passengers that they were compelled to sleep in the public areas of the ship, some on the decks, while Ismay stayed in seclusion, complete with a prominently posted "do not knock" sign on the door.

be slightly suspect though, as Lightoller was found to have stretched the truth in a number of places to shield his boss.

There are indications that Ismay may not have been as devastated as we have been led to believe. The morning of the rescue, at Captain Rostron's suggestion, Ismay wrote a Marconigram to Phillip Franklin- White Star's agent in New York. "Deeply regret advise you of *Titanic* sank this morning after collision iceberg, resulting serious loss of life. Full particulars later. Bruce Ismay." This was the Marconigram that was delayed.

Other decisions made by Ismay also tend to belie the idea he was almost irrational. Captain Haddock, of *Olympic*, had- via wireless- made the suggestion that she and *Carpathia* rendezvous at sea to transfer survivors, enabling their rapid return to Britain, but *Carpathia's* Captain, Arthur Rostron, was against it. His concern was that the last thing the survivors needed was to undergo another transfer at sea.

Ismay agreed, but for another reason. He felt that it would be extremely disconcerting to expose them to the sight of a ship almost identical to the one they had seen sink before their eyes.

However, Ismay may have overlooked one benefit of transferring to *Titanic's* older sister. He would be able to avoid the United States and the possibility that the Americans might want to ask embarrassing questions about the navigation of the ship, the inadequacy of the lifeboat provision, why so many people from steerage did not survive- and an assortment of others. The Americans might be rough with him too- they did not respect British class distinctions- in fact they seemed to have a pronounced distaste for them.

To Ismay, and people of his background, the United States must have appeared to be a manifestly odd country. The Americans seemed to somehow invest nobility in their commonness, and they would be unlikely to treat Ismay with the kid glove courtesy he had learned to expect in Britain.[116]

Ismay, if you accepted and followed his reasoning, could hide from some of the fallout from the disaster. After all, he was just an officer of White Star- not *Titanic*. So, technically, he was not actually in charge of the ship. He had just been along for the ride. The voyage could be viewed- at the most- as a glorified busman's holiday for him.

His conversations with Captain Smith- if Ismay even acknowledged having participated in them- about an early arrival in New York had been nothing more than well intentioned "suggestions."

Anything that had to do with navigation had been the responsibility of the Captain and of course, as a passenger, Ismay could not answer any questions about that. At the time of the collision he had been tucked into bed- fast asleep.

---

[116] He would be surprised- the British Inquiry was less than gentle with him either.

However, there was one question that he knew he could not avoid, and it was one that would surely be asked. It was obvious.

How could it be, Mr. Ismay, that you were fortunate enough to find a seat in a lifeboat while a large number of your paying passengers- many of them women and children- the very people who relied on your company to ensure their safe passage- did not?

Please correct us if this is not true, but is it not a fact that you boarded this boat from the boat deck? Maybe we missed that part of your story. You did not, perchance, have to jump into the sea and swim to a lifeboat like second officer Lightoller did- or even some of your passengers- like Colonel Gracie or Jack Thayer? How fortunate for you that you did not even have to get your feet wet. Could you please explain the circumstances of your rescue to us? By all means, Mr. Ismay, take your time.

Ismay could rightfully expect to be roasted alive. Hardly a sympathetic character- Ismay was instead cold and distant. Most of his acquaintances were businessmen and only a few of these would admit to having any fondness for him. Ismay owed his position within White Star to inheritance, and therefore had never had to develop any political skills.

Unaccustomed with gaining the cooperation of others in order to achieve his ends, Ismay was used to issuing commands to subordinates, expecting no discussion or debate. Therefore, he could be very direct- and intense. Part of his power stemmed from his physical presence. He was much taller than average- about 6' 4", and sported an impressive waxed handlebar moustache.

There probably were a number of people- many undoubtedly within his own company- who must have delighted in his discomfiture. His act of boarding a lifeboat- while women and children were still aboard - and left to perish in the icy sea- looked like a cowardly- if not criminal- act. J. "Brute" Ismay- as the press would shortly, and somewhat unimaginatively, dub him- would become the incarnation of evil in the disaster- whether he actually deserved the role or not.[117]

Captain Smith, whether by design or destiny, had gone down with the ship- and since it had always been thought to be bad form to speak ill of the dead- that left Ismay squarely in the crosshairs.

Unfortunately, in most histories of the *Titanic* disaster, Ismay has been portrayed as a two-dimensional character- with these proportions being greed and insensitivity. His depiction has invariably been one of a heartless, cigar smoking, shifty-eyed, SOB who thought more of profit than of human life.

It was he- against what was now perceived as fundamental common sense- who decided that the ship would be equipped with far fewer lifeboats than she required, and it was he who pressured Captain Smith to

---

[117] Ismay was not alone. Virtually every adult male passenger who managed to find his way into a boat suffered damage to his reputation. They were branded as cowards and there were accusations that some had disguised themselves as women in order to desert the liner (no evidence of this has ever surfaced). Major Arthur Peuchen, who offered to help manage a short-staffed boat due to his experience as a "yachtsman" and was ordered in by Lightoller, sought out *Titanic's* second officer on the *Carpathia* and obtained a signed letter from him stating such.

push her to speeds that again- in the light of what happened- seem to be reckless in the extreme.

It was he who also equivocated about both later.

He's also been depicted as a selfish coward who, exactly like a rat, deserted the sinking and in the process deprived an innocent passenger, usually represented as a soulful-eyed flaxen-haired little girl, of his or her rightful place in a lifeboat.

These assertions are not entirely true.

Ismay had a complicated personality. Until he became infamous, he had to content himself with the fact that his father had been the well known member of the family.

Thomas Ismay had built the Oceanic Steam Navigation Company, which was popularly called the White Star line, from virtually nothing. He had also forged the link between White Star and Harland and Wolff and in the process had formed a close relationship with Harland and Wolff's owner, Lord Pirrie.

White Star, under previous owners, originally had served Australia and India from Britain, but toward the end of the 19th century it shifted much of its operations to the North Atlantic, the place where the money was. The traffic was heavy, and because the distance between Liverpool and New York was much shorter, it could be served with far fewer ships than were required to make the long voyages to Asia.

As may be expected, there were already several established lines competing on the North Atlantic and the competition was intense and the new route proved to be the undoing of the company. White Star soon went bankrupt. All of its assets were purchased by Thomas Ismay.

Ismay proved to be a talented manager, and turned what had been a weak sister into a contender. Within a few years White Star was one of the leading shipping companies in the Western Hemisphere, serving destinations worldwide.

But Thomas Ismay was not the only person who had noted the potential of the route between Europe and North America, so had J.P. Morgan. Morgan was an American banker who, as we have mentioned, had made the practice of creating monopolies, or "trusts" as they were called, into an art form.[118] He had achieved most of his success taking over railroads in the United States. His business triumphs had led to strong anti-trust legislation being passed in the United States which broke up his empire and forced him to look elsewhere to satisfy his desire for conquest. Quickly, he realized that his opportunity lay at sea where regulations regarding monopolies were largely non-existent, or because of the number of countries involved, extremely difficult to enforce.

Morgan, like the classic predator, looked for a weakened victim, setting his sights on the British-owned Inman line, a company that had been on the threshold of collapse for several years. By seizing Inman, Morgan would not only have an instant fleet, but more importantly, he would also have the infrastructure- piers, warehouses, and employees- to begin his campaign to

---

[118] Morgan was the person who coined the phrase "If you have to ask, you can't afford it." He was speaking of the cost of his yacht, *Corsair*. Corsair, in French, means "pirate."

consolidate every line into the corporation he would call the International Mercantile Marine.

Thomas Ismay was quick to see what Morgan was attempting, and tried to enlist his competitors in helping him to beat Morgan to Inman, but the response was indifferent. Ismay was unable to convince them of the threat of allowing this American banker with the deep pockets into their business. Everyone believed that he was overreacting and exaggerating the danger. To them, Inman was a seriously weak sister- a money pit. The arrogant Yankee would be quickly overwhelmed and taught a lasting lesson.

But Morgan taught them one. When Inman fell to Morgan what had been a competitive, but somewhat gentlemanly, industry soon became a cutthroat and vicious brawl. As each line toppled, Morgan- and the IMM- were there to catch it.

As a child, Joseph Bruce Ismay was largely shielded from his father's problems. Born in 1862 into a world of privilege, Bruce attended fashionable schools, and built a reputation as being a skilled athlete. But unlike the majority of his schoolmates, he shied away from team sports, preferring tennis and other solitary pursuits such as hunting and fishing, which more suited his personality. He proved to be a somewhat private man- avoiding publicity when he could- and preferring to remain in the background.

When he came of age, he joined his father's business, and was soon sent to North America to represent the company.[119] It was here that Ismay met and married his wife, a pharmaceutical heiress from New England. In 1899, when the elder Ismay died, Bruce inherited the business and was installed as White Star's Chairman.

Morgan sensed that the son did not possess the tenacity and stubbornness of the father. It was time to begin turning up the heat to amalgamate White Star into his massive combine.

---

[119] There is an oft repeated story that young Bruce left his hat and coat in his father's office the first day on the job. Thomas Ismay loudly let it be known that the "new office boy" needed to find somewhere else to stow them while he was at work. Although this story is usually presented as humorous, the incident undoubtedly must have wounded the younger Ismay. There probably were many slights similar to this one that the Father directed at his son.

Bruce knew that his father had fought for years to keep IMM at bay, but was unsure as to what course of action was best for the company.

He turned to his father's old friend, Lord Pirrie- of Harland and Wolff- for advice. Pirrie may have surprised Bruce with his recommendation. Instead of urging the younger Ismay to continue the fight against the IMM, Pirrie advocated White Star's sale.

Pirrie's argument was sound. White Star's incorporation into IMM was inevitable. White Star simply lacked the resources to keep up the struggle against such a dominant competitor. Ismay had a difficult choice, either he sold out to IMM or let Morgan's Cartel pick up the pieces after White Star failed. It would be preferable to make a deal while Ismay still held some cards.

Pirrie also had an ulterior motive for urging the buy-out- one that he probably did not bring to Ismay's attention. If White Star collapsed, Harland and Wolff would lose its primary, and best, customer. However, if Morgan was allowed to place White Star in his pocket, it would be accompanied by Pirrie's hand- money for new ships would no longer present a problem.

Harland and Wolff would be able to build the large liners for White Star that Pirrie envisioned. Pirrie probably also failed to mention to Ismay another idea of his- to install Harland and Wolff as the exclusive shipbuilder to IMM. This never came to fruition, for after *Titanic* was lost, IMM fortunes began a slow decline.[120]

The younger Ismay must have been reluctant to take Pirrie's advice, because he decided to wait, resisting the takeover until 1902. But when it became clear that Cunard had found a way to evade being engulfed by the combine by hiding in the government's skirts, Ismay finally relinquished control of White Star to IMM.

As a sop, Morgan installed Ismay as head of IMM and allowed him to remain chairman of White Star.

---

[120] Harland and Wolff would too be affected and, after finishing *Britannic*, would only build a few more ships for White Star, and none for the merged Cunard-White Star line. Eventually the gantries that supported the construction of the big ships would be demolished and the Belfast shipyard would be closed. The company still exists, but as only a shadow of what it once was.

But the position was largely a façade. Ismay was now nothing more than an employee of Morgan- again the "new office boy."

Shortly after the takeover, Pirrie invited Ismay to dinner at his home in London. It was here that it is generally held that the two conceived of the *Olympic* class liners, although the majority of historians believe that the ships were mostly Pirrie's idea. Ismay had very little to do with their design, except to approve their décor, luxurious appointments, and make adjustments in the plan of the ship, such as determining the "proper" number of lifeboats.[121]

A few hours after Ismay's first Marconigram was sent to New York, Franklin received a second. Instead of furnishing the "full particulars" of the disaster, as was promised- and incidentally never were supplied- this one

---

[121] Here is an interesting sidelight to the times. Ismay traveled aboard *Lusitania* and admired a certain type of sliding window installed aboard her- which he believed would be perfectly suited for the *Olympic* class liners. He wrote to Cunard asking them to supply him with the design details. Surprisingly, Cunard did.

contained instructions. "Very important you should hold *Cedric* daylight for *Titanic's* crew. Answer. YAMSI."

Since almost every wireless station within range on the east coast of the United States was listening in on the transmissions coming from *Carpathia*, most of the newspapers had the message before Franklin.[122]

Who was this mysterious "YAMSI" who was ordering Franklin to change the schedule of *Cedric*, one of White Star's smaller liners? We do not need to be cryptanalysts with the National Security Agency to quickly see that "YAMSI" is simply "ISMAY" spelled backward.

Unfortunately for Ismay, "YAMSI" was nothing more than his private signature to telegrams, and it was well-known throughout White Star. In fact, *Olympic* had

---

[122] Since wireless was a curiosity, there were stations in places that would seem somewhat odd today. One was located on the top floor of Wanamaker's department store in Philadelphia. One of their operators was a young man named David Sarnoff, who later went on to become Chairman of RCA. Radio was a popular hobby too. Crystal receivers could be made out of common materials and cost little. Transmitters were more expensive, but there were many who built their own sets and operated them. As noted, there was speculation that most of the erroneous information that was generated about *Titanic* came from these amateur operators.

earlier sent a wireless message to New York confirming that "YAMSI" was aboard *Carpathia*.

However, to many within the United States- particularly a U.S. Senator with the ironic last name of Smith- it appeared as if the "YAMSI" signature was an intentional, although rather inept, attempt at subterfuge.

To Senator William Alden Smith, it looked like the Chairman and his subordinates were going to try to use *Cedric* as a kind of nautical getaway car and that Ismay's wireless message was somewhat like him ordering Franklin to "keep the engine running."

The perception that Ismay was attempting to conceal his identity with this patently transparent ruse seemed to merely serve as confirmation of skullduggery afoot. It also prompted many to speculate about what he wished to hide. Steps would have to be taken quickly to prevent this attempt at escape.[123]

---

[123] There were several of these "YAMSI" messages. One concerned itself with Franklin securing some clothes and shoes for Ismay, (a seemingly petty item- which was quickly spread by the press) almost all the others were concerned with delaying *Cedric* so she could return the crew of *Titanic*, and Ismay, to Britain. Lightoller later attempted to take some of the responsibility for these messages, stating that he suggested sending them, as he wanted to keep the crew together

Senator Smith had already expressed his intention to undertake an investigation into the loss of *Titanic*, under the auspices of the Senate Commerce committee, of which he was a member. He issued instructions to have a revenue cutter intercept *Carpathia* as she entered the approaches to New York to prevent any monkey business.

When the Cunard liner docked in New York, Senator Smith was waiting on the pier, accompanied by a small army of Federal Marshals. Even before *Carpathia* had finished tying up, they boarded and dispersed, serving subpoenas to key members of *Titanic's* crew and many of her passengers.

Ismay did not escape; in fact he was singled out for special attention- Senator Smith served him personally. Ismay and the other members of the crew were instructed to remain in the United States until an investigation of *Titanic's* sinking was completed.

---

because they would be valuable witnesses at any investigation. Few believed it then either.

Of course, this caused an outcry in Britain about the presumptuousness of these upstart Americans. How *dare* they detain British subjects? There was a great deal of harrumphing about the legality of a foreign country conducting an investigation into the demise of a British ship- particularly one that had foundered in international waters.

It was an uncharted area legally, but the United States Senate was on firm footing. The International Mercantile Marine, who owned the White Star line, was American, so *Titanic* could be considered an American ship- once removed. And the old phrase, "possession is nine tenths of the law," also applied. Nobody was going anywhere until the investigation was complete.

Another, probably more important factor, at least politically, was that a large number of the people who died aboard *Titanic* were Americans, or they were seeking new lives in America. Since the British had obviously failed, it was up to the United States to see that others like them would be protected. That was enough.

Senator Smith had distinguished himself as a hard-nosed populist- just the type of person Ismay probably would have made a point to avoid. Smith was the embodiment of the common man from a state that was largely rural at that time.

The Senator, during his tenure in Congress, had shown himself to be a devoted enemy of "trusts," and a dedicated thorn in the side of J. P. Morgan- fighting to dissolve his railroad monopolies. Obviously, Smith suspected that some of his nemesis' business practices with IMM may have contributed to the death of *Titanic*. Morgan was in France- out of reach, but one Ismay in the hand was worth two Morgans in the bush.

Smith was determined to get to the bottom of why what had been considered to be the world's safest ocean liner was now lying wrecked on the floor of the Atlantic. He also wanted to know why the loss of life was so appalling.[124]

---

[124] Much was made, particularly in the British Press, of Senator Smith's seeming ignorance of marine matters. He asked one officer what an iceberg was made of (the answer was "Ice, I suppose.") He also asked whether people could have taken refuge in a watertight compartment

The Senator did not waste any time. He booked several rooms at New York's Waldorf Astoria hotel.[125] The hearings began the morning after *Carpathia* landed.[126]

Ismay was considered so vital to the American inquiry that he was the first witness called. His bearing was an odd mixture of arrogance, courtesy, and apparent bewilderment. He showed exaggerated respect to the Senators, made a show out of attempting to honestly answer their questions, and proved himself totally worthless as a witness.

After he was sworn in, and asked a few simple preliminary questions by Senator Smith regarding his

---

and sealed themselves in. He later asked a member of *Californian's* crew if the ship had anchored when she stopped. Smith might not have been a sailor, but he was a skilled lawyer, and believed that thorough questioning of witnesses would prevent surprises later. His debatably ignorant questions about the sea and ships generated a tremendous amount of public hostility toward his inquiry in Britain where the press dubbed him "Watertight Smith."

[125] Ironically, the Waldorf-Astoria was owned by the Astor family, and had been built by the same John Jacob Astor who had gone down on *Titanic*. In the 1930s, the hotel was torn down to make way for construction of the Empire State building.

[126] By chance, Marconi happened to be in New York and attended the hearing.

name, occupation and such, he began his testimony with a statement:

> "In the first place, I would like to express my sincere grief at this deplorable catastrophe. I understand that you gentlemen have been appointed as a committee of the Senate to inquire into the circumstances. So far as we are concerned, we welcome it. We court the fullest inquiry. We have nothing to conceal; nothing to hide."

Ismay then spent the remainder of his tenure on the stand attempting to do just that. And just like today when similar remarks are uttered by those at the focal point of any investigation, few believed that he, or anyone at White Star, truly encouraged "the fullest inquiry."

If one reads Ismay's initial testimony before the American Senate Committee, they may be left with the impression that White Star's Chairman just happened to be in Southampton at the time *Titanic* departed, and he was virtually shanghaied aboard her.

Ismay's account made it sound like he and Captain Smith were only casually acquainted, and during their chance meetings aboard during the voyage they did not discuss anything in particular.

Ismay's view was that he was just a passenger. He had no duties aboard *Titanic*, had no say about her navigation or speed, and was entirely unaware of the danger to the ship posed by the vast icefield.

According to his account, he remained in his cabin most of the voyage- and if he did venture out- it was only to dine with the ship's doctor, play bridge with some of the other passengers, or idle about the decks. He never left the first class areas aboard the ship.[127]

As far as explaining his presence in a lifeboat, Ismay stated that he sought refuge in the last lifeboat launched. There were no other passengers on deck at the time. Murdoch had even called for anyone else to board the boat. Ismay- who had been helping with the evacuation of the ship- seized his chance for life- and to his knowledge did not deprive anyone of a rightful place in the boat- at least no deserving woman or child.

---

[127] Ismay stated, amazingly, that the first time he even visited *Titanic's* bridge was after the collision. He had problems with this memory too. He seemed to be unsure of what his cabin number had been, or whether it had been on the port or starboard side of the ship.

Ismay's testimony is contradictory, detailed in places where there was no personal risk to him or his reputation and then exceedingly indistinct in areas where there was.

For instance, according to the Chairman, he had no real role aboard *Titanic*, but then contradicted himself later, stating that he was there to complete an inspection of the liner before she arrived in New York.

There were other contradictions too. He seemed to know, in detail, about the number of propeller revolutions the ship was making at different points in her voyage- indicating that he was more than aware of her speed- but he then was vague about the reasons behind why she was being sailed at those velocities.

According to Ismay, he had no conversations with Captain Smith about the ice danger ahead, but later admitted- after a passenger had told the Senators about it- that Captain Smith had given him an ice warning that the Chairman had carried around in his coat pocket for several hours and shown to some of his fellow first class passengers.[128] All in all, his testimony reeked of obscuration, distortion, omission, and intentional misstatement.

Ismay repeatedly fell back on his assertion that he had nothing to do with the navigation of the ship- that the line had hired competent officers, trusted them completely and did not question their judgment. Additionally, he had never had any discussions with Captain Smith or Chief Engineer Bell about the speed of the ship or her preferred time of arrival in New York.

Ismay's account of the disaster was equally muddled. He told the inquiry that he had talked to Bell shortly after the collision about the extent of the damage to *Titanic*.

According to Ismay, Chief Bell had assured him that the pumps would keep the ship afloat, but Ismay stated that he almost immediately began assisting the loading of the lifeboats.

---

[128] One passenger alleged that Ismay had "waved the ice message about at the dinner table."

He repeatedly reminded the Senators that *Titanic* had met the lifeboat requirements of the British Board of Trade, and that the United States had accepted them.

He was asked why White Star had gone to the expense of equipping *Olympic* and *Titanic* with the new electrically operated Wellin double-acting davits- which allowed multiple boats to be stowed under each- if the line had intended on only placing a single boat beneath each one. Ismay stated that White Star had expected that an update in the lifeboat regulations would require more lifeboats on each ship. They had simply wished to be prepared.

But, although it was never actually voiced at either official hearing, the question that Ismay was alive and well while so many of the people who had expected his company to see to their well-being were not hung in the air the whole time he testified.

And although the official inquiries shied away from asking the question, the press repeatedly posed it- on both sides of the Atlantic- and often in large headlines. The papers had a field day with the Chairman, publishing scathing stories, cartoons and even poorly-written rhymes about him. It would never be dropped. Ismay would be tarred, shunned, and defamed for the rest of his life by his decision to seek a seat in a lifeboat.

Was Ismay the scoundrel everyone believed him to be? Did he deserve the vilification he was forever to endure?

We cannot deny that White Star's Chairman was more than casually involved in the decision to under-equip the company's two largest liners with lifeboats, but the point has been made above that White Star was not the only company that had failed to provide enough boats for all aboard. Ismay's decision was undoubtedly influenced by the fact that he must have truly believed the two sisters to be unsinkable, as evidenced by his willingness to travel aboard both *Olympic* and *Titanic*.

He must have believed with certainty that the ships would never be subject to any damage that could present even the remotest chance that they could be involved in a disaster. It would have been a totally different matter if the Chairman had refused to travel aboard his own ships because of his concerns about their safety and inadequate lifesaving equipment. We can confirm this by his astonishment when he was informed that *Titanic* was going to sink.

Ismay also seemed- once he shook off his initial disbelief- to be one of the few people aboard who realized the urgency of filling and launching the lifeboats. Testimony revealed that he had been constantly present as the boats were being filled, urging women to board the boats and exhorting the crew to expedite the loading and lowering of them.

The previously mentioned dispute between Ismay and Fifth Officer Lowe needs to be briefly noted again because it serves to illustrate something further about Ismay. Lowe was unaware of the Chairman's identity, thinking he was merely an intrusive passenger. This provides confirmation of Ismay's reluctance to draw attention to himself. One would think that had Ismay been the traditional corporate leader, not only the officers, but *every* member of *Titanic's* crew would have been more than aware of his identity.

However, instead of seeing Ismay as an active participant in the evacuation of the ship, the popular portrayal of the Chairman is of a man who lurked in the shadows, waiting for a chance to escape, finally shouldering his way into a boat through a crowd of innocent passengers- composed principally of women and children. Sometimes we are even given the idea that he plucked a passenger from the boat and took their place. But it's an inaccurate picture of what actually happened.[129]

Ismay seemed somewhat surprised at the uproar his escape from *Titanic* triggered. After all, according to his account, he was virtually the last person off the ship aboard a lifeboat. It was not exactly true- but it almost was- and Ismay genuinely believed it to be until

---

[129] As an example of what is commonly stated, one text I consulted while researching this book, features a picture of Ismay. The caption below identifies him as "Bruce Ismay, general director of the of White Star line, survived to live in shame. Ismay jumped into the last lifeboat being lowered, taking the place of a woman."

he boarded Carpathia and learned otherwise. One other collapsible boat was launched from the port side of the ship after Ismay's boat departed from the starboard side. Ismay was almost certainly unaware of it.

Contrary to the legend, there was no "crowd" of passengers patiently awaiting their turn to board the boat, and there were none in the vicinity who were left behind. Furthermore, Ismay did not deprive a passenger of a seat. He did not even get the last one in the boat. *Thirty-nine* additional passengers could have been accommodated in the boat Ismay boarded. It was less than half full when lowered.

The boat, one of the collapsibles that had been removed from the top of the officer's quarters, had been assembled and fitted to the forward davits, just abaft the bridge. It was very near the water, and most of the remaining passengers had migrated aft as each boat had been lowered. The ship was rapidly sinking at this point- the bridge was now almost submerged- and as the water drew closer most people had abandoned the forward part of *Titanic*- seeking the perceived, but fleeting, safety of the stern.

Strangely, most written accounts of Ismay's departure from the ship are almost totally devoid of detail, usually confined to one line or maybe two at the most. One would think that such a pivotal and telling event would merit several paragraphs, if not pages. The few accounts that do provide details contradict one another- or supply such a wealth of information that they seem to be the product of imagination rather than research.

We have two movie versions of Ismay's boarding. One- in *A Night to Remember*- shows the frightened chairman standing alone on deck after Murdoch has informed the crowd of passengers that there is no more room in the boat.

We know that the ship is sinking rapidly now. The crew begins lowering the boat. Ismay looks about- almost timidly- and then plaintively calls "Is there no one else?" before he furtively scurries- exactly like a rat deserting the ship- into the boat as it's being lowered.

Murdoch calls to the crewmen to stop lowering. He fixes Ismay with a scornful look and then, the disgust clear in his voice, commands, “Lower away.” Ismay sits in the boat, wrapped in a blanket, with his back to Murdoch and the ship- portrayed as a cowardly figure, huddling- almost hiding- in the boat as it disappears into the darkness.[130]

In Cameron's *Titanic*, the boarding is essentially the same, except Ismay is portrayed as more calculating- absolutely in control of himself and aware of his actions. As Murdoch calls for any more “women and children,” Ismay- appearing almost as the personification of evil- looks slyly about and then jumps over the side of the ship into the boat. In this version too Murdoch stops the lowering of the boat so he may fix Ismay with a hard stare and, as the boat descends into the darkness, the

---

130 The portrayal of Ismay in *A Night to Remember* is one of the few faults of the film. The actor who plays Ismay, Frank Lawton, is short, moon faced, and rather round- completely missing the real Ismay. In fact, he plays the Chairman as, to use a British term, somewhat of a “twit.”

chairman seems to be transformed into a broken man as he realizes the import of his act.[131]

In reality, neither of these scenarios may be true.

Ismay had been darting about the deck, alternately helping and hindering the officers as they sought to launch the boats since the first one had been lowered at 12:45. It's impossible to say with any certainty what he was thinking as he moved about the liner.

If we are objective about his activities, he appears as totally selfless- trying to round up as many women and children as he could to fill the boats. He

---

[131] The 1953 *Titanic*, starring Clifton Webb and Barbara Stanwyck, makes no mention of Ismay at all, instead choosing to vilify a fictional character named Meeker, who spends most of the voyage attempting to cultivate favor with the socially prominent aboard and later sneaks into a lifeboat disguised as a woman. On the recent release of this movie on DVD, there is a commentary track that plays as the film unwinds. For some reason the producers decided to employ a writer named Sylvia Stoddard to provide the "historical commentary." Unfortunately, she apparently knows little to nothing about the disaster. The reason she offered as to why Ismay was not portrayed in the film was that "Sir Bruce" was still alive at the time and the producers were afraid of a lawsuit. As we will see, by 1953 Ismay had been dead sixteen years, and he was never knighted. However, Ms. Stoddard's credentials as a historian cannot be disputed, having written incisive and hard hitting volumes about the *Brady Bunch* and *Gilligan's Island*.

may have been awaiting his chance for escape, but if he did, he failed to mention it to anyone. As the collapsible was being readied and filled, he must have realized that his chances for survival were swiftly shrinking.

As the crew worked to fit the boat to the davits, Ismay may have discussed his departure with Murdoch. The 1st Officer may have even brought up the subject himself. The collapsible would probably be the last lifeboat launched on the starboard side.

There were two collapsibles remaining to be launched, but they were still stowed on the top of the officer's quarters, and the water was rising even more swiftly now. There would not be time to get these boats to the davits for loading. The only option would be to attempt to float them off as the ship sank. It seems a simple plan, and fairly easily done, but actually it would be fraught with significant risk. The boats were heavy and unwieldy, and no provision had been made for moving them from their position on the top of the deckhouse to the boat deck, except for some light rigging attached to the forward funnel.

Aside from this, there was always a chance that the liner would draw the boat down with her- the dreaded "suction" that supposedly occurred around any sinking ship. There were other risks too. The boat could become entangled in the ship's rigging or capsize.[132]

Murdoch may have told Ismay that they had both done all they could and the Chairman might as well take a seat in the collapsible if one was available. All evening, the First Officer had exhibited a significantly more liberal attitude toward boarding men on his side of the ship. If there was space in the boat and there were no women or children available, Murdoch had no qualms about filling the boat with anyone nearby. Entering a lifeboat would not have been something that a person

---

[132] *Titanic* had far more rigging than most people are aware. Not only were there lines used to stabilize and allow access to the masts, but there was also the Marconi aerial, which was suspended between them, and its associated wiring. The funnels also had multiple stays surrounding them. There is conjecture that some of the forward stays on the first funnel were cut to allow better access to the collapsible boats stowed below them, and this may have led to the funnel falling as the ship went down- killing many who were in the water. It may have happened, but the stays were made of thick steel cable, and would have been very difficult to sever. Additionally, with the cables under extreme tension, cutting one or more might have been exceedingly dangerous.

would have had to be talked into, unless he had strong convictions about his duty to the others aboard.

As Ismay himself stated repeatedly later, he was an officer of White Star, but not *Titanic*. The way he must have rationalized things, there was no reason to squander his life. After all, he may have reasoned, he had done all he could to assist in the evacuation of *Titanic*- more than many other people had done. He had had nothing to do with the ship colliding with the berg, and therefore had as much right to a seat in a lifeboat as any other male passenger- particularly when the boat was going to be lowered less than full.

Part of the above may be true- but I believe that Ismay, eager to seek some type of forgiveness afterward, would have mentioned Murdoch suggesting he leave the liner. However, whatever happened, Ismay must have justified his presence aboard the boat- at least to himself- probably viewing it as a straightforward matter of individual survival.

It's difficult, maybe impossible, to state with any certainty what any of us would do under similar circumstances. Would we have availed ourselves of a chance to live, or carefully weighed the potential damage we may have done to our reputations and passed it up? Would most of us even entertain a thought of what people would think of us if we were faced with making a life or death decision?

Ismay probably gave no consideration to the perceived correctness of his obtaining a seat in a boat. If he did, he may have thought that boarding the boat would draw no criticism at all- after all he may have reasoned that his going down with the ship would be no different than the owner of a burning building foolishly choosing to stay inside and perish with it. In Ismay's view, he had done all in his power to see passengers to the boats. Only an idiot would ignore an obvious path to safety and throw away his life.

We have an account of an alternative theory of how Ismay found himself in the boat, but it's almost certainly *not* true. During the course of the American Investigation, 2nd Officer Lightoller offered that he had been told that Chief Officer Wilde had "bundled" Ismay into the boat. According to Lightoller, Wilde was a large man, and it was impossible for Ismay to resist him.

At the time Ismay boarded the boat, Lightoller was occupied on the opposite side of the ship supervising the attachment of a collapsible boat to the forward davits and preparing to load and launch it. He admitted later that he had no first-hand knowledge of Ismay's departure from the ship, but had heard the story on *Carpathia*.

Chief Officer Wilde *was* assisting in loading and lowering the boat Ismay entered. But the crewman in charge of the boat, Quartermaster Thomas Rowe, later testified that Wilde had not even spoken with Ismay before the Chairman boarded the lifeboat.

Did Ismay deserve the abuse, scorn and derision to be heaped on him over the years, or was he merely a fall guy for all the mistakes that had been made in construction, administration, methods of navigation and even regulation over the years? Did he merely serve as a focus for the accumulated outrage of the public? To a certain extent, this may be true. But it's also true that Ismay did very little to help himself.

Would it even be possible for the Chairman to have escaped from *Titanic* with his life and not endured the damnation he experienced?

Let's begin with the primary act of Ismay that inflamed so many, the perception that he had taken a seat in a lifeboat that should have been occupied by a passenger. As we've already noted, the boat was not full even *after* Ismay boarded.

We must remember that at the time Ismay boarded the boat, *Titanic* was sinking quickly. She had less than fifteen minutes left to her- which is something that nobody present could have known. The ship was tilted at an alarming angle and could have taken her final plunge at any time. There simply was no time to seek out any more passengers. If they were not standing there waiting- they had literally missed the boat.

Ismay would have endured far less criticism if he had deserted the ship in the same manner Lightoller did. As the only surviving senior officer, Lightoller swam away from *Titanic* and spent a miserable night- part of it shivering as he and other survivors stood in ankle-deep water on the bottom of a capsized collapsible lifeboat that was slowly sinking. He was eventually able to attract the attention of another boat with his whistle, and so he and the others were able to vacate their precarious refuge.[133]

Had Ismay spent the same type of night- or even have jumped into the sea and swam to the boat he boarded, very few people would have been able to condemn his actions. He may have even been hailed as a hero.

Ismay's conduct after his rescue did not serve him either. As we've discussed above, he was less than helpful with the investigations looking into the demise of *Titanic*. According to Ismay, he was not responsible for anything involving the navigation of the ship or the provision of the lifesaving appliances aboard her. He

---

[133] Lightoller was almost drowned by water flooding the interior of the ship. He was briefly pinned against the grating of a ventilator- freed only by a chance blast of escaping air.

had assured himself that he was, in his belief, literally the last passenger off the ship.

But here we come to the primary sticking point in the whole matter- a small difference in perception between what Ismay maintained and what virtually everyone else believed. Should Ismay have been considered as just another passenger, or should he have been regarded as a member of the ships' company- obligated to remain aboard her until Captain Smith made the decision to release the crew from duty with the "every man for himself" order?

It's clear that the Chairman was in no way, "just another passenger." If John Jacob Astor or Colonel Gracie had asked Captain Smith to light additional boilers to make an earlier than anticipated arrival in New York, the response would undoubtedly have been a polite chuckle and a remark about the ship already making excellent time. Ismay's "suggestion" would have carried the weight of an order.

Ismay did not pay for his suite, which seems to be a small requirement for consideration as a "passenger," but on the other hand, he did not sign the ship's articles, which would have made him subject to Smith's orders and officially a member of the crew.[134]

So, we see that the haughty, remote, and calculating chairman of White Star seemed to be able to exist in, and freely move between, both spheres as it suited him.[135]

However, the consensus was that he should have elected to take his chances with the crew as the ship went down. Ismay's image was further damaged by the revelation that his male servant- who had accompanied him on the voyage- had perished with the ship.

Popular opinion was that Ismay deserved no place in the boat to begin with, and when it was discovered that he had been instrumental in the decision

---

[134] At the British Inquiry, Ismay was pressed on this subject- with the obvious goal of extracting an admission that he did not pay a fare- and therefore should have been considered part of the crew. However, Ismay countered by revealing that he never paid a fare aboard *any* ship, not even those of the competition.

[135] Walter Lord called Ismay a sort of "superpassenger." John Maxtone Graham called him a kind of "supercaptain." In either case, his wishes would be regarded as commands.

to equip with fewer boats that she required, that sealed his fate.

His evasions, omissions and misstatements did not serve him. But it's difficult to see how telling the truth would have helped either. If he had been frank about how frightened he was aboard the sinking *Titanic*, the fact that he had been unaware at the time that there were still women and children aboard, and how he had simply given thought to saving his own life, he may have escaped less harshly judged by the public. However, Ismay's image was always that of a person who lacked emotion, regret or remorse. People often did not believe Ismay even when he was truthful.

Ismay made some feeble attempts to repair his reputation. For instance, he immediately issued instructions to all lines owned by IMM to equip their ships with enough lifeboats to accommodate everyone aboard. But even *this* drew criticism, oddly from the *Board of Trade*. The BOT characterized his action as "precipitous" and cited the fact that Ismay had failed to consult with anyone, particularly marine architects and engineers, before making his decision.

It must be said, however, that Ismay had little choice. There had been a virtual mutiny aboard *Olympic*; most of her crew had deserted her after she arrived in Southampton, stating that they would not return until there were boats for all aboard. *Titanic's* boats, with anything that would indicate their origin carefully obliterated, would eventually be supplied to her older sister.[136]

Ismay soon discovered that nothing he did enabled him to atone for his perceived offenses. Never popular, people now had a reason to avoid him. Soon he found himself somewhat of a pariah. Invitations to social functions dried up almost instantly. He was shunned by his former acquaintances and people preferred not to do business with him- or White Star.

---

[136] Most anything removable that could associate the boat with *Titanic* had been taken by souvenir hunters aboard *Carpathia*. *Titanic's* painted name was sanded off in New York. But even her boats weren't sufficient to supply *Olympic*. She made do for a while with collapsibles, and finally had many more davits fitted to her boat deck with multiple boats beneath each.

Ismay was out of the company a little more than a year later- June 1913. Accounts diverge here, some stating that he had decided even before sailing on *Titanic* that he was going to leave; others state that he was asked to resign afterward. No matter what the reason, his public life was virtually over.

Ismay was still valued by a few for his business skills, and thus retained a few directorships within Britain. He kept a house in London, but essentially accepted exile to an estate in Ireland. When he did venture away from his property, he took measures to avoid contact with anyone. He would book an entire compartment on a train, so he would not have to share it. He even took pains to avoid the dining car by having a picnic hamper furnished to him.

Later in his life, Ismay made large donations to charities and engaged in other philanthropic work, but it seemed never to be enough to erase the stain on his reputation.

After a period of deteriorating health, in which he lost a leg to amputation, Ismay succumbed to a stroke in

1937, having never shed the stigma of surviving *Titanic*. He was buried in London, in a crypt that bears carvings of sailing ships.

Ironically, around the same time that Ismay departed, a ship to which his life had been inexorably linked, *Olympic*, was in the process of being scrapped in Scotland.

Unlike the former Chairman's funeral, which was lightly attended and scarcely mentioned in the press, *Olympic's* demise was chronicled all over Britain and sorely lamented. Hundreds, perhaps thousands, of people lined the banks of the river as she made her way to where she was dismantled.[137]

Ismay's wife was later quoted as saying- with the same apparent insensitivity that many attributed to Ismay- that *Titanic* "had ruined our lives."

---

[137] *Olympic* was actually scrapped in two different places. She first went to Jarrow, in Scotland, where she proved to be too large to be completely broken up. She then went to Iverkeithing, near Edinburgh, for final demolition.

Chapter Thirteen- Ice Warnings

Having set the stage and met those involved, we now need to go aboard *Titanic* and observe how the factors, conditions and personalities we have discussed interacted to contribute to the disaster.

The final voyage of *Titanic*, up to the moment the ice was sighted, is largely irrelevant to this discussion, except for a few incidents occurring before the collision.

The weather remained excellent throughout the trip. The winds were light, the sea was relatively calm and there were only a few isolated rain showers on the thirteenth.

Sailing day was warm for an April day in Southampton. The sky was overcast, but there were a few "sunny intervals," as the British optimistically like to refer to them.

Late in the morning, the boat train from London arrived and the embarkation of passengers began.

The ship must have been a delight to them as they boarded. Everything was new and *Titanic* was fragrant with the aromas of fresh paint, varnish, wood, pristine carpets, linoleum and furniture. Even veteran passengers must have felt a small thrill as they found their cabins.

Soon, a crowd began to gather on the various decks- depending on class of course- favoring the port side of the ship which was next to the pier.

From time to time Captain Smith could be seen on the bridge wings, accompanied by the pilot, George Bowyer.

Around noon, the gangways began to come off and the shell doors were secured. *Titanic* was now ready for sea.

The ship's whistle thundered over the crowd as the signal to cast off was made. Tugs approached the liner to assist her from her berth. *Titanic* had been moored stern-first at White Star's ocean dock to allow her swift departure.

Deep in the ship, the telegraphs began to ring in the engine room as the commands were sent down, Port engine- slow ahead, Starboard engine- dead slow ahead. The giant liner began to inch her way from the pier and into the channel. The decks began to tremble slightly as her massive engines began to turn.

Several minutes passed. "Uncle George," from his vantage on the bridge, satisfied that the ship was free of her moorings and clear of obstructions, rang down for an increase in engine revolutions.

Titanic began to make her way to the sea.

As she passed several smaller liners moored forward of her berth, sounds like rifle shots were heard to port, followed closely by the gasping of passengers lining the rail.

The source of the noises were lines on the liner *New York*, of the IMM owned American Line, snapping as *Titanic* passed alongside. The smaller ship heeled away from the pier, being dragged toward *Titanic* by the displacement of water by the larger vessel. It must have been a dramatic sight as *New York* left her berth, and in the process dropped two sixty-foot gangways into the water. Again, it appears that Smith and Bowyer had miscalculated the effect of a ship as large as *Titanic* had moving in a restricted space.

Titanic's starboard engine was immediately stopped and the port engine was reversed. Smith ordered the anchors be prepared to drop as a last ditch measure. They were not required, the reversed engine pushed *New York* away and a collision was narrowly averted. The smaller liner, which had drifted to within inches of *Titanic*, was eventually corralled. She was moved back to her berth by the tugs that had helped *Titanic* leave hers only minutes before.

Titanic began moving again, only to almost have the same effect on *Oceanic*- another White Star liner moored ahead of *New York*.[138] *Oceanic's* lines held and she only listed a few degrees before she was released by the pull of *Titanic* and returned to an even keel.

As soon as the smaller ships were cleared, speed was increased.

---

[138] Some accounts state that *New York* was moored outboard of *Oceanic* at the same pier- somewhat like she was double parked.

Off Cowes, a man equipped with a large format camera waited in a small boat. A local dentist named Becken; he had made it a habit to await each new liner as she sailed, in order to snap her picture.[139]

Smith ordered the whistle sounded. *Olympic* had almost run down Becken when she sailed on her maiden voyage the year before. Whether the whistle was intended as a warning to the photographer or serve as a friendly greeting, nobody knows.

Becken's image is probably the definitive photograph of *Titanic*, her graceful lines only marred by a few small streaks of rust on her white paintwork amidships.

Titanic negotiated the Bramble without incident and she then slowed to drop the pilot. Speed was increased as she entered the open ocean.

The first stop was Cherbourg, across the English Channel.

---

[139] Becken sold copies of his photographs, which became so popular that he began to photograph ships and boats as a living. His work- including the photograph he made of *Titanic*- continues to be sold.

Titanic waited in the harbor as tenders brought passengers and mail to her. Her stay was brief, only a few hours, and then she weighed anchor and proceeded to the port of Queenstown on the southern tip of Ireland.

As previously mentioned, during the passage to Ireland, Captain Smith ordered the ship to make a series of lazy "S" turns so he could judge her response to the rudder. Earlier, aboard *Olympic*, he had remarked to one of his junior officers that after commanding her on several voyages, he was finally beginning to be able to predict how she would react. These maneuvers were an apparent attempt to determine if *Titanic* would behave in a similar fashion.

Titanic anchored in the channel off Queenstown, and two tenders, named *Ireland* and *America*, brought passengers to her. She was also approached by what were called "bumboats." These were small vessels that carried locally made wares, such as fine Irish linen and lace to be peddled to passengers aboard the liner. The merchants set up shop on the boat deck and exhibited their goods to those who could most afford them. John

Jacob Astor was a customer, paying $1500 dollars for a single item.

During this pause in the voyage, there was a bit of a stir aboard. A stoker, believed to be seeking relief from the heat of the boiler rooms, had climbed the interior of the fourth funnel and stuck his head out to look at the crowd below. Some of the passengers who observed him were amused, but some others were disconcerted by the sight, and later called his appearance an “omen” of what was to come.

The vendors departed, along with the few passengers who had bought tickets only as far as Queenstown, and the ship was again readied for sea.

Following the departure from Ireland, the passengers quickly fell into the habits of a sea voyage. The crew did the same.

Thomas Andrews, *Titanic*'s builder, and the men who had accompanied him from Harland and Wolff had found the ship to be amazingly free of defects. Other than a piece of machinery in the first class galley refusing to function, and a trifling matter about coat hooks in some of the cabins being improperly secured, everyone aboard seemed to be more than satisfied with *Titanic's* performance. Even the notoriously unruly "black gang," who shoveled coal into *Titanic's* furnaces, characterized the ship as a "good job."

The only complication was the ice field that Smith knew lay ahead somewhere along *Titanic's* course.

One of the primary assertions made by many historians is that Smith, despite receiving numerous ice warnings which placed the danger squarely in his path, ignored them and knowingly drove her headlong into the area of risk.

Because this contention is so solidly embedded in the legend of the disaster, we must take some time and examine it.

Science defines "ice" as any one of fourteen different manifestations of frozen water. Some of these are common- others only exist in the laboratory, or in theory.

Simple ice, the form we are most familiar with, has one property that is not shared with most other frozen liquids. It expands as it freezes, and therefore is less dense than the liquid that it arises from. It floats.

The area to the east and southeast of Newfoundland had been known for years as a treacherous area requiring constant vigilance. Not only was there a danger from uncharted floating ice, it was further complicated by warm water carried north by the Gulf Stream which produced dense fogs as it came in contact with cold polar air- often reducing visibility to near zero.

Over the years the lines that served the North Atlantic had adopted a number of standardized courses which had evolved into eastbound and westbound shipping “lanes.” Ships were expected to stay within these course corridors to minimize the potential of collision.

However, the presence of drifting ice in these lanes imposed such a significant and almost ever-present danger to vessels in the North Atlantic that in

1898 the various lines serving it met in London and decided to move them south during the times of greatest hazard- which was most of the year. The area, somewhat paradoxically, was only known to be free of ice during the late autumn and winter. White Star had participated in the agreement. In fact, J. Bruce Ismay had chaired the meeting.

The Royal Navy also considered the area so dangerous that the Admiralty had included a section concerning North Atlantic ice in the sailing directions published by its Hydrographic department. These directions were undoubtedly aboard *Titanic*- probably in a brand new- and unopened- book in the chartroom.

They were specific.

"One of the chief dangers to which vessels are exposed in crossing the Atlantic lies in the probability of encountering masses of ice, both in the form of bergs and of extensive fields of solid compacted ice, released at the breaking up of winter in the Arctic regions, and drifting down the Labrador Current across their direct route. Ice is more likely to be encountered on this route between April and August, months inclusive, than at other times.

"The route chart of the North Atlantic, No. 2058, shows the limits within which both field ice and icebergs may be met with, and where it should be carefully looked out for at all times, but especially during the spring and summer seasons. From this chart it would appear that while the southern and eastern limits of field ice are about latitude 42 degrees north and longitude 45 degrees west, icebergs may be met with much farther from Newfoundland; in April, May and June they have been seen as far south as latitude 39 degrees north and as far east as latitude 38 degrees 30 minutes west. It is, in fact, impossible to give, within the outer limits named, any distinct idea of where ice may be expected, and no rule can be laid down to ensure safe navigation, as its position and the quantity met with differs so greatly in different seasons. Everything must depend on the vigilance, caution, and skill with which a vessel is navigated when crossing the dangerous ice bearing regions of the Atlantic Ocean."

Before wireless communication had come to sea, this section of ocean had claimed more than its share of ships- many of which disappeared without any trace.

Less than twenty years before the *Titanic* disaster, the most noted victim of this area was another White Star ship, *Naronic*. Like *Titanic*, she was similarly protected from collision. *Naronic* could remain afloat if two of her adjacent watertight compartments were breached, and the sea was "calm to moderate."

Naronic differed from *Titanic* in the respect that she was not a passenger ship, but a cargo vessel.

Information about *Naronic* and her fate is confused and somewhat contradictory. There is even disagreement about on what voyage she was lost.

Some accounts state that she was also on her maiden voyage, some say the seventh; some say the thirteenth.

There is even controversy about what kind of ship she was. But most accounts agree that she was a refrigerated cargo vessel- designed to carry cattle carcasses, and she had a small passenger accommodation. It was reported that she was lost with as many as eighty-four people aboard.

About the only thing certain about *Naronic* is that she sailed westbound- and disappeared. At the time she was lost, there was considerable debate, and speculation, about what caused her to founder. A collision with an iceberg was merely one theory. A shift in her cargo- or an explosion- was also advanced as a possible cause. Theories were as far as it got. No hard evidence was ever discovered and the mystery remains unclarified. Whatever claimed *Naronic*, all those aboard her had perished.

For many years afterward, bottles containing messages allegedly written aboard the foundering ship were found on both sides of the Atlantic. Messages in bottles supposedly from lost vessels are perhaps one of the oldest hoaxes known to man.

These were no different- all were eventually dismissed as fakes. The first was recovered only days after the ship was suspected lost, and could not have possibly drifted to where it was found in that time. All the other messages (except one which was not signed) bore names of people who were not aboard.

The only genuine artifacts found from *Naronic* were two of her lifeboats. They were adrift near where she had been presumed lost. One had capsized, the other was about half full of water. Neither boat had any survivors or bodies aboard. They were not recovered.

There had even been a previous accident in the area involving the "largest ship in the world"- a vessel named *Arizona*. In 1879, she sustained severe damage in a head-on collision with an iceberg while she was running at high speed though fog. She only just survived, managing to limp into St. Johns, Newfoundland.

Several other passenger ships had disappeared without a trace in the North Atlantic in the 20 years before *Titanic* sailed, with the loss of hundreds of lives. A collision with ice was often offered as a possible cause.

One commonly held belief about disaster is that the mass of ice that claimed the ship had only been there for a matter of a few days- appearing either around the time sailed or shortly after- but the truth is that it had been there for a month or more. Both the American Hydrographic Office and its British counterpart had issued warnings concerning the field.

It had already proven itself treacherous, almost sinking another liner- *Niagara*, of the French line. She had struck ice in the area less than two weeks before *Titanic*. *Niagara* had been seriously damaged- holed twice beneath her waterline. Her captain had even sent a wireless SOS call. This incident received almost no play in the newspapers until after *Titanic* disappeared.

There had been close calls to other ships during the same period. A Canadian Pacific liner, *Empress of*

India, had been forced to make a significant course change to the south, and a Cunard liner, *Carmania*, after finding herself in the field, spent several harrowing hours sailing slowly before she was able to successfully extract herself from the area of danger. Other ships in the vicinity during the time reported similar experiences.

Captain Smith had been made aware of the ice danger lurking in the North Atlantic shipping lanes before the ship sailed on April 10th. Fourth Officer Boxhall testified that the Captain had received, read, and discussed with his officers, the notices regarding the large area of floating ice. From what was known at the time *Titanic* sailed, the ice was in the vicinity of the Grand Banks. One of the officers- maybe Smith himself- had thought to leave a note on the chart with the penciled word “Ice” and its general position.

Ice in this area was not uncommon for April. The advisory probably did not trigger any apprehension, or even heightened concern, on the part of *Titanic's* officers. Ice was a fact of life in the North Atlantic- it was encountered as frequently as fog or bad weather. Smith, and other Captains under which he had served, had successfully evaded it for over thirty years, and there was no reason that he would have believed that this instance would be any different.

Smith was also aware that ice could assume many forms, and one of the more common was a slushy small-chunked type ice that would not damage the ship- only slow her progress as she plowed through it. This type of ice was often found in harbors- particularly in New York during the winter. Other types of ice, "pack ice" and "growlers" would present different concerns, as would an iceberg. All of these three- particularly the latter- would represent a serious collision hazard.

Smith's experience would have told him that ice moving into the warmer water of the Gulf Stream would disperse quickly, either melting away entirely or becoming "rotten," soft and slushy. However, he also would have known that the southern edge of an ice field was sometimes its most dangerous area. The last ice to melt would be the bergs, and sometimes they could be found miles south and east from the main body of ice.

On the other hand, they were usually easily seen and avoided.

The Captain weighed his options and plotted a course which he believed would carry *Titanic* well south of the region of reported danger, through an area of the sea that his experience told him should be ice-free.

What Smith was not told, mainly because no one was aware of it at the time, was that the polar winter had been much milder than it had been in the previous fifty years. An immense mass of ice, liberated by the warmer temperatures, was drifting down the Labrador Current into regions of the ocean where it had never been seen before, even by mariners with considerable experience sailing in the area.

The ice was a common topic on the wireless airwaves and *Titanic* began to receive ice reports from other ships shortly after she left Ireland.

The first recorded ice message received by *Titanic* was on April 12th, two days after she departed Southampton. It originated with the French Liner *La Touraine*. Her message detailed at least three hazards.

"My position 7 p.m., GMT, latitude 49.28 longitude. 26.28. Dense fog since this night. Crossed thick ice field latitude 44.58, longitude 50.40. *Paris* saw a derelict latitude 40.56, longitude 68.38. *Paris* please give me position. Best regards and Bon Voyage. Caussin."

This message had an abundance of bad news, noting not just the ice field, but also a floating wreck, and an area of extremely limited visibility- all of which would have indicated the necessity of increased vigilance and caution.

E.J. got the message- and *La Touraine* shortly received a response. Smith thanked them for the information, gave his position and told them that he was having "fine weather."

Smith probably looked at the coordinates- without even plotting them on a chart- and found reassurance that his assumptions about the extent of the ice were proving correct. The location of the ice defined by *La Touraine* was over two hundred miles north of *Titanic's* projected course, just about where Smith would have expected to find it this time of year.

Titanic received no messages regarding the field on April 13th, which may have reinforced Smith's perception that the ice danger was routine.

The next message regarding the hazard was sent at 0900 on April 14th from the Cunard liner *Caronia*. It was short and to the point. "Captain - *Titanic* Westbound steamers report bergs, growlers, and field ice in 42 degrees North from 49 degrees to 50 degrees west."

This message placed the ice danger much closer- a little over 30 miles north of *Titanic's* track. The lookouts would have to keep a sharp eye out, but based on the message, the ice was still a comfortable distance away.

At 1140 *Caronia* sent *Titanic* another message. It was relayed from another liner, *Noordam*- out of range for direct wireless transmission to *Titanic*. "Congratulations on new command. Had moderate westerly winds, fine weather, no fog, much ice reported in latitude 42 degrees 24 minutes to 42 degrees forty five minutes and longitude 49 degrees fifty minutes to fifty degrees twenty minutes."

This message seems to be a bit more comforting- at least the visibility had improved- Smith's lookouts would probably be able to spot the ice as the ship entered the area of danger, but it does state that there was "much" ice, but significantly, it placed the ice farther away than the original *Caronia* message- between 74 and 113 miles north of course.

Around 1300, another message came across the wireless- this time from *Baltic*- another White Star Liner. "Captain *Titanic*. Have had moderate, variable winds, and clear, fine weather since leaving. Greek steamer *Athenai* reports passing icebergs and large quantities of field ice today in latitude 49 degrees fifty one minutes north longitude 49 degrees 51 minutes west. Wish you and *Titanic* all success. Commander."

Smith made formal replies to all these transmissions, so we know he had received and read them.

Shortly after receiving the *Baltic* message, Smith encountered Ismay on “A” deck. Without comment or explanation, Smith took the Marconigram and handed it to the Chairman.

Ismay read it. However, instead of returning it to Smith, Ismay placed it in his coat pocket. It resided there- without being relayed to anyone else on the crew- for several hours.

Ismay was reported to have shown the message to a number of his fellow first-class passengers- as a sort of curiosity- before Smith retrieved it shortly before dinner. The Captain approached Ismay in the smoking room and asked for the message so he could post it in the chartroom “for the benefit of his officers.”

One may wonder why the Captain decided to leave the *Baltic* message with his boss, or if it had been his intent at all. Smith may have only tendered the message to the Chairman so he could read it and may have been somewhat surprised by Ismay’s decision to keep it. If Smith had any objection to Ismay keeping the message, he obviously decided not to make an issue of it, probably feeling that the other messages posted in the chartroom more than covered the ice danger.[140]

Over the years, many authors have singled out this "lost" message and the apparently casual attitude of Ismay and particularly Smith toward it. The obvious inference is made that instead of it being allowed to reside in Ismay's pocket, it should have been brought to the attention of Smith's subordinates- the assumption being that the information it contained may have prevented the loss of the ship.

However, the message *Baltic* relayed from *Athenai* was actually irrelevant. It placed the ice danger at over twice the distance of the *La Touraine* message- 550 miles away to the north.

But there *were* messages received by *Titanic* that accurately described the danger.

Shortly after *Baltic's* message was received, *Titanic's* wireless operators were asked to relay a

---

[140] There was testimony later that the message from *Caronia* was the only message posted in the chartroom. However, this is logical, as it was the one message that Smith saw that placed the ice closest to *Titanic's* course.

message from the German Liner *Amerika* to the United States Hydrographic office in Washington. "*Amerika* passed two large icebergs in 41 degrees twenty seven minutes north, 50 degrees eight minutes west, on April 14th."

If *Titanic* continued on course, she would pass nineteen miles *north* of where *Amerika* reported these icebergs to be.

Unfortunately, this message was never delivered to the bridge, and Captain Smith was never made aware of its contents.

The reason was chiefly due to the way Marconi categorized traffic. *Amerika's* ice report was not addressed to *Titanic* and it was classified as a "service" message, which required no action on the part of the operator other than to relay it. Senior operator Phillips took down the transmission, and since the contents of the message apparently meant nothing to him- he did not take it to the bridge. It sat on the wireless desk until almost 2100 when contact was made with Cape Race. It was then sent on, along with the other outgoing messages, and forgotten.

About 1930, *Titanic* intercepted another Marconigram. It was being transmitted to *Antillian* by *Californian*. "To Captain, *Antillian*. 18:30 apparent ship's time; latitude 42 degrees three minutes north, longitude 49 degrees nine minutes west. Three large bergs five miles to the southward of us." This message placed the ice around ninety miles north of course.

Although it was not addressed to *Titanic*, junior operator Bride took the initiative to deliver the message to the bridge. Bride also contacted *Californian* and informed operator Evans that he had listened in on the message and taken it down.

Smith could only form an opinion about the potential danger to his ship based on the information he was provided. The message that placed ice nearest the ship, from *Caronia*, was hours old. Here was a fresh message that indicated the danger at a distance almost three times farther away.

As most Captains would have done, Smith obviously decided to continue on course, and at his present speed, to await further developments or subsequent messages.

At 2140 on the 14th- less than two hours before the collision- *Titanic* received another wireless message. It was from a ship of the Atlantic Transport line- *Mesaba*:

"From *Mesaba* to *Titanic*. Ice report in latitude 42 degrees north to 41 degrees twenty five minutes north, Longitude 49 degrees to 50 degrees thirty minutes west. Saw much heavy pack ice and a great number large icebergs. Also field ice. Weather good, clear."

S. H. Adams, *Mesaba's* radio operator, received a curt "OKRD" from *Titanic*, wireless shorthand meaning "message received." He stated later that he stood by waiting for a more formal response, but there was nothing to indicate that the message had been delivered to Captain Smith or he had acknowledged it.

The *Mesaba's* ice report is the first message to mention the words "heavy" regarding the amount of ice and the assessment that there were a "great number" of icebergs. And, significantly, it placed the danger squarely astride *Titanic's* course. In fact, when the message was received, *Titanic* had already entered the western edge of the area defined by the message and it indicated the ice extended *sixty five miles south* of her intended path.

But Smith did not ignore this message.

He never saw it.

Nobody aboard *Titanic*, except for Jack Phillips- the wireless operator who took down the message from *Mesaba*- ever read it.

The prompt delivery of this communication would have been required by Marconi regulations, but Phillips apparently decided that the large amount of work he had before him was more pressing. Adams later stated that he heard *Titanic* again calling Cape Race immediately after Phillips responded to him.

Titanic's Marconi office had been unable to transmit a large amount of passenger messages that had been gathering all afternoon and evening because of an equipment failure. Her transmitter had failed either Saturday evening or Sunday morning (accounts disagree) and was out of service for almost seven hours as Harold Bride searched for the problem- which turned out to be an electrical short- and fixed it. As soon as the transmitter was repaired, he and Phillips had struggled to cope with the crush of unsent messages.

They then had a large backlog of incoming messages to deal with. Phillips began to laboriously take down the Marconigrams addressed to *Titanic* being transmitted by Cape Race.

During this period, operator Evans, aboard *Californian*, tried to contact *Titanic* again with a fresh ice warning, but Phillips rebuked him for interfering with his work and failed to record the message. This attempted transmission will be discussed in more detail later.

Phillips knew that *Titanic* had received several ice warnings and probably believed- as most of us would have- that the ship was in capable hands, adequate precautions were being taken, and there was no pressing need to relay this message to the bridge. He also, undoubtedly, had no idea of the ship's position.

To Phillips, the *Mesaba* message was just another ice report- the officers knew there was ice somewhere ahead. He may have intended to have Harold Bride deliver it to the bridge as soon as the junior operator rose from bed.[141]

The message from *Californian* never got through- and Phillips may not have identified it as a warning.

It appears that the officers aboard *Titanic*, including Smith, were relying on the wireless operators to relay messages regarding the ice, and it also appears that the wireless operators were equally expecting the ship's officers to anticipate and deal with the danger.

So does this lack of information absolve Captain Smith?

The Captain must have realized, particularly after receiving *Caronia* message- that placed the ice much closer than the others- that it would be reckless to

---

[141] Phillips told Lightoller about the *Mesaba* message shortly before he died clinging to overturned collapsible "C". Phillips told the 2nd officer that he had stuck it under a paperweight and forgotten about it.

assume that he had the full story about the threat to his ship.

Smith must have decided that it would be best to press on and assess the danger once the ship neared the field. He could alter course or reduce speed at that time, if he felt it was required. To Smith, visibility would have been the key factor, and he had been assured that it was excellent in the area of danger.

The Captain did implement some precautions. There is evidence that he or one of the other senior officers ordered a position fix made around 19:00 so the ship's distance from the reported ice could be confirmed.

Smith also ordered one other safety measure-delaying a course change. Ships sailing between Europe and North America could not sail an optimum great circle route because of Ireland and Newfoundland blocking their path, therefore they sailed a modified great circle until they reached a point to the southeast of Newfoundland. There they made a turn to the west to sail directly to New York. The area where they traditionally made the turn was informally referred to as the "corner," and it was called "turning the corner." Smith had postponed this change in course to take the ship farther south- estimated as anywhere between three and seventeen miles.

Smith must have believed that this delay in changing course would steer *Titanic* well away from the area of ice danger, and that no other precautions were required.

Oddly, although Smith seemed to be content that his lookouts were adequate, apparently nobody thought to check with them and assure they were ready. Had this happened, the matter regarding their lack of binoculars probably would have surfaced. The lookouts had complained earlier that they had no binoculars in the nest, but to Lightoller, not the Captain.

Smith could have been on the bridge at the time the encounter with the ice was expected. Instead, he decided to go to bed, leaving the task to his subordinates.

There was some debate among the officers about when the ship would reach the area where ice might be encountered. Lightoller believed that it would be as early as 20:00. Boxhall believed it would be later, around 23:00. However, Smith must have been aware that she would probably near the heaviest of the ice field sometime after dark on the 14th. He appeared on the bridge after dinner- sometime between 20:30 and 21:00 and discussed it with Lightoller, who was on duty.[142]

Smith reminded his junior about the ice warnings and told him to alert his lookouts. He also mentioned the possibility of fog or haze and remarked that the ship would have to reduce speed if conditions deteriorated.

---

[142] Smith had just come from a dinner party being thrown in the Ala Carte' restaurant in his honor by a couple named Widener. Those in attendance later dismissed allegations that Smith had liberally imbibed and was somewhat tipsy at the time of the accident. They all confirmed that Smith had consumed no alcohol at all. Some authors have used this dinner party as an illustration of how a Captain's duties could be divided aboard these large liners. Instead of attending to the safe navigation of the ship, Smith was keeping the customers happy. There was a White Star regulation that anticipated this problem, stating "Convivial intercourse with passengers is to be avoided." However Smith, and most of his contemporaries, regularly ignored this regulation, with the apparently tacit approval of the company.

After *Titanic* went down, White Star added another officer to the crew of each of its larger ships, an "Assistant" or "Staff" Captain. This officer was charged with seeing to the safety of the ship, organizing drills and administering her evacuation plans, lifeboat drills and other related matters. He was also given the task of taking the Captain's place at many of the social engagements aboard, freeing the Senior Captain to concentrate on the safe navigation of the vessel.

He then gave Lightoller vague instructions to call him at once if it became "doubtful." He told his second officer to pass on his concerns to the following watch, which would come on duty at 22:00.

Smith apparently believed that the key to the safety of the ship was visibility, but paradoxically- even aware of the possible danger to his ship- he failed to post additional lookouts.[143]

This is somewhat hard to understand- perhaps it was an oversight- or Smith, observing conditions himself, decided that the lookouts in place in the crow's nest and the officers on the bridge were a sufficient number of observers.

Lightoller later testified that visibility on the night of the disaster had been excellent, stating that is was possible to watch the setting of stars on the horizon.

---

[143] Here we are presented with another seeming inconsistency in Smith's actions. He mentioned the possibility of visibility problems, but he failed to take elementary precautions to detect or deal with them. It was common knowledge to lookouts that a light haze sometimes could not be detected from the crows nest, but it could be seen from deck- thus the employment of additional lookouts on the bow of the ship. In fact, lookouts posted on the bow were said to be stationed "in the eyes of the ship."

Smith commented to Lightoller about how unusually calm the sea was, which would be an obvious hindrance to spotting ice. He also would have been more than aware that there would be no moon during the hours of darkness,[144] and that any floating hazard would be lit only by starlight. Nevertheless, Smith must have thought that the visibility was adequate and no speed reduction was required. He must have felt that there needed to be additional elements, such as the appearance of fog, before it would be warranted.

An unanswered question is what Smith would have done if conditions *had* deteriorated. Would he have ordered a speed reduction?

The company, at least officially, would have sanctioned such a move. In the chartroom of each ship in White Star service was a framed notice detailing the formal duties of her officers.

---

[144] The moon had set in the afternoon. Even had it been shining at the time of the accident, it probably would have been little help- as only between nine and four percent of its disk was illuminated.

The first rule detailed "the vital importance of exercising the utmost caution in navigation, *safety outweighing every other consideration*." The emphasis is in the original document.

An additional entry on this notice also warned about the danger of "overconfidence," stating that it should be "especially guarded against."

The same notice specifically tasked the Chief Officer with the duty of warning the Captain if he felt the ship was not being sailed with proper regard to safety. However, had he been given the same information as Smith, Wilde would have most likely agreed with his superior. The other officers would have as well.

But White Star, like many corporations, displayed an inconsistency between what its procedures dictated and what was actually expected. These posted notices apparently received the same attention as the ice warnings.

In fact, if the White Star regulations are examined in relation to this accident, it appears that more than a few were ignored.

Unfortunately, Smith's thoughts on that night will be forever unknown, but it's clear that he must have considered the risk acceptable and also believed he had taken ample precautions.

Chapter Fourteen- The Warning that Never Was

Before we progress further, we need to pause for a few seconds and discuss another ice warning.

This message, which has now entered the lore of the accident, was allegedly transmitted to *Titanic* on the night of April 14th. It was not sent by wireless, but by Morse lamp (blinker), from a steamer named *Rappahannock* less than an hour before the collision. If this message was received aboard *Titanic*, then *all* the wireless messages warning her of the ice are reduced to irrelevancy. *Rappahannock's* message placed the ice danger in close proximity directly ahead of *Titanic*.

However, there are questions about this message, beginning with when it was sent. Geoffrey Marcus, in *The Maiden Voyage* stated that on April 14, around 2230- and about a half hour after 1st officer Murdoch took over from Lightoller and roughly an hour before the collision- a ship was sighted steering a nearly parallel- but opposite- course to *Titanic*. It was outbound from Halifax- also under the command of another

Captain named Smith- Albert E. Smith- of no relation to E.J.

It was *Rappahannock*, a ship owned by the Furness-Withy company. It had just exited the ice field. The traverse had been, to say the least, an experience for the crew of the smaller ship. Her Captain had been overcome by an ailment serious enough that Smith, who had been second in command, had been asked to take over for the remainder of the voyage.

The field was full of thick pack ice, growlers and large icebergs. Although Smith had taken *Rappahannock* cautiously through the area- at very low speed- she had been well beaten up- sustaining serious damage to her bow, propeller and rudder.

In the darkness, *Rappahannock's* blinker was seen aboard the speeding White Star Liner. "Have just passed through heavy field ice and several icebergs."

Titanic's response was brief. "Message received. Thanks. Good night."

Here, apparently, was one last ignored ice warning.

However, although *Rappahannock* message has been cited as a pivotal element in several books about the tragedy, there is debate as to when- or if- it occurred.

The first clue that there might be a problem with this story is a disagreement between other authors about when the message was sent. For instance, Walter Lord, in *The Night Lives On*, his second book about *Titanic*, stated that *Rappahannock's* message was transmitted to the doomed liner on the night *before* the collision, on *April 13th*.[145] However, the text of the message appeared to be essentially the same. This appears odd, because a message stating that *Rappahannock* had "just exited" the ice field- when it was at least a day's sailing behind the ship, would have been inaccurate and misleading.

It is obviously important to determine when the message was sent. If it were dispatched to *Titanic* less than an hour before the collision, then we have direct

---

[145] As we will shortly see why, there was no mention of the *Rappahannock* message in Lord's first book, "*A Night to Remember*" which was published in 1957.

evidence that her crew was negligent. If it were sent the night before, then it assumes much less importance. In fact, had it been sent the previous night, and no large ice field materialized, *Titanic*'s officers may have disregarded it entirely.

But there are serious doubts about whether the message from *Rappahannock* was sent at all.

There is no question that *Rappahannock* traversed the ice field, because one of her crew took photographs of it, but there is uncertainty about the position of the smaller ship in relation to *Titanic*.

The first word of *Rappahannock's* connection with the *Titanic* disaster came in a newspaper account, derived from an interview with Albert Smith- who is identified as, not her Captain or even her acting Captain, but as her *Chief Officer*.

Written shortly after the sinking, the story noted that the crew of *Rappahannock* had seen *Titanic* on April 13th as the smaller ship emerged from a rain squall.

Apparently the news value of the piece lay simply in that the crew of *Rappahannock* was presumed to be the last people to have seen *Titanic* before she sank- nothing more.

The article spends time noting Smith's impressions of the ice field and how large it was, but- astonishingly- it fails to mention anything of the dramatic last warning message transmitted on his order to the liner regarding the ice danger that lay in such close proximity.

However, it appears that by 1962- when Smith was over eighty- his memory had improved, and sometime during the interim he had received a retroactive promotion.

In a letter written to a London newspaper, Smith reported that he, as *Captain* of *Rappahannock*, directed that the Morse message be sent to *Titanic* regarding the peril posed by the ice directly in her path. Smith stated that the message was sent at 22:30 on the night of the disaster and that the larger ship had acknowledged it.

If the story is true, then why did *Titanic* ignore such a compelling warning? As Smith related the contents, *Rappahannock's* message could not be misinterpreted. *Titanic* was steering into a dangerous ice field. Why did Murdoch fail to address this with Captain Smith? If he did, why was the decision made to continue with no course change or speed reduction?

The answer lies in that Murdoch, and *Titanic*, never received *any* warning from *Rappahannock*.

There are numerous discrepancies between the 1912 account Smith gave the newspaper and the letter he mailed forty years later which supposedly recounted the same events.

Simple calculations reveal that *Rappahannock's* April 14th position, as reported by Smith, is in conflict with other facts known about her voyage.

Rappahannock departed Halifax on April 9th and arrived at her destination, Gravesend, a port on the Thames near London, ten days later. These dates may be confirmed by consulting archived newspapers in both Halifax and London, which recorded the arrival and departures of ships as a matter of routine.

The time interval required to make this voyage was consistent with others she made between the two ports- indicating an average speed of about 11 knots- or about 265 nautical miles a day.

Titanic's wreck is located approximately 600 miles east of Halifax, and elementary arithmetic indicates that the Rappahannock would have passed this area sometime on April 12th- not two days later.

If *Rappahannock* actually was near where *Titanic* struck the berg, her average speed could not have exceeded five knots during the five days following her departure from Halifax.

The point may be made that *Rappahannock* could have been significantly slowed by the ice pack in the area and this would have greatly diminished her average speed. However, if we accept this premise, then we must also believe that, to make her April 19th arrival, the ship then had to complete her voyage at an average speed of 19 knots.

Rappahannock was only capable of thirteen.

There are other unresolved questions.

If the dates in both accounts are correct, *Rappahannock* would have had to be in two places at once, in mid Atlantic- having encountered *Titanic* on the 13th, and also much farther to the west- having encountered her again the day afterward. She would have had to have reversed course, outrun the liner, and then reversed course again. Obviously this would have been impossible.

If *Rappahannock* was seriously damaged it would seem prudent that her Captain- and it appears doubtful that Smith was actually in command- would have sought repair at the nearest port, somewhere in Ireland or on the West coast of England- or if the damage was severe- even the southeastern coast of Newfoundland.

However, the ship continued on her way, across the Atlantic, around the southern tip of Britain, up the English Channel and on to the Thames estuary, which is on the East coast of England.

There was no recorded observation of *Rappahannock*- or of any message, by any of the surviving members of *Titanic*'s crew or passengers, nor any of *Rappahannock's* crew- other than Smith.

In an age where newspapers paid substantial fortunes for exclusive stories regarding major events, did it just slip Smith's mind that he and his ship had sent a last warning message to *Titanic* that could have saved her?

Chapter Fifteen- The Collision

Unfortunately, the first accurate warning of ice received by *Titanic*, and acted upon by her officers, was also her last one.

Lookout Fredrick Fleet had been on duty for a little under an hour and a half. He and his companion in the crow's nest, Reginald Lee, were nearing the end of their two hours on- and four hours off- watch at midnight.[146]

Being a lookout on a North Atlantic Liner- particularly one like *Titanic*- was a position of some prestige. It involved no physical work- save climbing the ladder inside *Titanic*'s foremast- but it paid more than a regular deckhand's job.

The extra money was not just a meaningless perk- lookouts were exposed to the elements throughout

---

[146] Traditionally, shipboard watches begin every four hours- at twelve, four, and eight- either AM or PM. The time of the watches are struck with ships bells. The clock strikes one the first half-hour of each watch, and then strikes an additional bell each half hour until it reaches a total of eight at the watch change. The bells are struck in pairs, giving the ship's clock its distinctive "ding-ding, ding-ding," sound. However, White Star apparently did not observe the traditional watch times, instead beginning at six, ten and two.

the duration of their duty. This frequently meant standing their watches in lashing rain, wind, sleet, snow, or at the other end of the spectrum- blazing sun and heat. The duty could be miserable, interminably long, and often it was excruciatingly boring.

Tonight, the duty was not all that unpleasant, the biggest drawback was the cold- the temperature was hovering around 32 degrees Fahrenheit- and the eye-watering twenty-two knot wind blowing aft- caused by *Titanic* shearing through the still night air- produced a wind chill of about four degrees in the crow's nest. It was a bone-chilling and finger-numbing cold. But, it could have been worse. At least the night was dry and the visibility was good.[147]

When the watch changed at 22:00, the previous lookouts had passed on something about being alert for

---

[147] Both Fleet and Lee later testified about a light haze being in the air at the time they came on watch. One of the lookouts on the previous watch also mentioned it, but apparently neither bothered to report this visibility problem to the bridge. There has always been some debate about whether this "haze" actually existed, or it was an invention of the lookouts to shift some of the blame for not spotting the iceberg sooner away from them. Fleet spent the rest of his life in torment resulting from his role in the loss of *Titanic*.

small ice and growlers- 2nd officer Lightoller had been concerned enough to call the crow's nest and ask them to relay the warning to Fleet and Lee.

However, it's a matter of debate about how much impact this warning had. It appears that being told to watch for "small ice and growlers" may have somewhat of a joke to North Atlantic lookouts (something like "don't take any wooden nickels.") It may have not carried any weight at all.

It did not seem as if Mr. Murdoch and Mr. Moody, who were now on watch, were as worried about the ice as Lightoller had been- in fact there had been nothing from the bridge since the watch had changed. Ordinarily, there was not a great deal of communication between the bridge and the crow's nest, so it could be that the bulk of the danger was already behind the ship, but it did not hurt to be sharp.

Mr. Murdoch was not totally unconcerned about the danger- he had sent a crewman forward a short time earlier to close a hatch that had been giving off some light and possibly spoiling their night vision.

From his perch above the deck, Fleet could see over two miles farther than the men on the darkened bridge behind him, but paradoxically, even though *Titanic* was faster and more difficult to stop than most other ships, her design would actually impair the visibility of her lookouts.

Since it simply would not do to have passengers stumbling blindly around the exterior decks at night, liners had to provide light for those aboard. If left in the dark they could easily be injured- or even fall overboard. So while a freighter might have no external lighting at all, save for her navigation and masthead lights, *Titanic* was literally ablaze. The glass domes over the two first class stairways were dazzlingly illuminated. The promenade and boats decks were also brightly lit, and the pale color of the funnels that towered behind the lookouts reflected much of this light forward. The sea also mirrored light from the ship.

Additionally, the lookouts were required to periodically examine the ship's running lights and inform the bridge of their function. Even a glance at a light would impair night vision for a few moments.

Occasionally, Fleet would turn aft and see Murdoch, clad in his heavy bridge coat, standing on the wing- scanning the horizon with his binoculars, and probably wondering why he, a lookout- of all people aboard- was without a pair.

However, there was some debate, even among the lookouts themselves, about whether binoculars provided any advantage. There were two schools of thought. One maintained that binoculars narrowed the field of view too sharply, and a broader picture of the area ahead of the ship was required. That may have been true, particularly in seeing moving objects, such as other ships.

The other side of the debate thought that the light gathering power of binoculars enhanced the probability of spotting objects on dark nights and would be invaluable in detecting them at long range. Tonight, binoculars may have been useful as Fleet and Lee were watching for stationary hazards- icebergs- and the night was dark. It may have been a moot point though. Fleet stated, at the American hearing, that most lookouts used their binoculars only *after* an object was sighted in the path of the ship- to confirm its identity. Fleet added that the binoculars furnished by White Star were often of such low quality that they were virtually useless.[148]

Even with good binoculars, sighting icebergs could be tricky under the best of conditions. Most often the bergs were coarse-surfaced and snow white- the traditional way an iceberg is depicted. But there was a different- more dangerous- variant, a glassy smooth berg that was a deep cobalt blue. Called "black (or blue)

---

[148] In fact, White Star had ceased provisioning binoculars to the lookouts aboard their ships in 1895. Instead, the line deemed it to be the responsibility of the officers who essentially had to supply the binoculars with money from their own pockets. Since good binoculars were frequently "lost" (stolen and sold) by the lookouts, the officers soon began to buy cheaper pairs.

On *Titanic*, the original 2nd officer, David Blair, had provided the binoculars, but when he was bumped from the ship by the last minute insertion of Wilde as Chief, he retrieved them and locked them away in his cabin- apparently not informing Lightoller, who had taken his position. Lightoller later looked for them, but searched for them in Murdoch's cabin instead of his own. It's been stated that Blair left the ship carrying the key to the locker where he stowed the binoculars, and therefore they could not be retrieved. Blair undoubtedly expected to return to *Titanic* after her maiden voyage, and probably wanted to assure himself that his property would still be aboard when he did.

bergs," they resulted from an iceberg breaking up and exposing either a fresh, unweathered surface, or because of melting, the iceberg's center of gravity would change and it would roll over, exposing a side that had been previously underwater. These bergs were virtually invisible at night- particularly one without a moon like the night of April 14, 1912.[149]

Experienced lookouts had developed techniques, some of questionable effectiveness, to cope with this problem. One trick was to watch for waves breaking along the base of the bergs. Another was to look for areas of the sky that seemed to be "blacked out," indicating their presence. Unfortunately, the second method was unreliable- because it required the berg to be large and near the horizon, and the first method was useless tonight. There was no discernible

---

[149] "Black" bergs are exceedingly rare. Many mariners who regularly sail in areas where ice is common will never see such a berg during their career. It is unknown if the berg that sank the *Titanic* was such, but it appears that it was not. According to Walter Lord in *A Night To Remember*, a German ship, *Prinz Adelbert*, was near the scene of the accident on April 15. An iceberg was sighted, and photographed, that was different than the others that had been seen that day. This one had an immense scar of red paint near the base.

wave action. Some lookouts maintained that they could "smell" ice[150] or that bergs could be expected if there was a sharp drop in air temperature- indicating they were near- but most seamen found these methods extremely unreliable. If all else failed- bergs could sometimes be seen in reflected starlight.

In fact, there *had* been a significant drop in temperature- of over ten degrees- during the two hours before the ship encountered the ice. Thermometers aboard *Titanic* were showing a sea temperature of 31 degrees, and an air temperature of 32, prompting Lightoller to alert the engine room and the ship's carpenters to see to the ship's fresh water supplies to keep them from freezing. There was no reason to alert the lookouts to the plunge in temperature but exposed to the unremitting chill breeze generated by the ship's momentum, they were undoubtedly aware of it.

---

[150] An assertion that's not as strange as it sounds. Some icebergs contain a large amount of frozen organic matter and as the berg thaws, this substance begins to decay. This gives the berg a distinctly foul odor. Melting icebergs often emit a fresh water aroma, somewhat like that of approaching rain, so depending on the direction and the speed of the wind; it is possible at times to "smell" ice.

Titanic- amply warned- and almost totally unprepared- plowed steadily through the sea, her bow slicing through the glassy water at full speed.

Suddenly, Fleet thought he saw something. He looked again- it was not his imagination. He nudged Lee and pointed toward it. Almost without thinking, he grasped the lanyard on the crow's nest bell- sounding it three times as he reached for the telephone.

A seeming eternity passed. Finally the telephone clicked and the voice of 4th officer Moody was heard. "What did you see?" he asked.

"Iceberg- right ahead!" called Fleet.

"Thank you." To Fleet, the voice sounded strangely detached and unconcerned.[151] The phone clicked again. Moody had replaced the receiver. Fleet and Lee now watched as the mass of ice steadily became larger and larger.

---

[151] Moody's reply, "Thank you," shocked many at the time Fleet related the response in his testimony. One newspaper even headlined it. To them it seemed to illustrate the lack of concern displayed by the officers aboard *Titanic*. As noted above, Moody did not survive *Titanic*, so we only have Fleet's word for what was said.

The ship continued on- then at what seemed to be the very last second- her bow began to slowly swing to port. Maybe they were going to clear. If they did, it was going to be close- really close. Both lookouts found themselves tightly gripping the rim of the nest and holding their breaths.

Fleet later told Senate Investigators that the iceberg originally looked extremely small- like two of the tables in the hotel suite being used for the hearing placed next to each other, but by the time the ship came alongside, it towered fifty feet or more over the deck. He said it looked like *Titanic* was going to miss the berg, but as she brushed past- ice showered the fore and well decks and there was a pronounced shimmer felt though the ship. She soon stopped.

We cannot, with any certainty, determine how far the iceberg was from *Titanic* when Fleet first saw it, but we may make some assumptions. Both lookouts estimated that the berg was less than a mile ahead of the ship when it was first seen. This appears to be confirmed by the fact that *Titanic* had begun her turn when she struck the berg.

Obviously, to 1st officer Murdoch, there were only two courses of action open to him- reverse engines to slow or stop the ship before she came into contact with the ice- or trying to steer the ship clear.

With only seconds to make a decision, he undoubtedly did what his instincts and years of experience told him to do. He ordered "hard a-starboard" (which at that time actually ordered a hard turn to port) and signaled the engine room to reverse the engines- and he's been second-guessed ever since by people who have had all the time they needed to decide what they would have done.

And, there is one factor that it appears that no one has considered before. Murdoch had absolutely no idea how long it would take *Titanic*'s rudder to make a full deflection, how rapidly she would react to the change in rudder angle, and even what her turning radius would be.

Murdoch, in fact, had asked *Titanic* to make a maneuver that nobody else had ever attempted- not even with *Olympic*- a hard turn at high speed with a loaded ship- the engines ordered full astern.[152]

And, unfortunately, Murdoch's experience in handling *Titanic* would have been absolutely zero. He was not on the bridge to observe her behavior as she exited Southampton. Instead he was stationed aft- on the docking bridge. When the ship departed Cherbourg or Queenstown, there would have been almost no maneuvering required, as the ship was anchored offshore instead of docked. Smith would have rung down for engines and the wheel would be shifted until the desired course was being steered. Murdoch's actions were totally based on how smaller, and more maneuverable, ships had reacted before.

---

[152] Both of the big liners had undergone brief acceptance trials in Belfast Lough prior to their acceptance by White Star. Each ship was brought full astern from full ahead and made hard turns at high speed. These trials were made with light loads- almost no loaded stores, no passengers, and because of the coal strike, *Titanic* had very little coal aboard.

Murdoch's experience on *Olympic* would have probably been much the same. Unfortunately, the only skill a watch-keeping officer aboard either of the big White Star liners would have would be to maintain course, and occasionally ordering a gentle turn to avoid another ship.

Even Captain Smith may have been unable to reliably predict how *Titanic* would react to the combination of rudder and engine commands that Murdoch ordered at the time the iceberg was sighted, because the only experience he had with either ship was at low speeds, and generally she was under pilot during those times.

The "perfect" course of action does not exist- a solution that guarantees undamaged survival of the ship. There are a few alternatives that may have resulted in less damage than the ship actually sustained, and her survival, but none guarantee it. There are far too many variables and unknowns to accurately forecast what harm *Titanic* would have experienced in these different scenarios.

What if *Titanic* had managed to turn sooner- or her turn had been tighter? She may have missed the iceberg completely. If there had been a collision, the iceberg may have contacted the ship further aft, leaving some of the forward compartments intact and able to furnish buoyancy. The ship may have remained afloat- depending on what damage she actually incurred. There may have been some additional damage as water flooded into her boiler rooms and possibly her engine spaces. She may have suffered boiler explosions as the cold seawater flooded into the bottom of the ship, but if the rate of flooding was similar to what actually was experienced, the boiler room crews may have been able to draw the fires and exhaust the steam from the boilers before the water reached them.[153] *Titanic* may have found herself without power and unable to maneuver, but she may have survived.

---

[153] The reader may wonder how a boiler can explode when it comes into contact with cold seawater- it sounds somewhat counterintuitive. However, steel is easily fractured by virtually instant cooling. This would allow the boiler to explode.

Let's go the other way now. What if *Titanic* had turned slower or she did not turn at all? Had she sustained damage to only one or two forward compartments, she would have remained afloat and her passengers would have lived. Her maiden voyage would have been marred, Ismay would have gotten a different set of headlines than he wanted, but the ship would have lived to sail out her career.

If *Titanic* had hit the iceberg head-on there probably would have been casualties- steerage males and crew who occupied cabins in the forward part of the ship, but again, the ship may have survived. Damage would have been extensive, but the *Olympic* class ships had been designed to cope with just such collisions. Even had she breached her first four compartments, *Titanic* would have settled at the bow, probably to an alarming angle, but again, she would have remained afloat. If Murdoch had been able to reduce her speed significantly before she struck the berg- the damage would obviously have been less.[154]

Unfortunately, hitting an object the size of what was estimated later to be a "medium" sized iceberg would have been exactly like driving the ship against a sheer rock face.[155] An iceberg of these dimensions would weigh in at anywhere from 500,000 to 750,000 tons. A 45,000 ton ship striking this berg head on would be almost like a fly striking a brick. The berg would not have yielded. There may have been wholesale shearing of rivets all along the sides of the ship, and it may have even "telescoped" the hull in places (where plates unable to withstand the pressure would rip free and slide under adjacent ones.)

---

[154] To illustrate some of the more flagrant examples of second guessing, some newspapers opined after the accident that Murdoch should have stuck to his course and rammed the iceberg squarely. Did anyone actually believe that anyone would do something like that intentionally?

[155] Just seven years earlier, during a trans-Atlantic yacht race called the "Kaiser's cup," an immense iceberg was observed by one of the competitors, a sailing ship named *Atlantic*, in the same general area that *Titanic* foundered. It was estimated to be over 300 feet tall and almost a half mile in length. One of the observers was a man named Hoyt. Hoyt perished on *Titanic*.

Now let's discuss Murdoch's other decision- to reverse engines as he attempted to steer *Titanic* clear of the ice.

Ships' engines cannot be brought astern instantly, and *Titanic*'s were particularly unsuited for swift reversal- primarily because of their immense size. As previously mentioned, the reciprocating engines aboard the *Olympic* class liners were the largest ever installed aboard a ship. They were three decks tall. Their moving components, pistons, connecting rods, and crankshafts literally weighed tons, as did the propellers and propeller shafts. It took a great deal of power to merely overcome the inertia of these moving masses, much less to stop them and then send them working in the other direction.

When the command came down from the bridge, it undoubtedly must have taken the engineers on duty by surprise. Since none of them survived, we may only speculate what was occurring in the engine room, but it was undoubtedly the routine of a new ship at sea- working off minor problems and tending to usual maintenance matters- a normal Sunday night. It is customary for the bridge to advise the engine room to anticipate commands in areas where there may be danger, but tonight there had been nothing from above.

This last factor assumes some importance in this discussion, because had the bridge ordered the engine room to stand by, one or more of the engineers would have been stationed at the engine control platform, ready to react.

Abruptly, the sharp clang of the engine telegraphs pierces the subdued din of the engine room- startling the personnel on duty. The command is full astern. *Full astern!* Something very out of the ordinary is going on. Speed in responding to the command is essential. The first step is to go to the engine control platform and answer the bells- letting the bridge know that the command has been received and acknowledged.

The second step is to close the throttle valves on the engines to stop them. However it is inadvisable to shut the valves instantly. There is a risk of damage to the engines unless they are allowed to slow smoothly to a stop. This process might take as long as twenty seconds. The valve controlling exhaust steam from the reciprocating engines also has to be repositioned to stop sending steam to the turbine and instead divert it to the condensers.

After the main engines stop, a "reversing engine" is employed- a small engine that uses high-pressure steam to start the bigger engine in the opposite direction. Once the main engine begins to reverse, the throttle valves are reopened and the propellers begin to revolve in the opposite direction. The whole process may have consumed a minute or more.

On *Titanic* it may have taken even longer, because we continue to see the factor of crew unfamiliarity with the ship. Some of the engineers had served aboard *Olympic*- but others- just like the deck officers- had come from other White Star ships which obviously would have had different engine room layouts.[156]

Titanic had gone to full astern once- during her trials in Belfast loch. However, at that time the command was expected, everyone was ready, and there were technicians from Harland and Wolff aboard to assist. Here, again, we have men who were almost totally unprepared.

We also must consider the factor that a full reversal of engines at high speed was something that very few of the engineers would have been familiar with, because it almost never happened.

Now, let's examine the physics of engine reversal.

Earlier we mentioned that one advantage that a reciprocating engine had over a turbine was that these types of engines could apply full power astern, but that's not exactly correct.

---

[156] Sixth officer Moody gives us an example. He told his sister- in a letter- that it had taken him almost a week to confidently find his way around *Titanic*, which he called "the big omnibus."

As fixed pitch propellers reverse, they waste a great deal of power as they cavitate- a phenomenon where the passage of the blades through the water lowers the pressure at their trailing edges to the point where the water actually boils and produces bubbles.

Cavitation occurs with almost all propellers- creating the swirl of foam behind any boat or ship under power. However, cavitation is more pronounced when propellers are reversed. Propellers are designed somewhat like airfoils, with a thick, rounded leading edge to bite into the water and a finely tapered trailing edge to minimize turbulence as it flows back into place.

However, when the propellers go astern, the design goes out the window. It's almost like trying to back an airplane into the air. Everything is haywire, and because the former leading edge of the propeller leaves a large area of low pressure behind it- cavitation becomes quite pronounced, robbing the ship of much of its stopping power.[157]

---

[157] Many modern ships are equipped with variable pitch propellers- somewhat like those on airplanes- that allow the blades to be oriented

Also mentioned earlier, *Titanic* had a small rudder, and a large component of her maneuverability relied on the wash of the ship's center propeller passing over it- the rudder directing it- almost like a vectored thrust jet engine nozzle- to change the course of the ship. When Murdoch ordered the reciprocating engines reversed, steam was cut off to the turbine driving the center propeller. It stopped, and so did the propeller. The vectored thrust effect was lost, and the rudder became far less effective.

What if Murdoch had only reduced speed, left the engines alone, or only reversed the port engine? Would *Titanic* have turned more swiftly? Would she have been able to avoid the berg altogether?

---

in reverse without stopping the engines and preserving the airfoil shape of the blades. These propellers may be almost instantly reversed. Additionally, many new ships- including *Queen Mary 2*- are being equipped with "Azipod" propulsion. The propellers are housed in assemblies that may be rotated, serving as thrusters and because the propellers may be directed, they assist in steering the ship to a much greater degree. In fact, *Queen Mary 2* has no rudder, but is instead steered by computer command of her Azipod units and thrusters. Strangely, Rolls-Royce, who built the units, calls them "Mermaids", but the controls for them on the bridge are clearly labeled "Azipod."

From what we can discern about the accident, the berg only grazed the starboard side of the ship, not even ripping a hole in her, as such, but merely buckling plates and popping rivets. The total area of the "hole" in the ship was later calculated by a Marine Architect named Edward Wilding- who worked for Harland and Wolff and had access to *Titanic*'s plans- to be about twelve square feet- or the size of an average refrigerator door.

It appears, tragically, that Murdoch chose the precise course of action that ensured the maximum amount of damage to the ship.

Had the berg been sighted earlier- or later- had the ship reacted to her rudder more swiftly, or more slowly, had the engines been left at full speed- merely slowed- or if Murdoch had chosen to only reverse the port engine- it may not have exposed the unprotected flank of the first six watertight compartments to the ice.

After the *Titanic* disaster, *Olympic* returned to Belfast Loch and was put through a series of tests to determine her handling characteristics. It was found that she took approximately 37 seconds to make a 20 degree change in heading, and during that time she had traveled 1,300 feet- or a little over a sixth of a nautical mile. She was also asked to make stops by reversing engines from 21.5 knots. This took three minutes, 15 seconds, and the ship required around 3,000 feet to do so, about half a nautical mile. However, significantly- and somewhat surprisingly- no test was conducted asking the ship to duplicate the commands Murdoch had issued, or at the speed *Titanic* had been sailing.

Even these tests have to be considered in the context they were performed. As we discussed before, when the trials of *Olympic/Titanic* were conducted, everyone was ready- and again, the ship had no cargo or passengers aboard. Undoubtedly, the length of time required for *Titanic* to have made these same maneuvers on the night she sank would have taken more time.

Before we begin this discussion, we have to remember that we are hampered by one severe handicap. Nobody can state with certainty what the visibility was on the night of the collision, or how far the ship was from the iceberg when it was seen.

Unlike today's ships, with their synchronized digital data and voice recorders which reveal virtually every facet of an accident, *Titanic* had nothing- not even a paper roll that logged her heading. The only data we have to work with are the recollections of those aboard who survived. And because human memory is exceedingly unreliable, we may only speculate as to what happened and how long it took.

Let's look at the sequence of events, using what we know and making reasoned assumptions about what is unknown.

We do know that *Titanic* was cutting through the mirror-like sea at a velocity of 22.5 knots, or about thirty-eight feet per second. At this speed, *Titanic* travels her own length every twenty-three seconds.

Fleet sees the iceberg and takes another look to make sure. He then fumbles for the lanyard to ring the bell in the crow's nest to alert the bridge.

Murdoch and Moody undoubtedly hear the alarm, as the bridge of *Titanic* is sheltered, but open on the sides. Moody, who is probably closer to the bridge telephone than Murdoch, goes to answer it.

Murdoch most likely moves to the nearest bridge wing or the forward windows to look at the area ahead of the ship with his binoculars. He knows that the bell in the crow's nest is only sounded when there is something in the path of the ship. He swings his glasses through a narrow arc ahead, and now he also sees the iceberg.

"Iceberg right ahead!" calls Moody from the telephone station, confirming Murdoch's observation.

As many as twenty seconds have now transpired. The ship has traveled about 760 feet.

Murdoch quickly judges the clearances. It must have appeared that the ship would have a better chance if he attempted to steer the ship to the left, but a collision was probably inevitable. He barks orders: "Hard a starboard! Full astern both!"[158]

---

[158] The command "Hard a starboard," actually meant to steer the ship the opposite direction, to port. This is another point of contention

Quartermaster Robert Hitchens, at the helm, spins the wheel left until it stops.

At the stern of the ship, one of two powerful steam engines dedicated solely to moving the massive rudder receives an electrical signal from the telemotor on the bridge, and begins to turn the mechanism to swing the rudder to the ordered position.[159] Unfortunately, Hitchens' swiftness in spinning the helm has no effect in hastening the deflection of the rudder. The telemotor upon which the wheel is mounted in the wheelhouse is simply an electrical switch that tells the rudder how far to

---

between maritime historians, and several theories have been advanced. The most reasonable states that the command was a holdover from the days when boats were steered with rudders connected to tillers. The command of "hard a starboard" would have meant to move the tiller to the right and thus turn the rudder to port. Murdoch's decision to turn the ship to port may also have been influenced by the driving habits of the British- who drive on the left side of the road. Just as an American officer would be inclined to steer to the right, a British officer would go left. In 2010, Lightoller's granddaughter stated that Lightoller had told her that the helmsman had steered *Titanic* the wrong way, and this had led to her loss. However, Murdoch undoubtedly would have visually confirmed the turning of the wheel and if it had been shifted the wrong direction; he would have instantly corrected it. Another factor that might lead us to question this statement is another assertion she made, that Ismay had ordered Smith to continue at full speed after the collision.

[159] One steam engine served as the primary and the other was a backup, and it was the practice to regularly alternate them.

turn- not how quickly- and it made no difference if Hitchens spun the helm to its stop, or gently turned it until the rudder had moved to the limit. It's impossible to swiftly move an object that weighs fifty-four tons. It probably takes the rudder as long as ten seconds to move into position.

During this time *Titanic* has traveled another 380 feet- 1,140 feet since the iceberg was seen.

Meanwhile, as we discussed earlier, there is a scramble in the engine room to stop and reverse the engines. It probably took at least twenty seconds to stop them, and likely longer.

The ship has now traveled 1,900 feet since the alarm was first sounded- almost a quarter of a nautical mile.

Now the engines are placed in reverse and brought back to speed. Again, this may have taken twenty seconds or more. After only a minute of reacting and attempting to evade the danger, the ship has traveled 2,280 feet before anything begins to really happen, except for perhaps a slight change in heading.

And significantly, we cannot be sure that the engineers actually ever achieved full astern. There is evidence that the engines either reversed slowly, or they never came astern at all.

Although none of the engineering officers survived *Titanic*, a few members of the engine room crew did. A trimmer named Thomas Dillon was in the reciprocating engine room at the time of the collision. His normal duty was to bring coal to one of the reserve boilers, but it was unused that night, so he was instead assisting in "cleaning the gear" in the engine room.

Dillon testified at the British Inquiry that when the command came down from the bridge to reverse engines, there was a great clamor in the engine room as the personnel on duty hurried to comply with the order. The engines never had time to come to full reverse and had only achieved "slow astern" before the impact with the berg was felt. Dillon stated that it had taken two minutes to stop and reverse the engines.

There is indirect evidence confirming Dillon's story. When a ship traveling at high speed reverses her engines, it is usually accompanied by high amplitude vibrations, almost as if the ship is trying to shake herself to pieces- particularly aft. Nobody aboard *Titanic* reported *any* vibration- other than that caused by the brush with the berg, and that was invariably described as lasting only a few seconds.[160]

It's not possible to calculate the exact amount *Titanic* had changed course by the time she struck the berg because the *Olympic* tests were done with the engines turning ahead, the wash of the center propeller aided the turn, and we are unable to determine with any accuracy *Titanic*'s actual distance from the ice when she began her maneuver.

However, we may make a reasoned assumption that her rate of turn would be less than half it would be with engine assistance, so *Titanic* had

---

[160] *Olympic* made a similar emergency stop during her career. The strong vibrations absent aboard *Titanic were* felt aboard her. Another example reveals the strength of these vibrations. When *QE2* was undergoing builder's trials, a full astern command from speed caused several bulkheads in the crew's quarters aft to collapse.

probably only turned five degrees or less before she struck the berg.

Shortly after this, time ran out. William Murdoch, despite his experience, had failed.

Now let's take a few seconds to address another decision made by Captain Smith- the speed at which *Titanic* was being driven.

Chapter Sixteen –The Question of Speed

The subject of *Titanic*'s speed on the night of April 14th has always been one of the most controversial topics concerning the disaster, so it will be discussed in some detail.

We have noted above that under Smith's orders *Titanic* had steadily increased speed throughout her voyage and it had been anticipated that if the weather held, she would be driven at her maximum the following day.

It has been a recurring theme in that the ship was being sailed at a speed inconsistent with her safety. It is said that had the ship been traveling a few knots slower, then the iceberg would have been seen earlier and avoided.

It cannot be debated that *Titanic* was, in effect, "overdriving her lights," unable to stop in the distance she could see, but her crew was obviously unaware of this.

But why was she traveling so rapidly? Or, in fact, was the speed at which she was sailing *really* excessive?

This question needs to be examined from many angles, some of which have already been mentioned.

Perhaps the most enduring theory regarding *Titanic*'s speed has to do with the desire of J. Bruce Ismay to make a noteworthy passage, and Smith's reluctance to disappoint his chief.

The most commonly advanced, and accepted, idea is that Ismay was pressuring, almost browbeating, Captain Smith to push *Titanic*- not to wrest the blue riband from his Cunard rivals- which was impossible- but to beat, or at least equal, *Olympic's* best time.

There are a number of problems with this theory, one having to do with Smith himself. While not absolute- the evidence suggests that the Captain was making his last voyage in the employ of White Star, intending to retire after his return to Britain. Therefore it would appear that he would be largely immune from being pressured into doing something that the believed to be unsafe.

However, there is good evidence that Smith, instead of being a reluctant pawn in the scheme of his superior, may have been a willing conspirator. The Captain may have even suggested the record-breaking voyage himself.

When Smith brought *Olympic* over on her maiden voyage the previous year, everyone had been surprised that she had proven to be faster and considerably more fuel-efficient than designed. She cut several hours off the time projected for her crossing-arriving the evening of the day before her scheduled arrival, which delighted the officers of White Star, including Ismay, who was aboard.

Her early arrival received more than its share of lavish praise from the press, who added her unexpected swiftness to her list of superlatives.

When Smith was asked by reporters if *Olympic* might be capable of an even faster passage, the Captain assured them that the liner would always be a

“Wednesday ship,” which meant that she could be expected to arrive, on schedule, the Wednesday following her departure from Southampton- no earlier.

Olympic then proceeded to arrive on Tuesday evening on her next westbound voyage and significantly, Ismay was *not* aboard this time. This again garnered positive press for the ship, Captain Smith, and White Star. *Olympic* made several early arrivals; in fact, her schedule was soon adjusted to capitalize on her unexpected speed.

Another unforeseen dividend was the discovery that the ship proved to be the most free of vibration when she was steaming at 21.5 knots. This was soon adopted as her standard cruising speed.

We have no data regarding vibration aboard *Titanic*, but it suggests yet another alternative theory about her speed. We know that there was a team from Harland and Wolff aboard led by Thomas Andrews. Instead of being aboard *Titanic*, as many authors have suggested, merely making small repairs and correcting problems, it makes more sense to think that they were examining all facets of the ship's performance- which they undoubtedly were.

This would include evaluating her engines, assessing her fuel consumption, and examining the efficiency of her housekeeping systems, such as her electrical plant, pumps, heating- a large array of items.

It is also reasonable to suggest that they were also making detailed observations of how *Titanic* behaved at different speeds, particularly how much vibration her engines produced, and where in the ship it most manifested itself. It is also logical to suggest that they had asked for the gradual increase speed over a day or two so that they could accurately assess how *Titanic* responded to differences in engine revolutions.[161]

But ultimately, the final decision would have been Captain Smith's.

---

[161] This also may explain the seemingly odd fate of Thomas Andrews. After playing a major part in the evacuation of the ship, Andrews then withdrew. Shortly before *Titanic* went down, he was seen in one of the public rooms staring vacantly at a painting. When he was asked if he was going to make an effort to save himself, he did not respond or even react to the question. He perished with the ship. Andrews had no reason to feel any guilt concerning *Titanic*, unless he had somehow been instrumental in the speed she was making on the night of the collision.

If we entertain the idea that Smith was unopposed to the idea of making a triumphant early entry into New York on his last voyage, it neatly resolves some mysteries surrounding the speed of the ship- particularly the question of why, if Smith was planning to retire after the crossing- why he just did not tell Ismay that he felt the high speed run was inadvisable and refuse to take the risk.

It's unlikely that Ismay, even given his imperious manner, would have pressed the speed issue with the Captain, particularly had Smith been insistent on not increasing speed and outlined his reasons for the decision. What was Ismay going to do, fire him?

We will never know the extent, or content, of any conversations conducted between the Chairman of the White Star line and his senior Captain regarding *Titanic*'s speed. Smith went down with the ship and Ismay maintained to his death that he had not participated in, or interfered with, the navigation of the liner.

But we do have testimony that they discussed the subject. A passenger named Edith Lyons stated that she had overheard the pair in the first class lounge talking about the speed of the ship a day or two before the collision.

Ismay, again, was not being obtuse. He realized that the second ship in the trio would be like the middle child in a family. She needed to draw some attention to herself, and the Chairman could think of no better way to do this than to have her make a proud entry, ahead of schedule, into New York harbor, garnering positive press about the latest addition to the White Star Fleet. She could be advertised as not only luxurious, but swift as well- maybe even more than her older sister.

Ismay may have been ignorant of the ice strewn in *Titanic*'s path at this time. We only know for certain that he became aware of the danger when the *Baltic* message was handed to him on the afternoon before the collision. Captain Smith may have informed him earlier, but we cannot be sure. So again we see an allegation being made on thin to non-existent proof.

Although the idea has taken hold that *Titanic* had been pushed to a foolhardy and reckless velocity on the night of the disaster, she was only traveling about one knot faster than had *Olympic* on her maiden voyage, and *Olympic* had made a subsequent voyage under Smith at 22.5 knots- the speed *Titanic* was making the night of the collision.

The difference in velocity was negligible- only about *eighteen inches* per second more than if she had been traveling at 21.5 knots.

The dissimilarity in speed probably had no effect on the outcome of the collision at all.

Smith apparently had decided to assure himself that the ice danger was behind the ship before attempting to push her any faster. He may have consulted with Ismay and the two decided that it was a prudent precaution.

But maybe *Titanic* was not going *fast enough*.

Perhaps it was a mistake to have waited- possibly *Titanic* should have been pushed to *higher speeds earlier in the voyage*, being worked up to at least the speed on the night of the collision and maybe more.

While this theory may seem odd, it makes sense when examined.

An assessment of the distance covered by *Titanic* before the collision and the time required to so, shows us that the ship was averaging about 21.5 knots during the voyage, but had she been pushed to 22.5 knots at the beginning of the voyage, and averaged that speed throughout, it may have changed her fate.

If *Titanic* had averaged 22.5 knots, it may have placed her anywhere up to seventy miles further along her course by 23:30 on April 14th. She would have entered the area of ice danger almost three hours earlier- at about 19:30, which coincidentally is about the time that darkness set in at that latitude on that evening. Icebergs ahead of the ship would have been silhouetted by the setting sun or the residual glow on the horizon as twilight closed in.

Conceivably, the ice would have been seen in time and avoided.

Nevertheless, and all speculation aside, Smith must have believed that 22.5 knots *was* a safe speed for the ship the night of April 14.

But, given what we know now- what speed really would have been safe?

Since the iceberg receded out of sight aft after the collision, we must assume that when the order was given to reverse engines, it was less than three thousand feet from the ship. What speed would have allowed *Titanic* to have stopped before it struck, given the factors that we have?

First, let's discuss her rate of deceleration. *Titanic*, from 22.5 knots, would have slowed about .01 feet per second when her engines were stopped. This works out to a loss in velocity of about *one and a half inches per second* per second.

Now we must make some reasoned assumptions. For the sake of this argument, let's say that the iceberg was lost to sight one quarter to one half ship length aft of *Titanic*, and that she came to rest about the same time. This makes the "overrun" of the ship somewhere between 1200 and 1400 feet- which leaves us a distance of up to 1600 feet to stop the ship before she strikes the berg.

What initial speed would have allowed the ship to stop in that distance?

Titanic could only have made a full stop, in the space that we have calculated, if she had been traveling at less than 16 knots- and it would have been extremely unlikely that Smith, or any other officer, would have reduced speed so significantly when the visibility was perceived as being excellent and he believed the ice to be miles north of his track.

Chapter Seventeen- The First Moments

It appears that, unfortunately, the berg struck by *Titanic* was standing almost like a sentry at the eastern edge of the ice field. There is no record of any ice sighted by her crew prior to seeing it.[162] Perhaps if she had initially come in contact with lighter ice or large bergs had been sighted off her track- anything to convince the officers on her bridge that the danger was real and present- her speed would have been sharply reduced and care would have been taken in traversing the ice field or sailing around it. Tragically, the first ice sighted by her crew sank her.[163]

---

[162] There is one largely unsubstantiated report that ice was sighted and reported to *Titanic*'s bridge at least three times before the iceberg was observed. There may be some truth to this, but the record, and common sense, indicates otherwise. None of the four lookouts who were on duty prior to the collision reported seeing any ice, and there was no real reason that they would have kept it to themselves if they had. Fleet, the lookout who sighted the iceberg, had a great deal of guilt that his failure to see the ice in time had doomed the ship- and he felt that a number of people blamed him for her loss. Obviously, Fleet would have quickly wanted to assure everyone that it had not been his failure that sank *Titanic*; it instead was the result of the officers ignoring repeated warnings.

[163] There are many unintentionally humorous statements regarding the ice made by passengers (or made up by eager reporters) after the accident. One stated that the ship had been steaming through ice almost all day Sunday; another said that the iceberg was visible for

It is unknown if Captain Smith had retired for the night at the time of the collision, but it appears that he had not- because he was on the bridge almost instantly afterward, still partially dressed in his uniform.[164] He immediately ordered the watertight doors closed, and finding that this had already been done- briefly queried First Officer Murdoch about the collision. The junior officer started to explain, but it appears that the Captain either was not listening or only wanted Murdoch's snap assessment of damage.

The Captain went to the starboard bridge wing and looked aft to get a look at the iceberg, which was rapidly receding into the darkness. He could see what it had left behind aboard his ship- several tons of ice on the fore and well decks on the starboard side.

---

over an hour before the ship struck it. Another story stated that passengers had saved themselves by floating on a cake of ice near the ship.

[164] There is debate about where Smith was during the collision. Most accounts state that he was in his cabin- which was directly abaft the bridge. Others state he was napping in the chartroom, which was nearby. In either instance he was not in a position to have altered events.

Smith ordered the engines stopped and immediately set about to determine the damage to his vessel.

Fourth Officer Boxhall, who had arrived on the bridge almost as soon as Smith, was dispatched below to inspect and ascertain what harm had been done. Boxhall's examination must have been cursory in the extreme- for he shortly returned to the bridge and informed Smith that he had found nothing- it looked like a close shave- that was all.[165]

Smith illustrated his skepticism by showing the junior officer the commutator in the wheelhouse- an instrument that displays how deeply a ship is rolling. The sea was almost still- like a millpond- and *Titanic* was motionless. However, the instrument indicated a five degree starboard list.

Boxhall speculated optimistically that the list might be produced by the weight of the ice on the foredeck, but Smith was unconvinced. To him it was

---

[165] Some accounts state that Boxhall found some flooding, but assessed it as minor.

clear that the ship was taking on water and the angle indicated by the commutator looked to him as if the flooding might be serious. He is reported as exclaiming "My God!" when he first noted the reading.

The Captain ordered Boxhall to find one of the ship's carpenters and have the ship sounded- checking for water in each compartment. That proved unnecessary. One appeared on the bridge around this time and informed the Captain that he had just completed the task.[166] His assessment was radically different from Boxhall's. He told Smith that *Titanic* was rapidly filling all the way from her forepeak- at the very bow- aft to boiler room number five.[167]

Now Smith had two different versions of how much damage his ship had sustained. Based on his earlier statements regarding his perception of her safety,

---

[166] One source states that the Carpenter (who is thought to have been Hutchison) seemed almost panicked by what he had found.

[167] Lamp Trimmer Samuel Hemming testified that water was rushing into the bow with such velocity that it was causing air to hiss as it escaped from a hatch cover on deck.

he may have been uncertain of whether she was fatally wounded.

What he needed now was an accurate appraisal of how badly hurt his ship was- something concrete. He sent for Thomas Andrews. There could not be any better judge of *Titanic*'s condition. As mentioned, Andrews had participated in the design of the ship and he had supervised her construction. Here was a third chance for Smith to make a personal inspection of his ship, but he declined to accompany Andrews as *Titanic*'s builder went below.

Andrews made a quick tour and confirmed what the Carpenter had found- extensive and relatively rapid flooding. His recommendation was that Smith needed to prepare for the worst. Andrews gave the ship about two hours, at the most, to remain afloat.

The word was spreading. Most of the officers had now gathered on the bridge. J. Bruce Ismay soon joined them. He arrived in his pajamas, overcoat and slippers, demanding to know why the ship had stopped and wanting answers- particularly an estimate of how long it would be before they would get underway again.

White Star's chairman was extremely unhappy. This unscheduled stop was going to throw a wrench into his plan for a triumphant early entry into New York, particularly if the ship was damaged seriously enough that it would affect her speed or- the worst case as far as Ismay was concerned- if she would be forced to return to Belfast for repairs. No dry dock in North America could accommodate a vessel of her size.

Ismay knew too that the news of the collision would be instantly exploited by the newspapers on both sides of the Atlantic, obliterating any positive publicity he had sought to generate about *Titanic*. Her reputation, and White Star's, would inevitably be damaged.

The last thing he needed were the newspapers carrying stories, and photographs, of the ship limping into New York, or some nearer haven- although there were no other ports on the east coast of North America that would be able to accommodate *Titanic*'s draft.[168] In fact, if she settled seriously, she would not be able to dock in New York either- as the harbor had been dredged to allow her only a few feet of clearance. This could easily become an enormous problem.

In the long run, *Titanic* might even come to be regarded as a "jinxed" ship, which, given the superstitions of the sea, might lead to problems crewing her and filling her with passengers.

Smith told him that it was far worse than that. *Titanic* was going down- Andrews had told him so.[169]

---

[168] New York City had expressed its displeasure with White Star when plans for building *Olympic* were announced. The ship would require longer piers, and extensive harbor dredging to accommodate her draft. It was to cost the port authority several hundred thousand dollars, but there was no real chance that the work would not be done. Boston was more than eager to take the Atlantic trade away from New York and White Star would simply shift its operations there.

[169] In *A Night to Remember* there is a scene where Andrews and Smith repair to Andrews' cabin to examine the ship's blueprints, and he offers his gloomy assessment of her fate. Evidence suggests that this never happened- that the news was conveyed to both Smith and Ismay on the bridge. Andrews' cabin was far aft, and it's unlikely that Andrews needed to consult plans to confirm what he undoubtedly already knew. After the discussion, Andrews and Ismay departed, and the three never conversed as a group again.

Initially, Ismay seemed incapable of accepting the news. She could not founder, it was impossible! Surely everyone was mistaken- the ship was unsinkable! The watertight bulkheads would prevent the rest of the ship from flooding. Maybe she would settle a little at the bow- but she would remain afloat.

Andrews patiently explained to him that before this night the amount of damage he had observed below had been inconceivable to a ship the size of *Titanic*. The iceberg had opened the starboard side of the ship- a breach almost three hundred feet long- a third of *Titanic*'s length. "Unsinkable" or not- *Titanic* could not survive that kind of damage. Five forward compartments were flooding. She could only float with four being flooded at one time.

The watertight bulkheads in the succeeding compartments would not save the ship. They rose only ten feet above the normal waterline, and *Titanic*'s watertight compartments were not *really* watertight. A true watertight compartment is sealed in all dimensions, but *Titanic*'s were open at the top. As the ship sank lower at the bow, the top of each watertight bulkhead would be pulled down below the water level in the adjacent compartment and water would pour over the top. The sequence would be repeated with the next compartment, and the next, as each compartment filled in series. Andrews called it a "mathematical certainty"- almost as if he were explaining an engineering exercise.

At this point, there must have also been a discussion regarding what- if anything- could be done to either prevent the ship from sinking, or delay it as long as possible.

In the next chapter we will examine what- if anything- could have been done to save *Titanic*.

Chapter Eighteen- Could the Ship have been saved?

When a ship is damaged to the extent that it may sink, there are only a few options open to those aboard.

The first is to beach her, a viable alternative only if the ship is in or near an area of shallows where she may settle to the bottom, allowing her upper works to remain above the water. Unfortunately, this was unavailable to *Titanic*, as the nearest place where shallow water could be found was over a day's steaming- at full speed- to the northwest.

The second option is to stem the influx of water- some type of repair. Could anything have been done to save *Titanic*, or at least delay her sinking to allow enough time for rescue ships to arrive and help evacuate her passengers? *Was* anything done?

Unfortunately for this discussion, all the members of the crew who could have voiced opinions or suggested ways to save the ship were lost with her. The men who knew her best- the experts from Harland and

Wolff, including Thomas Andrews, also went down with the ship. So, it follows, that anything we explore in the next few pages must be of a speculative nature, based on what we know about the crew and the ship.

Since none of these men survived the sinking- and none of the survivors had any contact with them- except in the initial stages of the disaster- we may only surmise what action they took and how they spent their final moments.

Another aspect we must consider is how much damage the ship sustained, and therefore how much repair would be required- and whether it would have been possible.

In the mid-1990s, an expedition to *Titanic* used sonar to determine what had happened during the collision. Later, other scientists diving on the wreck found a small amount of visible damage. The findings suggested that as the ship grazed the iceberg, rivets sheared and snapped, allowing seams to open between the buckling hull plates. Metallurgical tests performed on salvaged rivets revealed that there was a wide range in their quality. Some were laced with impurities which would have reduced their strength to dangerously low levels. The flaws in the rivets would have been exaggerated by the low temperature of the sea water on the night of the collision.

Was the ship beyond hope from the start or could anything have been done to save her?

A primary requirement would have been an accurate and rapid survey of where the ship was taking on water and decisions made about where the most strategic employment of available resources should be employed. This may have been impossible.

As discussed previously, the damage to *Titanic* is thought to have been approximately a third of her length- or roughly 300 feet- and it was calculated that the total opening in the ship's hull was about twelve square feet. Logic suggests the gash in the starboard side of the ship would not have been a uniform width, but instead was a series of various sized openings that allowed the water to flood into the compartments.[170] The sonar survey mentioned above has confirmed this.

Titanic was not a warship, with a well-planned and practiced damage control strategy and a crew trained to implement it, and even if she had been, as we have mentioned before, nobody thought the amount of damage she sustained was possible.[171]

She had not been designed to allow rapid access to the spaces near her outside skin. The way would have been blocked by machinery, boilers, cargo, stores and piping. It would have been difficult to exactly determine where the water was entering the ship.

The suggestion has been made that the crew should have concentrated its efforts in repairing the leak in the number five boiler room, keeping it from filling and

---

[170] In the course of researching this book, I have seen several artists' depictions of what the damage was thought to have been, most showing a massive tear in the ship's hull- several feet wide. Damage of this magnitude would have sunk the ship in a matter of only a few minutes.

[171] Throughout the history of technology, we see again and again that engineers attempt to plan for every eventuality just to be surprised by something that nobody imagined could happen. The Apollo 13 mission illustrates this, as does the Three Mile Island accident.

keeping the ship alive long enough for rescue to arrive. Unfortunately, most of the damage here was deep inside a coal bunker, which would have taken hours to clear.[172]

The accounts of those who survived from the lower decks during the collision all state that the water "erupted" or "exploded" into the damaged compartments and in fact, water entered the ship at an estimated 400 tons per minute. Some of the damage was quickly hidden by the rising water, and in some compartments the water rose so rapidly that there was little choice other to abandon the spaces. The pressure and temperature of the inrushing water would have made even an attempt at stemming the leak difficult or impossible.[173]

---

[172] Boiler room number five- the boiler room directly aft of six- was the site of a coal bunker fire that had been burning since the ship left Southampton. A special crew was embarked in Britain to rake out the bunker and extinguish the fire. They finally completed their work sometime either Saturday night or Sunday morning. Some authors have made an issue of this event, speculating that the fire weakened the watertight bulkhead allowing it to collapse and allowing the ship to sink even more rapidly.

[173] Free water within the hull would have been just as cold as the sea beyond the ship. It would have numbed, and killed, anyone who spent any time in it.

Even if she had sufficient material to enable an attempt at repair, it would have been imperative that the spaces be pumped dry- or at least the flooding brought under control until the leaks were sealed.

But before we discuss what could have been done, let's examine how the crew was organized aboard the liner, their duties, and possibly as a surprise to the reader, who actually would have been asked to evaluate the damage to the ship and repair her.

In the 19th Century, ships had evolved from relatively small wooden sailing vessels dependent on the wind for motion, and on human strength for almost everything else- into steel-hulled, steam powered giants that required a complex internal infrastructure to service their propulsion plants.

On sailing ships, the Captain and officers were experts in all aspects of the vessel. Years of experience told them exactly the amount of sail they should carry, how the lines should be tensioned, and the course they should steer to obtain the best result from the combination. Often they could tell simply from the noises the ship was producing whether she was in her best trim.

However, by 1912, many Captains and deck officers had lost touch with the sea in a number of respects. All they had to know now was that ringing down for engines produced headway and many of them probably had little idea, and less inclination, to find out what enabled them to set any course they chose.

As ships had evolved and became far more mechanical, a new class of crewmen, engineers- so called because their primary duty was to tend to the engines- began to appear.[174]

At first, the engineers simply maintained the propulsion plant, often doing double duty stoking the furnace beneath the boiler and making whatever repairs were required to keep the engine working. They, like their engine, were often afterthoughts on most ships, the engineer frequently berthing in the same space as the machinery.

---

[174] The original meaning of the word "Engineer" allegedly was "Man of Genius."

By 1912, the task of the engineer had expanded to include the maintenance of virtually everything of a mechanical nature aboard the ship, not just the engines, but her generators, pumps, heating and electrical system. While many have assumed that the engineers would have been responsible for stemming leaks, somewhat surprisingly, the engineering staff actually would have had little to do with her physical structure.

Instead- officially- repairs to the hull would have been the responsibility of the ship's carpenters. On *Titanic*, these were only two individuals- James Maxwell and John Hutchinson.

As with the engineers, the role of the carpenter had evolved in the 19th Century too, but in reverse. As the importance of engineers had expanded, the carpenter's had diminished.

On a wooden vessel, the carpenter was a vital crewmember. He was expected to keep the ship watertight and to make repairs to her structure, often under demanding conditions, and with limited resources. On older ships, the carpenter frequently had more than his hands full. He had to be inventive and ingenious to ensure his own survival.

But on a ship like *Titanic*, which was made mostly of steel, the carpenter's lot was significantly less arduous- and in fact the job was somewhat of an anachronism.[175]

Although the carpenter still performed some traditional duties, such as sounding the ship for leaks, most of his time was spent adjusting doors, repairing furniture and woodwork, and securing loose decking.[176] Earlier in the evening of the collision, Lightoller had called their attention to the dropping temperature and instructed them to keep an eye on the fresh water tanks to prevent them from freezing.

---

[175] The nadir of the carpenter's position came with the maiden voyage of *SS United States* in 1951. The only wood aboard her, other than balsa filling her bilge keels- which was inaccessible- was the chef's butcher block and the Steinway piano. The ship's designer, William Francis Gibbs, was a fanatic about fireproofing.

[176] It may surprise the reader to know that *Titanic* probably had a number of small leaks in her hull throughout the voyage. Any riveted ship would have imperfectly joined plates which would admit small amounts of water until corrosion sealed them. Although she had been afloat for almost a year before her maiden voyage, the vibration imparted to her structure by her engines would have exposed the few remaining places where water could have entered the hull.

We know little about either carpenter, but neither were very old- Maxwell being 31 and Hutchinson 28. Unlike the officers of the ship, who were permanent White Star employees, most other crewmen were hired on a different basis- often voyage to voyage- so we have little idea of what kind of experience either man had at sea. However, it would be safe to assume that both were skilled and would be more than aware of repair techniques.

What would have been available to them?

The traditional method would be to stem the leak from the inside of the ship by placing planking over the area of damage and securing it with shoring timbers- where the phrase "shoring up," comes from. This option was usually employed in situations where small leaks had developed. Here it would clearly require a prohibitive amount of planking, timber, and time- plus a dedicated and skilled crew to place the patches, so it would have been rapidly dismissed as an option.

Another alternative involves sealing the leak from the *outside* of the ship. One method of accomplishing this, called "fothering," requires a basket mounted on a long pole. The basket is filled with sawdust, ashes, pieces of oakum, or whatever else is handy. The basket is then covered with a loose piece of canvas and rapidly plunged into the water near the area of the presumed leak. The idea is that the debris in the basket will be drawn into the leak by the water flowing into the ship and thus slowing or stopping the flow. It is almost certain that this method- if it was even advanced- was also rejected.

A variant to this option would involve rigging an external patch. The idea would be to place a large section of canvas or other suitable heavy cloth over the area of damage by maneuvering it into position with lines tied to the corners. Water pressure would then draw the patch firmly to the side of the ship. The lines would then be tightened to ensure that it would remain in place.

White Star's *Republic*, mentioned above, was kept afloat for several hours because her crew had rigged just such a patch, using a large piece of sailcloth.

This last method may have received some consideration, but it's difficult to accurately determine if it would have been a workable alternative. *Titanic*, like any ship, would have had an ample supply of lines of all sizes- particularly heavy mooring lines- and she would also have had a large supply of cloth, not necessarily canvas, but sheets, blankets, even *carpets* removed from public rooms or passageways. It would have not been a requirement that the leak be covered completely- at least to begin with. The initial patches could have been strategically positioned to stem critical flooding, allowing others to be put in place later if they were needed.

The obvious problem with this idea is the time and manpower it would have required.

Maxwell and Hutchinson could not have done it alone. It would have required a large crew of men to accomplish the repair- first to obtain the materials to be used in the patches, and then to fashion and correctly position them. Who could they have called upon?

The deck crew- the actual seamen aboard- were almost all occupied in launching and manning the boats, and the engineers had their hands full too. All they could have mustered would have been idle stokers and various members of the passenger staff- waiters, stewards, cooks, and the like- many of who were out of pocket. Of course, there would probably have been more than enough willing and able-bodied passengers who could also be employed.

The second problem the Carpenters would have encountered was the sheer size of the ship. Lines would have to be attached to the patches and then these lines would have had to be drawn under the keel so they could be placed against the hull. The only effective way to do this would have been to pull the lines to the bow and slip them over her stem, drawing them tightly into position over the damaged areas.

It appears that this might be very difficult, if not impossible. However, it also seems that if someone stopped and thought about it for a moment, virtually all the required equipment was already in place, and, tantalizingly, the ship may have been saved- or at least her sinking may have been delayed long enough for rescue ships to arrive and those aboard safety transferred to them.

Located on the foredeck of *Titanic* were several powerful winches, called capstans, used when the ship was being docked. These winches would be used to retract mooring lines as the ship was being made fast. They could have easily been employed to draw the patching lines to the bow of the ship. Once a sufficient amount of line had been brought forward, it could be dropped into the sea and walked aft until it was in the proper position. Once the lines were in the water, their buoyancy would allow them to become much easier to handle. The line that was to be placed under the ship could have been weighted to allow it to slip beneath the keel.

Once these lines were brought back to the area of the leak, then they could be moved into position and tightened. Here, again, there would have been equipment in place to assist this effort. There were two large cargo cranes located on the foredeck just forward of the bridge, and there were *lifeboat davits*- which are essentially cranes- located directly above the area that would have required the patches. The winches on the davits would have enabled the patch to be moved in relation to the leak and tightened once it was in the proper place. The leak could be either stopped or reduced to the point where the pumps in the area could deal with it.

This now brings us to the third option when a ship is in danger of sinking- pumping. This option was probably the first considered- and it was undoubtedly employed- but unfortunately *Titanic* was taking on water at a rate that was impossible to control with the equipment aboard.

The ship was flooding at the approximate rate of seven tons of water *per second* (1,700 gallons- or enough to fill an average in-ground pool in about eleven seconds). Even modern high-capacity pumps would be daunted by this volume of water. Pumps of this size require enormous amounts of power- on the order or five to seven thousand horsepower each- the equivalent power produced by two large modern diesel railroad locomotives. They also require that the flow of water remain constant through them- otherwise cavitation will tear them apart.

Titanic's pumps were archaic and inefficient by today's standards. Instead of being of centrifugal design, where water is moved by a rotating impeller and produces a constant flow, most of *Titanic*'s pumps employed pistons.

There was no pump- or even a combination of pumps- aboard *Titanic* that could have coped with the inrush of water. Most of the large pumps within the ship were part of the propulsion plant, and would not have been able to be rigged to discharge free water within the hull.

These pumps could not be removed from the duties for with they were designed- such as those that were required to supply the boilers with water, or assuring a flow of cooling water through the condensers- both of which were necessary for powering the ship.[177]

In the motion picture *A Night To Remember*, we see crewmen deploying a portable pump in an effort to slow the rising water. However, there was no such equipment aboard the ship.

Harland and Wolfe had supplied *Titanic* with five large bilge pumps, which at the time were thought to be more than adequate for any eventuality.

These pumps were designed for and dedicated to removing free water within the hull. As on any ship, this water could accumulate from a number of sources, condensation from escaped steam within the boiler rooms and engine spaces, piping leaks and bursts, and even small imperfections in the hull.

The *Olympic* class ships had been provided with seemingly more than ample capacity to remove this

---

[177] The pumps that supplied cooling water to the condensers, one of the few of centrifugal design, could be rigged to draft from the bilges in the engine rooms if they were needed to remove water from this area. Unfortunately, their intakes could not be moved forward and the engines spaces only flooded as the ship made her final plunge.

water. Two of the pumps had capacities of 250 tons per hour, the remaining three could discharge 150 tons of water each, for a total of 950 tons of water an hour. Unfortunately, *Titanic* was taking on that amount of water about every *two minutes*. *Titanic* simply could not have pumped out the amount of water that was flowing into her hull.

The arrangement of pumps aboard *Titanic* was rather complicated. Each compartment was equipped with "suctions" or hard-plumbed pipes dedicated to removing free water. These suctions ranged in diameter from three to eighteen inches and they could, through an assortment of valves, be connected to two pumps at one time.

Unfortunately, the smaller pumps were located forward, where the ship was flooding, and the larger pumps were aft. And, although the forward spaces were equipped with as many as four suctions per compartment, none of them exceeded five inches in diameter.

Another significant detail we must factor into this discussion is that even this limited amount of total pumping capacity could not be brought to bear simultaneously. The bilge pumps were installed throughout the length of the ship, with both large pumps located in the engine rooms and three smaller pumps evenly spaced forward. There was no provision for linking the pumps, or allowing them to draw water from forward compartments. The two large bilge pumps aft were probably never brought online because they remained in a dry area until just moments before the ship broke in two and sank.[178]

The reader may be wondering why, with the hazard of collision being most likely at the bow, the large pumps were not located in this area. It appears that the men who designed the *Olympic* class liners believed that

---

[178] As mentioned previously, *Olympic* was extensively rebuilt following the *Titanic* disaster. One of the modifications made to her was the installation of a large conduit that would allow all her pumps to be brought to bear simultaneously. However, even had *Titanic* been equipped with a similar arrangement, it would have made little to no difference.

it was more important to protect the engine spaces. Without the engines, and the associated generators, the ship would be helpless. There was also the possibility of a serious breach in the condenser system. The condensers are units- somewhat like large radiators- which use seawater pumped into the ship to cool exhaust steam and return it to the liquid state to be sent back to the boilers. Each condenser unit used a lattice of hollow tubes, cooled externally by seawater, through which the steam would flow. A leak in this system- particularly one that allowed sea water to enter the hull- could introduce catastrophic flooding in the engine rooms. If such a leak were not quickly controlled, the ship would lose power. It also appears that damaged compartments forward would be allowed to flood- relying totally on the watertight subdivision of the ship to protect it.

One author has suggested that the ash ejection systems aboard- used to clear the boiler rooms of coal ashes- could have been employed to remove water from the ship. Under normal conditions, these systems used pumps to jettison a slurry of water and coal ash overboard. However, while they may have helped for a time, they would have soon been engulfed too.

Titanic's pumps probably played no significant role in keeping her afloat. They were simply overwhelmed.

The reader may be wondering how *Titanic* survived for any appreciable length of time- much less for the almost three hours she did- if she was filling at such an enormous rate, but we must consider her size.

Titanic had thousands of cubic feet of enclosed space. If water was entering the ship at the rate of seven tons per second, she would be filling at about 224 cubic feet of water per second, with a cubic foot of water weighing about 62.5 pounds. At this rate, it would take about six seconds to fill a twelve by twelve room- provided it had a ten foot ceiling. An average 1500 square foot house would fill in a little over a minute.

We must assume that this rate of flooding continued until the ship became submerged to where her upper decks were awash and this allowed water to enter the ship through doors and other places where there was no provision for watertight integrity.[179]

Obviously, after making an assessment of the damage and the options available to them; Andrews, Maxwell, Hutchinson and Bell must have shaken their heads and decided that the only real choice open to them was the last- abandoning ship.

---

[179] There were probably a few open portholes in the forward part of the ship as well, so the area of iceberg damage may not have been as extensive as it has been assumed. When *Titanic*'s younger sister, *Britannic*, foundered during the First World War it was later determined that her extensive watertight protection had been virtually eliminated by portholes that had been left open to ventilate the ship.

Chapter Nineteen- The Failed Evacuation

One component of the *Titanic* disaster that most histories of the event accurately recount is the inexcusable lack of planning and coordination in her abandonment.

Only a few passengers had still been awake at the time of the collision- some die-hard card players in the smoking room- one or two of them who were suspected of being professional gamblers- but most were tucked into bed.[180]

The collision had been relatively gentle, so it had roused only the lightest sleepers, but many more were awakened by the *absence* of noise. When the engines stopped an abnormal hush descended over the ship.

Those who had the initiative to investigate were initially shooed back to their cabins by stewards who- if they knew anything about why the ship had stopped- told

---

[180] White Star had a regulation forbidding the playing of cards on Sundays, but the rule had been suspended on April 14th aboard *Titanic*. Almost every large ship on the North Atlantic carried its share of "boatmen," card sharps, and many made a good living fleecing the wealthy men with whom they played.

them various stories- almost all of them comforting and unintentionally untrue.

One steward was reported to have told a woman that there “was talk of an iceberg” and he thought that the ship had stopped to avoid hitting it. Another passenger was told to return to her cabin- there was nothing to see on deck and she would surely catch her “death of cold” if she insisted on going out on deck in her nightdress.

A story that the ship had “cut a whale in two” made the rounds, along with one about her merely dropping a propeller blade- undoubtedly started by crewmembers who had previously been aboard *Olympic*.

A small number of passengers were told the truth- the ship had struck a berg- but then the story diverged and softened somewhat. They had stopped so an inspection could be made. The damage was assuredly minor and the ship would be underway again as soon as the crew made the necessary repairs.

Henry Sleeper Harper, a first class passenger traveling with his wife, had been having a miserable voyage. Ill and confined to his bed, he noticed that the ship had stopped and that there was unusual activity outside his cabin. He rose and started to dress-intending to find out what was happening.

Harper's wife, alarmed that exposure to the cold night air would only aggravate his condition, summoned the ship's doctor. Dr. O'Loughlin told Harper to put his pajamas back on and get back into bed, that the damage was not serious.

Harper did not believe him. O'Loughlin decided to compromise with his impatient patient, telling him that he would go and check. The doctor returned in a few minutes. "They tell me that trunks are floating around in the hold, so you may as well go up on deck." Harper's concern well served him; he, his wife, and his *dog* were all saved. O'Loughlin was not.

Finally, the word came down that all passengers were to be awakened, told to dress warmly, don their lifejackets and report on deck. The stewards were to see to it, even if people had to be dragged out of bed. Of course, the first class passengers would not be subjected to this type of treatment. The stewards would resort to gentle persuasion with them.

By the time this measure was implemented, almost forty-five minutes of Andrews' optimistic two-hour estimate had ticked away.[181]

Even after the decision was made to muster the passengers and get them ready to abandon ship, most of them seemed to have trouble grasping the fact that the ship- and they- were in significant peril.

Passengers who had not been told the truth- the majority of those aboard- tried to make sense out of what was happening. If the ship was truly unsinkable, what was the purpose of all this?

Most believed that White Star was unnecessarily inconveniencing them, running a sort of pointless drill, and of course, in that era- people did not merely pull on

---

[181] Preparing the boats for launch consumed some time too. Each had a heavy canvas cover lashed over its top. Instead of merely cutting the lashings, the seamen detailed to remove the covers laboriously untied each cover, and some even went to the trouble of folding and stowing them. They then had to release the boat from its cradle. There were other chores too, such as assuring that drain plugs were replaced in each boat before it was launched, and assuring that lights stowed within the boats were in working order.

a pair of jeans and a jacket, they had to dress properly. For the men that meant coats and ties, and for the women that meant layers of underpinnings, corsets, stockings, hats, etc. Some men took time to shave and several women asked the stewards to draw baths for them. They were gently told that there was no time. It was essential they report to the boat deck without delay.

Once there, most of the women recoiled at the thought of trading the perceived safety of the large, warm, well-lit, and seemingly undamaged ship for a seat in a tiny lifeboat adrift in a vast, dark ocean. Most of the men who accompanied them either decided not to press the issue or failed to grasp the seriousness of the situation.

It was unpleasant enough to be on deck- it would be much colder in a lifeboat. *Titanic* was sinking slowly at this point, and there was little indication that she was in any real danger, other than an almost imperceptible tilt of her decks toward the bow. Many of the passengers decided that it was senseless to stand idly shivering on the deck, and the best plan was to go back inside, where it was warm, and await developments.

Part of the problem with filling the boats had to do with some well-intentioned deceit on the part of the male passengers and crew. This was an era where it was thought that women had to be sheltered from life- spared from cruel realities- and it was believed to be better to shield them from the truth about the ship, so even those men who had been told or suspected the truth hesitated to reveal it.

Instead, the women were told that *Titanic* was not *really* sinking, but Captain Smith was being stuffily conservative and doing his duty. Filling and launching the lifeboats was termed a “formality,” a “precaution,” and even a “necessary inconvenience.”

Even if the weather had been pleasant it would not have been an inviting prospect for the women to know that they were to be herded into lifeboats in the company of strangers- without their husbands- and launched into what appeared to be a bottomless void.

It was a long way from the boat deck down to the water- almost like standing on the roof of a seven-story building. The descent was literally like dropping into a black hole, and few women took pleasure in the idea of dangling over what must have seemed like an abyss. Just stepping from the deck into the boat was like standing at the edge of a precipice.

The area around the ship was not brilliantly lit like it appears in movies- it was dark- almost impenetrably. Once the boats were out of the small puddle of light produced by the liner they would be engulfed in a night darker than many of those aboard had ever experienced.

They were out of sight of land, in the middle of the Atlantic ocean- and they would literally be on their own- some of them packed like sardines- under the command of one or two seamen, if they were available. Some boats had to make do with whoever was handy at the time they were launched, sometimes passenger or even kitchen staff.

There was needless confusion too- people did not know if they were in the "right" boat or they decided to wait to go with friends or family. Some thought that there were designated "first class" boats, or that there should be, appalled at finding that they were being seated with people below their station. Some expressed their intention to pen strong letters to the management of the White Star Line complaining of the poor service it was providing.

And yet there continued to be no definitive word as to what was really happening.

Most of the ship's senior officers were occupied with organizing and implementing the evacuation and therefore had little time to converse with the passengers- so the latter had to content themselves with bits and pieces of what they could pick up from other members of the crew- stewards, stewardesses, dining room staff and the like.

However, most of these crewmen knew little more than the passengers. They filled the gaps with uninformed speculation, much of it positive, comforting, and false. It would have been a cardinal sin for them to have intentionally upset the customers- and of course, they must have wanted to believe the best too. And, as in any situation where rumor is the foundation of belief, the "facts" changed as they went from person to person.

The story that generally became accepted- at least at first- was that nobody could be sure how fast *Titanic* was sinking, so the women and children were being evacuated first to assure their survival. The men would shortly follow. There was no cause for concern- there were enough boats for everyone. *Titanic* had so many superlatives; she had to have enough lifeboats too- it was expected.

And because the ship had one of the most advanced wireless installations at sea- there had to be rescue ships on the way. Surely, these ships would arrive in plenty of time. Even if *Titanic* were destined to sink- it would not happen for a matter of hours, so it would be a simple affair of boarding a boat and being rowed to another ship.

Unfortunately, most of the men who told their wives these stories also believed them- attributing the "women and children first" order as simply Edwardian chivalry- "good form" on the part of the Captain. Few- if any- of the passengers knew that there were a limited number of boats. This misconception about boat capacity further hampered abandoning the ship because many women decided to wait and go with their husbands.

Although a few of the women either had the intelligence to note the discrepancies between what they were seeing and what they were being told- or saw through the deception and boarded the boats, many took it at face value- only realizing their peril when it was too late.

Meanwhile, on the bridge, Smith seemed to be as fuddled as Ismay- almost to the point where he appeared paralyzed by the enormity of what was happening. He too seemed unable to grasp the fact that the ship was actually sinking. He had ordered the boats swung out, but had not issued a command to start filling them. Twice, 2nd officer Lightoller asked Chief Officer Wilde about beginning the evacuation and both times he was told to wait for the order.

Lightoller could not understand what was causing the delay, but it was obvious to him that valuable time was being squandered. He finally decided to ignore Wilde and the chain of command. He went to the bridge to appeal directly to Smith. The 2nd officer pointedly asked the Captain if he wanted to start filling the boats with passengers.

Smith, at last, issued the order to abandon ship. The first boat was lowered to the sea at 12:45- *a full hour and fifteen minutes after the collision*.

There was a problem with the boats. As previously discussed, there were not near enough. *Titanic* had 2207 people aboard tonight- passengers and crew, with room in the boats for only 1178. Before tonight the disparity between the number of people aboard the ship and the number who could be evacuated in the boats was thought to be irrelevant.

Ismay must have reflected on his participation in the meetings where the number of boats was cut from sixty-four to forty-eight and finally to twenty. And of these, only sixteen of these were fitted to the davits. The remaining four were "collapsible" boats that were not readily available. Instead of being stowed on the boat deck, they were carried on top of the officers' quarters abaft the bridge.

Now this was coming home to roost. Even with perfect organization, and the cooperation of everyone, there was only room in the boats for about half the people aboard. It was only good fortune that the ship was not carrying her full passenger capacity for the boats would have held only about a third of that number.

But this night would not see a textbook, well organized, evacuation because White Star had never produced a textbook, and even if it had, it's doubtful that anyone would have read it.

Some of the confusion could have been eliminated by conducting a boat drill shortly after the ship left Ireland. By coincidence, one had been scheduled for the afternoon the day of the collision, but the weather had been beautiful and Smith was reluctant to spoil it, so the drill had been canceled.[182] Because *Titanic* was brand-new, no previous boat drills had *ever* been conducted aboard her. So, nobody- crew or passenger- knew to which boat they were assigned- or even if they *were* assigned.

Previous works on the *Titanic* disaster draw the seemingly obvious inference that the cancellation of this drill was instrumental in the appalling loss of life- that had everyone been rehearsed in their assignments, things would have transpired more positively.

However, examination reveals that the cancellation of the drill was largely irrelevant. Had *Titanic* conducted a boat drill on the afternoon prior to the disaster, the outcome would most likely been identical to what actually happened.

---

[182] This also was a violation of White Star directives. The rule stated that "The Regulations as to inspection of watertight doors, and fire and boat drill are to be carefully observed." The British hearing attributed the cancellation of the boat drill to the recalcitrance of stokers, who did not wish to participate in it. If this is true, they proved more than willing to participate in the actual abandonment of *Titanic*, having the largest proportion saved from the entire crew.

On the face of it, this assertion may appear astonishing, but let's examine the facts.

One seemingly obvious question- and one that appears to have been almost universally ignored by historians- arises at this point: How does one conduct a boat drill aboard a ship that *does not have enough boats*?

It would seem that such a drill would pointedly drive home to some passengers that the ship lacked the equipment to save the full complement of people aboard, but as strange as it may seem, there is strong evidence that prior to the sinking of *Titanic*, boat drills *did not involve the passengers*, but were intended only for the benefit of the crew.

Boat lists would be posted in crew areas, assigning crewmen to individual boats, and the "drill" usually did not involve anything more than swinging out a boat or two, checking the gear and then returning them to the deck- if even that much. Many sources also indicate that the cancellation of the boat drill was fairly common, and if a drill was conducted, it would usually occur in port, when there were no passengers aboard.

A boat drill requiring passenger participation would also necessitate allowing steerage passengers access to the boat deck- which was off limits to them.

There were problems with the crew too. As has been stated, very few of them knew how to operate the modern electrically-driven Welin Davits- except the indeterminable handful that had come from *Olympic.* Additionally, there were very few actual seamen aboard- less than 50 out of a crew of almost 900. The remainder was mostly passenger staff- waiters, stewards, cooks, bakers, etc.-many who had never been to sea before, so manning the boats was also going to be a difficulty.

Smith was more than aware of the shortage of boats, so he issued orders to Murdoch on the starboard side and Lightoller on the port side to board women and children first. Unfortunately for many of the male passengers aboard- Lightoller apparently misinterpreted this order as "women and children *only*" sending several boats away less than full because he could find no women or children willing or available to board them.[183]

On deck it had become difficult to communicate. The safety valves on the boilers had lifted shortly after the ship had stopped and now steam was roaring off from all four funnels- making even shouted conversation difficult.[184] Initially the officers and crew working to lower and fill the boats had to use hand signals to communicate with each other. Filling the boats went slowly at first.

The noise may have frightened some people briefly, but the excess steam was soon exhausted, the valves closed and more soothing sounds were heard. The ship's combined orchestra had convened on deck

---

[183] Lightoller's reputation has suffered over the years because of this mistake. However, the real fault has to lie in the order issued by Smith that apparently was ambiguous enough to allow it to happen and his lack of oversight in filling the boats to assure that the order was being followed correctly.

[184] There has been speculation that the engines of *Titanic* were left in "full astern" for an indefinite period after the collision, actually moving the ship from the area of the accident. The safety valves lifting belie this notion. Once the engines stopped steam pressure increased and lifted the valves, despite the efforts of those below to draw the fires under the boilers.

and began to play an assortment of lively tunes. There is no evidence that they were directed to do this, but instead had assembled on their own initiative with the intent to calm the passengers. This has always been presented as an unselfish, and ultimately heroic act, as the musicians were all lost, but it may have backfired to a certain extent- having an unintentional negative effect on filling the boats. We may easily visualize concerned passengers talking among themselves. "How serious can this be? If the ship is really going down, why is the orchestra playing *Alexander's Rag Time Band*?"[185]

Another problem in filling the boats was that neither Lightoller nor Murdoch trusted their rated capacities. The boats were certified to carry sixty-eight

---

[185] Even this is in dispute. Some survivors stated that the ship's orchestra played light tunes; some others say that they played hymns. There is even debate about the last selection that was played before the ship sank. Walter Lord stated in *A Night to Remember* that the final work played by the orchestra was an Episcopal Hymn called *Autumn*. However, in a later book he stated that he may have been in error about this, and instead the selection may have been a bright tune called *Song de Autumn*. There is even debate about whether *Nearer my God to Thee* was actually played, and if it was, whether it was the British or American version.

passengers each[186], but nobody seemed to know if that number could be boarded from the boat deck. There were concerns about the keels of the boats buckling if that number of people were seated in the boat before it was lowered.

Thomas Andrews- who seemed to be one of the few persons of responsibility aboard that night who actually grasped the seriousness of the situation- was appalled when he observed boats being lowered less than full. He quickly informed both officers that the boats could be loaded to capacity-and maybe even beyond. They had been tested in Belfast- filled with shipyard workers who surely weighed more than the women and children being boarded.[187]

---

[186] Some accounts say sixty-five. There is an additional complication in determining the absolute lifeboat capacity of *Titanic*, as she was equipped with two smaller lifeboats called "emergency boats," which were not identical. These boats were affixed to the davits just abaft the bridge and were to be used in situations where a boat might be launched to retrieve someone from the water. They had capacities of around forty people. The collapsibles were also smaller than the regular lifeboats.

[187] To give Lightoller and Murdoch some credit, they both decided, independently, to attempt to fill the boats from gangway ports farther down on the side of the ship once the boats entered the water.

Another reason that the boats left the ship without full loads had to do with the odd way the passengers congregated on the deck that night. While Lightoller had his hands full on the port side of the ship- with large crowds surging around each boat as it was lowered- the starboard side of the ship was somewhat deserted. Murdoch simply could not find people to fill some of his boats.[188]

An ironic factor is that the steerage passengers probably would have had taken to the boats with alacrity, but they were denied seats in them- even deprived access to the boat deck itself- at least at first. These people did not need convincing that the ship was going down. Many of them were quartered near the bow of the ship, and their cabin floors were now under several inches of swiftly rising water.

Lightoller sent a group of seamen, led by the ship's boson, below to open the doors. They were never seen again.

[188] This disparity was probably the result of one of the few commands we know was issued by Chief Officer Wilde. He noted that as she was sinking, *Titanic* seemed to be listing somewhat to starboard, so he ordered "everyone to the port side to straighten her up." Afterward, many passengers remained there and therefore missed an opportunity to board a boat.

Spooked rats had emerged from their hiding places and were scurrying over the decks below. There was little doubt in steerage that the ship was sinking- and as always seemed to be true in the life of the underprivileged classes- their part of the ship was going down first and there was nothing they could do to escape. However, even in steerage, there were a few who seemed unconcerned. Several men from third class had appeared on the well deck forward- their "promenade" space- and started an impromptu British football match, using a chunk of ice as the "ball."

Over the years it has been suggested that people were locked in steerage because of class distinctions, racism, hatred for the Irish, or a variety of other reasons.[189] Some accounts almost go to the point of accusing *Titanic*'s officers and crew of deliberate murder. The real reason is much simpler, and it again had to do with the absence of an evacuation plan for the

---

[189] Most histories of the *Titanic* disaster lead the reader to believe that almost all the steerage passengers aboard her were from Ireland, but they comprised only about a seventh of those aboard. There were passengers from all over the world, even a few from India and Asia.

ship, the perception that she was unsinkable- and partially with the fact that nothing official ever came from the officers about unlocking the gates- and once they were, the routes from the steerage areas to the boat deck were unmarked and confusing.

American immigration laws had established strict requirements about the segregation of steerage passengers. The concern was the spread of communicable diseases that many of them were suspected to carry. After all- it was thought- they came from some of the less desirable regions of Europe and more than one epidemic that had ravaged New York had been suspected to originate with immigrants. If the steerage passengers had been allowed to go to the boat deck with those of first and second-class and mingle freely- and the ship had survived- the officials in New York may have required everyone aboard to go through quarantine- and inspection.

Unfortunately, it seems that in the confusion the senior officers simply forgot about steerage- or, as we see again and again throughout all phases of this disaster, assumed that someone else was seeing to them. Under normal circumstances the ship's officers would have little to no contact with third class- except in the completion of rounds aboard the ship. If they gave the lower deck passengers any thought at all, they must have assumed that those responsible were dealing with the situation.

So, the crewmen assigned to steerage continued to wait for some word about their increasingly impatient charges. They were determined not to incur the wrath of the company by taking the initiative of opening the gates and allowing the third class passengers access to the rest of the ship and were obviously as ill-informed about the ship's true condition as their shipmates in the other classes.

Once it became apparent that the liner really was doomed, the barriers came down and the steerage passengers were allowed up on deck. However, even at this late hour, a few had to be broken down by force from within, and harried stewards, fearful of losing their jobs, vainly tried to collect the names of those who destroyed the gates so the line could recover damages. However, no matter how the steerage passengers escaped, by the time they reached the boat deck, most of the boats were gone.[190] Ultimately, it would have been Smith's decision to order the gates unlocked and the steerage passengers brought up to board the boats. This order was never given.

Steerage was not the only class denied access to the boats to begin with. Several second-class passengers attempted to gain access to the forward boat deck shortly after the order was passed to abandon ship- which would have required allowing them into the first class promenade area. They were stopped by stewards

---

[190] It cannot be denied that there was an undercurrent of racism aboard the ship. There was also some concern about an undisciplined "flood" of steerage passengers- who represented the largest group aboard- "rushing" the boats and interfering with the evacuation of the ship. So it does appear that in some cases there were people who made conscious decisions to evacuate first and second class before the others. Later, at the American Hearings, the Italian Ambassador was so disturbed by Fifth officer Lowe's characterization of Italians- who Lowe repeatedly described as cowardly "dagoes" - that the envoy demanded Lowe retract his statements and instead refer to the passengers in question as being of "Latin extraction."

and told that they were to report to the “second class” area of the boat deck, which was aft.

Now we must return to our discussion of the number of boats.

Let’s begin by looking at some figures. The total capacity of the boats aboard *Titanic*, including the collapsibles, was 1178 people. The total number aboard *Titanic* the night of the collision was 2228, so that means that at least 1050 people lost their lives in the disaster. But that’s not the true number. Since the sea was so calm, each boat could be conservatively “overloaded” by up to ten people, particularly if these people were children, so an additional 200 people were saved, or a total of 1378 people.

Unfortunately, these numbers are hypothetical. The real numbers went the other direction. Only *705* people were saved, or less than 60% of those that could have been had the crew strictly observed the rated capacity of the boats.

473 people died unnecessarily.[191]

There was space in the boats for them, but somehow they did not make it into one. We know that there were two collapsible boats that were not properly launched before the ship went down. One capsized and the other was swamped by the falling forward funnel.

That leaves room in the other boats for 1048 people- but again we are faced with a large disparity between the actual number saved and the number that could have been. Given the conditions of the night of April 14/15, 1912, was there any excuse that every boat was not filled to capacity?

The obvious answer lies in the indefensible squandering of time by the crew between the time of the collision and the moment the first boat left the ship. It was an incredible *one hour and fifteen minutes*. Even more unbelievable is that the crew gave no thought to retrieving and launching the collapsible boats until near

---

[191] These numbers are probably in error. There are at least three different generally accepted totals for those aboard, those saved and those lost. They do not differ significantly and they do not affect this discussion.

the end, and had to employ whoever was nearby to move the boats into position. Additionally, as we saw above, most of the passengers had fled to the stern when these boats were made ready for launch, and therefore there were only a handful of people in each.

How long would have been a reasonable amount of time between the collision and the launching of the boats? It should have been more of the order of thirty minutes or even less. Had the launching of boats begun sooner, all the boats would have been in the sea and away from the ship at the time the ship finally sank.

Smith should have ordered the passengers awakened and assembled as soon as the ship stopped- even before her damage was assessed. It would have been much easier to send them back to bed if it proved to be minor.

Let's do some calculations. The ship launched eighteen lifeboats, some filled to beyond their rated capacity and some virtually empty, but giving us an unbelievably low average of only *thirty-nine* people in each boat.[192]

If *Titanic* had been equipped with sixty-four boats, even using the low actual ratio of passengers to boats, then a grand total of 2506 passengers and crew could have been saved- 278 more people than were aboard that night. So even with the reduced numbers of people actually boarded in the boats the night of the collision, everyone would have been saved if there had been sixty-four boats- right?

Before we make that judgment, let's look at some more numbers, and examine one fact that almost everyone who has casually examined this disaster has seemed to overlook- *the crew was only able to launch eighteen of the twenty lifeboats aboard Titanic before she sank.*

It would not have made any difference if *Titanic* had been equipped with a dedicated boat for *each individual passenger*.

---

[192] One boat was launched with only twelve people in it, seven of them *male crewmembers*.

If all the external factors bearing on launching the boats were the same as on the night of the disaster, a *Titanic* equipped with sixty-four boats would have gone down with forty-six boats still aboard. Maybe a few could have been floated off the deck as she settled- with a handful of survivors aboard each, but we may only speculate as to what would have actually happened and how many would have escaped the ship alive.

The first boat launched was in the water at 12:45. The last boat was launched at 02:05. That gives us a period of one hour and twenty minutes to launch the boats that were loaded from the davits, with an average time of about four minutes and 30 seconds to launch each boat. Of course, we must remember that boats were being loaded on both sides of the ship so the actual times of filling each boat and lowering would have been longer. Nevertheless, even if we double the time for lowering each boat to nine minutes- the time of loading and launching remains respectable.

However, at the rate of loading and launching a boat every four minutes thirty seconds, calculation gives us a total time of four hours and seven minutes to launch sixty-four boats. The ship remained afloat for two hours and fifty minutes after striking the iceberg. Even if boat launching had commenced within seconds of the collision, the ship still would have been about one hour short of the time required to get all the boats into the water.

So, even if there were enough boats, could everyone have been saved? It looks like a gloomy prospect, but it could have been done. However, some of the other factors bearing on the evacuation of the ship would have had to have been significantly different.

For the purpose of our discussion, let's equip our *Titanic* with sixty-four boats, four under each set of davits, nested within each other. Let's also make them standard boats, not collapsibles- which required some assembly before they could be loaded.[193] This

---

[193] Collapsible boats consisted of a standard wooden lifeboat keel and bottom, but had canvas skirts that were stretched upward from the bottom over a heavy wire framework to bring the gunwales (sides) of the boat to the proper height. After *Titanic* went down, the shipping lines were forced to scramble to equip their ships with enough boats. Collapsibles were a popular choice, as they were lighter, cheaper, and required far less deck space. However, the sea was usually unkind to

configuration is what Harland and Wolff originally intended the ship to have.

We've already discussed the reason that they boats went away with less than full loads. What could have been done to change that?

Captain Smith should have taken charge. He failed to do this to any real extent. His classic portrayal in films, such as the 1953 *Titanic* and *A Night to Remember*, show him as a cool, clear-thinking officer who instantly and accurately sized up the situation and began to prepare for the worst- issuing concise orders and supervising the abandonment of the ship.[194]

But the real Edward Smith was a lot less decisive. In fact, Smith seemed at times to be almost incapacitated by the enormity of what was happening. There was no leadership aboard *Titanic* the night she

---

the canvas components- which required periodic replacement. Many lines neglected to do this, and the boats were essentially rendered useless. Even some attempts at maintaining the boats backfired. Some were painted to protect them, and so many coats were eventually applied that the canvas became a solid mass. For these reasons collapsible boats were eventually outlawed.

[194] Actually, in the 1953 version of *Titanic*, Captain Smith, as played by actor Brian Aherne, seems to be more competent *after* the collision.

went down, except in isolated places where officers, other members of the crew, or even passengers took charge.

Another obvious problem was communication. The gates that barred passengers from the first and second-class areas of the ship should have immediately been unlocked and everyone should have had access to the boat deck.

Stewards should not only have been dispatched to awaken passengers, but they should have been briefed beforehand as fully and realistically on the condition of the ship as possible, and they should have been ordered to be truthful with the passengers about their prospects of survival.

However, on the night of the collision, the people who knew the severity of the situation seemed to be quite reluctant to disclose this information to any of the passengers.

Of course, the oft-repeated reason is that the responsible parties aboard *Titanic* wanted to prevent panic, but it appears that nobody was thinking that far ahead that night, and that this reason may have been invented later to explain the inaction of the crew.

There was no plan; no strategy for evacuation of the ship, except what was cobbled together by the officers as events began to unfold. Even if the contention of preventing panic were true, it may have been better to risk some alarm to ensure that the boats left with full loads. In fact, there would have been a greater probability of panic if the passengers were able to recognize that nobody aboard had even the slightest idea of how to handle the situation.

Far from being panicked, the passengers seemed to be so blasé during the initial stages of the evacuation that they failed to grasp that they were in mortal danger. Some were actually angry that they had been awakened and told to report to the boat deck. They perceived nothing happening, and returned to their cabins. Some even went back to bed.

Those passengers who chose to remain on deck stood about in small groups talking to one another, and in the absence of any factual information about the damage *Titanic* had sustained, they resorted to speculation. Since the ship, at least in the beginning, seemed to be largely unaffected by the collision, they felt little need to board the boats. Many left the deck to warm up inside the ship.

Smith, the one person who indeed knew his ship was doomed, did little. Instead, he seemed to be rooted to the bridge during the initial part of the evacuation. The argument may be made that he was coordinating the abandonment of *Titanic* from that location, but there was little to manage. Aside from issuing some vague orders, Smith really did very little in the actual launching of the boats.

The one time he did seize the initiative, apparently realizing that several of the lifeboats that were already in the water were less than full, he called to them to return to the ship- and was ignored.[195]

---

[195] Almost universally, the occupants of these boats- when questioned later- stated that they did not return to the ship because they feared the "suction" *Titanic* was sure to produce when she sank. It is not hard to appreciate their apprehension. Nobody in the world had experience with such a large ship going down. In Number one Emergency Boat- the one that left the ship with only twelve people aboard- there was a story that the embarked Duff-Gordons had paid off the crew in the boat

It may have served everyone better if Smith had been more visible during this period. If it came to it, he should have addressed the passengers directly, telling them that the ship was indeed sinking, had less than two hours to live, and they needed to step to the boats as quickly as possible. It would be strictly women and children first until they were all off the ship, then the men would go.

All that would have been needed to prevent panic- at least in the initial stages of the evacuation- would be to tell the passengers that rescue ships were on the way, but it was not certain when they would arrive, thus everyone needed to leave the ship as soon as possible. Both of these would have been true.

But let's return to the matter of the boat drill. A drill- that required the participation of the passengers- would have benefitted all- eliminating the tremendous

---

not to row back to the ship. The story offered by the Duff-Gordons was different. They had taken pity on the crewmen in their boat- the sailors had lost everything and their pay had stopped when *Titanic* sank. The Duff-Gordons had offered to supply each with five pounds (about $250 in today's money) so they could replace some of their losses.

amount of confusion that attended the abandonment of *Titanic*. Instead of wandering the ship, looking for an opportunity to get in a boat, each passenger would have had a specific boat station where they could have waited until the boats were ready for them. Passengers could then be led to their boat and boarded. It would be far more orderly and it would allow families to stay together.[196]

But this still fails to address the problem of limited time. How do you get sixty-four filled boats into the water before the ship goes down?

As we've explored before, there would be no requirement to launch all the boats if the ship was not filled to capacity. There were 2228 people aboard *Titanic* on the night she sank, so only about 35 of the boats would have had to be launched if they were properly loaded. Unfortunately, that's about double the

---

[196] Today, evacuation drills are conducted before the ship leaves the pier and passengers are required to attend them. Ships are mandated to have several contingency plans too- that take into account damage to lifeboats or the inability to launch them due to list, etc. Each ship also carries a large number of large, enclosed rafts that inflate automatically when released from their canisters and dropped into the sea.

number that actually got away from the ship. So, it appears that even with more boats, many of the passengers aboard *Titanic* would still be doomed.

But again, that's not necessarily true. If Smith had detailed four crews- instead of two- to load boats, then thirty-six could have been launched before the ship made her final plunge. It probably would have been best to start at both ends of the boat deck and work toward the middle. In this way, the boats at the extreme ends of the deck would have been launched before the ship reached a point it became difficult to put them in the water. This idea is neither novel nor ingenious- it surely would have occurred to anyone who was detailed to devise a practical evacuation plan.

Conceivably, all the required boats could have been in the water and away from the ship by the time she broke in two and left the surface. Everyone could have been saved.

As we know, the majority of *Titanic*'s passengers and crew were left aboard as she foundered, either trapped inside as she plunged to the bottom, or left to perish in the frigid waters, either by drowning or freezing.

Afterward, many considered it to be a manifestation of providence as to who had survived and who had not.

However, as the newspapers began to tally the numbers, the idea that class distinctions governed those who were saved began to take hold. Although much had been made of Smith's command of "women and children first," there had been a good number of men saved. In fact, there had been more men from first class saved than steerage children- almost twice as many.

However, the numbers also revealed some other interesting facts, which the newspapers largely ignored. There actually were more males saved from *steerage* than first class. In fact, it appears that your chances of being saved were the worst if you were a male traveling in second class. Only fourteen of 168 aboard were saved.

As mentioned, almost every man who survived the *Titanic* disaster- unless he was a crewmember who had been assigned to a boat, or had been one of the few who had swam away from the ship before being taken into one- was branded as a coward and made to live with the stigma of taking a place in a lifeboat that could have saved a woman or child.

But there were actually enough empty seats in the boats to have saved *all* the women and children who were left aboard. No man who was saved deprived anyone of a seat- not even Ismay.

The women and children who died aboard *Titanic* were lost because there was no plan to save them.

Chapter Twenty- Rescue

As mentioned previously, some of the passengers had been told, or had simply surmised, that rescue ships had been summoned and were speeding to their aid. That was true- to an extent. Unfortunately, Phillips and Bride had been unable to find one near enough to make any difference, and it did not help any that Smith had insisted on exhibiting his talent for wasting valuable time.

The Captain went to the wireless shack shortly after the collision. Chief operator Phillips had just turned the key over to Harold Bride, the junior operator, and was preparing to go to bed. There was an unusual amount of commotion on deck for the hour. Phillips remarked that the ship had stopped, but he did not know why. He speculated that it might involve a return to Belfast for repairs. Neither radioman took pleasure in this thought, because they would surely be doubly swamped with messages.

The Captain stuck his head in the door and by clearing up one mystery- created another. "We've struck an iceberg, and I'm having an inspection made to tell us what it has done to us. You must be ready to send out a call for assistance, but do not send it until I tell you." Smith then left.

That explained why the ship had stopped, but the "call for assistance"? What was that all about? What would an unsinkable ship need with assistance? Maybe the collision had damaged the engines or boilers or some other vital part of the ship and she could not get underway again. Well, whatever it was that had happened- it had not affected the electrical power. The lights were still burning brightly and the wireless spark was still strong.

Phillips must have thought that there was little chance of him getting any sleep, so he abandoned his plans for bed and began to reconcile the "accounts."

Smith reappeared. "Send the call for assistance!" he ordered.

The Captain's command must have confused Phillips. What kind of "assistance" did he want?

"What call should I send?"

"The regular international call for assistance," Smith responded. "Just that."

At 0015, *forty-five minutes* after the collision, *Titanic* finally let the outside world know that she was in trouble. Phillips sent the letters "CQD" six times followed by "MGY", *Titanic*'s radio call sign.[197] He then sent "Have struck an iceberg. We are badly damaged. *Titanic*. Position 41 degrees 44 minutes north, 50 degrees 24 minutes west."

Several ships heard this call. It was also picked up by the Marconi shore station at Cape Race, Newfoundland.

The mood in the wireless room was somewhat lighthearted to begin with, with Bride suggesting that Phillips send "SOS" because it was the new call- and it might be his last chance to send it. Bride later testified

---

197 *Titanic* was originally assigned "MUC" as a call sign, but because her fitting out was delayed by the repairs to *Olympic*, the sign was given to an American ship named *Yale*. So, if things had stayed the same, the title of this book could have been *SOS-MUC*. Somehow, it just does not have the same ring to it.

that he and Phillips said "all kinds of funny things to each other," during these first few minutes.

The distress call drew quick responses from other ships. The first was from the North German Lloyd liner *Frankfurt* at 0018. Phillips gave her operator more information when he returned from informing his Captain. Unfortunately *Frankfurt* was over 150 miles away to the southwest- it would take her several hours to reach *Titanic's* reported position.[198]

Another ship responded. She was much closer. Her name was *Carpathia*.

It had been a somewhat slow night aboard the Cunarder and her lone wireless operator, Harold Cottam, had been on the bridge talking to one of the watch

---

[198] The story that Phillips was looking for a Marconi equipped ship to aid *Titanic* and therefore rudely dismissed *Frankfurt*- which used the German Telefunken system- is false. Telefunken and Marconi had business agreements that allied them. The truth is that *Frankfurt* was too distant to have made any difference and instead of her operator realizing this and staying off the air, he became a pest- repeatedly asking Phillips for details of the collision and interfering with communication with other ships. Phillips finally told him, less than politely, to stay off the air. Cyril Evans, of *Californian*, stated later that *Frankfurt's* operator made a nuisance of himself again early on the morning of April 15th, when he jammed signals between *Californian* and *Carpathia*.

officers. He had returned to his cabin and prepared to go to bed. Earlier he had tuned his radio to a different frequency and listened in on the transmissions from one of Marconi's shore stations.

There were messages for *Titanic*, but Cottam did not hear her on the frequency. Knowing that she should be within range, he decided, before he switched off his set for the night, to call her and ask her if she knew there were some Marconigrams awaiting her.

Cottam was shocked to find out that *Titanic* had struck an iceberg and was sinking. He quickly took down her position and ran to the bridge.

Once there, the officers on duty did not believe him. It appears that Cottam may have had a reputation for being a bit of a practical joker, and they thought he was playing a trick on them.

Sure! An unsinkable ship was sending a distress call! Of course! Let's all go and make fools of ourselves by waking up the Captain and telling him! Cottam did not waste any time trying to convince them.

Instead, he ran to the cabin of Captain Arthur Rostron, who had turned in for the night.

Cottam burst into the Captain's cabin and quickly explained what was happening. Rostron, although initially disturbed at the radio operator's unannounced entry, immediately ordered the ship turned around and headed North North West. It was not a joke.

Phillips now had a corrected position. Smith had ordered fourth officer Boxhall- who, while he might not be the best at determining damage, was reputed to be the best navigator aboard- to recalculate their location. [199]

"CQD CQD SOS SOS CQD SOS. Come at once. We have struck a berg. CQD OM (Wireless shorthand meaning 'It's a CQD old man'). Position 41

---

[199] Boxhall's position was calculated from the star observations that were made about 19:30 that evening. The latitude was almost right, but the longitude was wrong, suggesting that *Titanic*'s chronometer was off by a few minutes. The wreckage of the ship was found several miles southeast of where he calculated her to be. After Boxhall died, he had left instructions that his cremated remains be scattered at *Titanic's* last calculated position. He died before the wreck was discovered, so he never knew of his error.

degrees 46 minutes north, fifty degrees 14 minutes west. CQD SOS."

Apparently it now became impossible for Phillips to hear any response because of the safety valves lifting. *Ypiranga*, a German Hamburg American liner, heard *Titanic* repeating the same general message several times- maybe as many as twenty.[200] The text of the message varied slightly each time, but it followed a general pattern. "MGY CQD (or SOS)." Phillips gave her position, and then "Require immediate assistance. We have collided with iceberg. Sinking. Can hear nothing for noise of steam."

Cottam now had returned to his set aboard *Carpathia* and received the corrected position. He relayed it to Rostron, who changed course accordingly. Unfortunately, *Carpathia* was slow. Her regular route this time of year was from Italy to New York- carrying Hungarian immigrants westbound- hardly a run requiring an ocean greyhound.

---

[200] The odd name of the ship was derived from a city in Brazil.

Unlike her bigger cousins, *Mauretania* and *Lusitania*, who could steam at speeds of 28 knots, *Carpathia's* regular cruising speed was half that- 14. Tonight, eastbound, she was somewhere around fifty-eight miles away from *Titanic*'s reported position.

Rostron ordered his engineers to do whatever was required to boost *Carpathia's* speed. They pulled out the stops, shutting off almost anything that would consume steam- including heat to the ship. They also took some serious liberties with her power plant- even resorting to circumventing the safety valves on her boilers to allow her engines to operate at a higher steam pressure. They probably managed to coax her to somewhere around fifteen knots.[201]

Even at this increased pace; it would still take about four hours to cover the distance between her and

---

[201] The widely accepted estimate of *Carpathia's* boosted speed is around seventeen knots, but it was unlikely that the little Cunarder was capable of that velocity. The speed calculation was based on the distance between the dead reckoned position of *Carpathia* at the time the distress call came in and the erroneous position *Titanic* supplied, which was almost thirteen miles to the northwest of where the wreck was located, so her actual speed during the rescue dash cannot be determined.

Titanic. By that time it would be too late for most of the people aboard the sinking ship. It did not help that *Carpathia* had to backtrack the ten to twelve nautical miles that she had sailed between the time of the collision and the first distress call.

There had to be someone closer!

Now in the night, *Titanic*'s sister called. *Olympic* was also eastbound, but she was almost ten times farther away than *Carpathia* -over 500 miles- more than a full day's steaming.

Like the majority of people that night- *Olympic's* officers seemed to have problems realizing the seriousness of *Titanic*'s plight. She asked about the weather in the vicinity of *Titanic* and asked, "Are you steaming south to meet us?"

Smith's response did not dispel the confusion to any degree, he asked Captain Haddock, master of *Olympic*, to have his boats ready.[202] Despite powerful

---

[202] Haddock is virtually unknown today, but he was almost a maritime superstar in his time. During the First World War, he was cited by the Royal Navy for his courageous attempt to tow the torpedoed Royal Navy battleship *Audacious* to safety with *Olympic*. Unfortunately, the

wireless sets aboard both the White Star sisters, *Olympic's* operator was having trouble hearing his counterparts aboard *Titanic*. He later testified that there were problems with atmospherics and interference from the number of ships transmitting in between the two liners.

Meanwhile, on deck, the lookouts- who oddly were still manning *Titanic*'s crow's nest- sounded their bell and rang the bridge. Had anyone noticed the light off the starboard bow?

There *was* a light off in that direction- it appeared to be a small steamer of some kind. Boxhall began to try to signal her with the Morse lamp. He observed her closely with his binoculars, and thought she might be responding, but the message was

---

warship sank before she could be saved. All of *Olympic's* passengers were sworn to secrecy about the fate of the battleship, which did little to keep the word from getting out (actually the Germans knew about it before the British public.) Later, Haddock was tapped to command a "phantom fleet" of merchant ships that had been altered to resemble a large squadron of warships in order to decoy the Germans- who were not fooled.

unreadable. He finally assumed that it must be the smaller ship's masthead light flickering.[203]

Harold Bride appeared on the bridge with an update about the rescue fleet on the way to *Titanic*'s position. The news was not good- none of the responding ships were near enough to make any difference. Smith took Bride to the bridge wing and pointed out the mysterious light off the bow. There was a ship close enough! What about her? Had they tried to contact it?

---

[203] An Able Seaman named Buley, aboard *Titanic*, told the American Inquiry that he was certain that a ship had steamed within three miles of the sinking liner and had remained off her bow for three hours before she sailed away. Since *Titanic* sank less than three hours after the collision, and nobody else reported seeing lights so close to the ship, this may serve as an indication of how unreliable eyewitness testimony can be. In fact, there were a number of people aboard *Titanic* who later stated that they had observed lights at different bearings all about the ship- giving the impression that the liner had been surrounded by potential rescue vessels. However, to the inexperienced eye, celestial bodies, particularly in the extremely dark conditions on the night of April 14th, would appear to be lights of nearby ships. If they set below the western horizon, the natural assumption would be that they had "sailed away." The author, employing a computer and an astronomy software program, was able to approximate the night sky in the general area *Titanic* went down. There were several bright stars near the horizon during the time of the sinking. In fact, Stanley Lord, Captain of *Californian* stated later that he and his crew had experienced problems with misidentified celestial bodies on the night *Titanic* went down.

Bride was puzzled. There was no way the other ship could have missed *Titanic*'s SOS if her operator was monitoring his wireless. The big liner's distress call would have arrived like thunder over his headset- obliterating any other signals he might be hearing. Bride could only speculate as to why the steamer had not responded. Not all ships had wireless, or maybe she was not able to keep a twenty-four hour watch.

The light was maddening- it seemed so close! The other ship appeared to be so near that Smith ordered word to be passed to officers lowering the lifeboats to instruct them to row toward it after they were launched- unload their passengers and return.

The other ship seemed to be oblivious of *Titanic* and her predicament. Somehow they would have to attract her attention.

Around this time the telephone on the bridge rang again. This time it was Quartermaster George Rowe calling from his duty station- the docking bridge at the stern of the ship. He was perplexed. Did the bridge know that there was a lifeboat in the water? The officers looked at each other in disbelief- didn't Rowe know what was going on? Apparently not, but they quickly found a job for him.

Titanic had one more method at her disposal for seeking assistance. Rowe was sent to the pyrotechnics locker. He removed twelve rockets and took them to the port bridge wing. Captain Smith ordered the first one fired a little before 0100 and told Rowe to fire the rest of them at six to eight minute intervals. Maybe that would wake up the officers of the other ship.

Only time would tell.

Chapter Twenty One- the Lights on the Horizon

In 1912, The International Mercantile Marine Corporation was well on its way to eliminating competition on the North Atlantic. Their strategy in the acquisition of properties was simple. If a competing line represented a threat- or appeared vulnerable- an offer was made. If the line resisted, the IMM would undercut them on their routes until they capitulated or were put out of business. By 1912, IMM had absorbed almost twenty-five lines, including the relatively small concern of Frederick Leyland.

The upper management of IMM, many of them who had experience in building monopolies in other businesses, knew only too well the headaches that could be produced if acquired companies were merged into one large entity, so most of IMM's subsidiaries were allowed to function as autonomous units. Therefore, while Leyland and White Star might both be IMM owned companies, they did not share procedures.

The evening of April 14, 1912 found the Leyland Liner *Californian* stopped on the eastern edge of the ice field. Whether she actually was a "liner" is open to debate. A more accurate definition of the ship would be that she was a small, slow, cargo vessel equipped with Spartan accommodations for forty passengers.

Californian was middle-aged for a ship- having been built in 1901 in Scotland to carry cotton. She had no regular run, but instead served ports all over the east coast of the United States from Britain.

When IMM had absorbed Leyland, *Californian* had been modified to include more passenger accommodations, but tonight, like many of her voyages, there were none aboard.

Californian's destination was Boston, but she had stopped when her lookouts reported what appeared to be a solid field of ice ahead. Her Captain- Stanley Lord- wanted no part of it, deciding to work his way through the area of danger after the sun rose the next morning.

Lord was a relatively young- only thirty-five- and he had been in command of *Californian* a little over a year. *Californian* had entered the fringes of the ice field earlier. It was not unexpected, as the ship was equipped with wireless and she had received many of the same messages as had *Titanic*. Lord had posted extra lookouts at the bow of the ship who had reported thickening ice all evening.

Californian had even transmitted wireless ice warnings to other ships- one of which *Titanic* had intercepted.

It's unclear what time Lord left the bridge for the night. He stated that he left sometime around 23:00, but his officers said that it was earlier- before 21:00. Actually, in light of later events, the time he left was irrelevant. Lord assured himself that all was in hand, turned the watch over to his officers and went below.

About 23:00, the crew of *Californian* observed a ship approaching from the east. She was traveling west and, if she continued on course, would pass south of their position. It seemed that this vessel must have spotted the ice field because at about 23:30, she too stopped.

From what the officers on *Californian* could make of her- she seemed to be a passenger ship, and, like they, had apparently decided to wait until morning to make a traverse of the ice field. It also appeared that she had turned off most of her lights. One of the officers aboard *Californian* thought that it was rather odd for a ship to do this, but another had been previously employed by a line where it was common practice to extinguish the deck lights around midnight to encourage passengers to go to bed. Maybe this ship was doing the same thing.

The officer on watch, Charles Groves, decided to contact the other ship to determine her identity. He brought the Morse lamp to the bridge and plugged it in. He sent the word "What?" (meaning "what ship") several times, but it seemed as if the other vessel was oblivious to his signals.

At about this time, Captain Lord reappeared on the bridge and joined in the discussion about the other vessel. The debate concerned itself with what kind of ship she was. Lord examined her through his binoculars and informed his officers that his verdict was that she was merely another freighter. Groves explained to the Captain that the ship in question had extinguished her deck lights after she stopped and that he was sure that she was a passenger liner.

Lord, still looking at the other ship with his glasses, noted a flickering light aboard her. "There- he's answering you," he said.

None of the officers on the bridge could make any sense of the sequence of flashes and finally deciding it was the other ship's masthead light malfunctioning.

Groves asked the Lord if there were any passenger steamers known to be in the area.

"Only *Titanic*," the Captain replied. He then left the bridge.

The watch that came on duty at 24:00 (or 00:00 if you prefer) was informed of the lights on the horizon.

Around 01:00, the mystery ship began to fire rockets, and to- to use the words of the observers aboard *Californian*- look "queer in the water."

Maybe this was something that Captain Lord needed to be advised of, and if you look closely, it may reveal something about the interplay between the officers on *Californian*. Other than the usual relationship between ship's officers, it appears that there may have been some undercurrents that night aboard the small steamer.

One seems to show Lord as one of those masters who had to have the last word on every issue- and if that included being awakened for what might seem to be a trivial item- so be it. It also might indicate that Second officer Herbert Stone- on watch with an apprentice named James Gibson- sent Gibson to the chartroom, where Lord was resting on a sofa, to give him a rather pointed hint that *Californian* might want to check out the odd doings to the south.[204]

---

[204] Many of *Californian's* crew admitted later that most everyone aboard the ship was afraid of the Captain. It may have been Lord's

The Captain had been asleep. Exhausted when he turned in, he awoke groggy and it soon became clear that he was disinclined to investigate. He asked a couple of questions- about the color of the rockets (white) and the number that had been fired (a total of eight). Lord's assessment was that his officers were probably observing nothing more than the other ship using some kind of "company" signal, perhaps sending a message to another vessel out of sight of *Californian*- over the horizon.

Lord either did not ask the right questions, did not absorb what he was told, or Gibson failed to properly communicate what he had seen to the Captain. Had Lord been on the bridge, things may have been different. He advised Gibson to tell Stone to continue attempting to establish contact with the other ship with the Morse lamp.

"Company signals" were a holdover from the days before the invention of wireless, when ships could

---

nature to intimidate his crew, but it could be something as simple as a chronic lack of sleep that gave him his sour disposition.

only communicate if they had one another in sight. Each shipping line had adopted a unique rocket display to for identification at night. For instance, a White Star ship would fire two green rockets at once. The Leyland line identified its ships with three red rockets fired in succession. Each ship carried a book that detailed these signals. *Californian* had such a volume in her chartroom.

However, no company identified its ships with white rockets of the type fired from *Titanic*. Had the officers of *Californian* taken the initiative- or Lord had exercised the elementary precaution to order them to check the book, they would have discovered this.

The Merchant Shipping Act of 1894 (Great Britain) established that a ship in trouble could signify such by the following:

"When a ship is in distress and requires assistance from other ships or from the shore, the following shall be the signals to be used or displayed by her, either together or separately.
1. A gun fired at intervals of about one minute;
2. Flames on the ship (as from a burning tar barrel, oil barrel, etc.)

3. Rockets or shells, throwing stars of any color or description, fired one at a time, at short intervals."

There has been discussion over the years that *Californian* failed to act because the rockets should have been red, but we must note that the above states that a distress rocket could be of *any color.* The only specification made is that the rockets "throw stars", meaning that the rocket should detonate at the top of its flight, emitting a pyrotechnic burst- like a fourth of July display. It was this type of rocket that *Titanic* fired.[205]

Lord was only told that the mystery ship was firing "white rockets."

There is another item in the above that may have some bearing. Although the act specifies that if a ship chooses to employ a gun to signal distress, it should be fired at intervals of about a minute- it becomes vague when it comes to the launching of rockets, only

---

[205] Some sources state that these "rockets" were actually projectiles launched from a mortar-type device called a "socket signal." The delivery mechanism is irrelevant; the display above the ship would have been the same and would have made no difference in the observation of it.

saying that they should be fired at “short “intervals. As to what constituted such a period was left up to either the person firing the rockets or the person observing them.

Out of her total store of thirty-six- *Titanic* launched only eight detonating rockets. Rowe fired the rockets irregularly- every five to eight minutes. This was either his or Smith’s definition of a short time. Unfortunately, in later testimony, neither his American or British questioners thought to ask Rowe why only eight rockets were fired nor why there was such a significant interval between them. The only inference that may be drawn from reading the testimony is that they fired only eight because they ran out of time.[206]

---

[206] It often becomes almost infuriating to read the hearing transcripts- of either investigation. Questions that should have been asked weren’t, vague answers were not clarified with follow-up questions, and sometimes, when it appeared that someone was on the path to discover something important, another person (usually one of the lawyers) interrupted to ask something else or discuss some obscure legal point. When the questions resumed, the original thread of the discussion was lost and it then proceeded off on an irrelevant tangent. Some authors have attributed this (particularly in the case of the British Inquiry) as being done intentionally to avoid sensitive issues.

If- for argument- these rockets had been fired one each minute and all thirty-six had been fired, perhaps the officers of *Californian* would have interpreted them for what they were. No company signal specified that a ship would fire that number of rockets or in so short a span. It is quite likely that had Lord been told that a ship had been observed firing thirty-six rockets in a little over a half hour- he would have surmised that something was wrong and investigated.

The one man who could clear up the mystery was never consulted. Apparently nobody thought to wake up Cyril Evans- the wireless operator- or if they did, they never voiced it. Evans had switched off his set, and turned in around 2300, which was around the time he normally went to bed. However, his role in the *Titanic* disaster began earlier in the evening.

Shortly after nightfall, Evans had noticed that *Californian* had stopped and went to the bridge to find out why. There he encountered Captain Lord. Lord told Evans that there was ice ahead and asked if there were any ships nearby.

The nearest vessel with wireless- in Evans' estimation- was *Titanic*, which, based on her signal strength, was less than one hundred miles to east- probably nearer. He had been listening in on her transmissions to the Cape Race Marconi station. For a good part of the evening it had all been private traffic- people sending telegrams to friends, family, and business associates ashore.

Lord told Evans to call *Titanic* and warn her about the ice.

Evans could have transmitted the warning as a "Master's Service Message," a class of communication sent in situations when the safety of the ship, or other ships, was believed to be involved, and it was to be handled with utmost seriousness. Operators aboard *Titanic*- no matter how busy they might be- would have been compelled to drop what they were doing, take down the message, and immediately deliver it to the Captain. An acknowledgement would then be transmitted to the originating ship.

However, a Master's Service Message was only sent at the Captain's direction. It was not Evans' prerogative, Lord did not order it, and Evans apparently did not suggest it. If he did, Lord must have decided against doing so.

So, Evans sent the message informally, breaking in on *Titanic*'s operator, Jack Phillips, conversationally, beginning his transmission with the letters "SOM", which in wireless shorthand meant, "Say, Old Man." He followed it with "we are surrounded by ice and stopped."

Phillips was furious. He had been taking down inbound messages from Cape Race and not only had Evans interrupted the message he had been copying- requiring retransmission- but also the proximity of *Californian* to *Titanic* almost deafened him.

Titanic's senior operator responded angrily, telling Evans, "Shut up, shut up, I am busy; I am working Cape Race. You are jamming me." He then called Cape Race again, "Sorry, please repeat; jammed."

It may appear that Evans committed a rookie mistake breaking in on *Titanic* in this fashion, but he later stated that he was unaware that Phillips had been receiving messages from Cape Race. Evans' set was unable to pick up the shore station, so to him it would have sounded like the airwaves were quiet.

Earlier in the evening, Evans had been contacted by second operator Bride, and he may have thought that he was transmitting to him. The way he prefaced his message with SOM (Say old man) may indicate that he may have had two purposes in contacting the bigger ship.

The first was to obviously warn *Titanic* of the ice, the second may have been to spend some time "chatting" with another operator. It's obvious that the message- as sent- did not conform to accepted Marconi practice. It's possible that Phillips only heard the first three letters of the transmission, and because the message was literally blasting him with noise, he may have removed his headsets until he was certain the transmission had ended. He may have not heard anything about the ice at all. However, even if he had, he had no idea of where the message had originated, and he never asked.

Evans stated that he did not take Phillips' rebuke personally, since, as he later testified, such things happened frequently because of *Californian's* unsophisticated wireless apparatus.

Evans decided not to press the issue, so he figuratively shrugged his shoulders, shut down his set for the night and went to bed. However, in doing so, he was in direct contradiction of Marconi regulations, which required operators to remain on duty during periods of danger- and the ice field could be construed as such- particularly to a large passenger liner steaming at full speed toward it.

But Evans' seeming negligence is a matter for debate. Unfortunately, the Marconi regulations- like so many others we have seen bearing on this event- were somewhat inexact. There was no clear definition of the constitution of "danger."

Evans, like Phillips, was not a seaman, and to him, there would have been no danger. His ship was drifting peacefully, and safely, at the edge of an ice field that had been sighted by her crew. It must have never occurred to him that *Titanic* might be unable to sight the ice in time.

From Evans point of view, *Titanic* had been amply warned about the ice. Evans undoubtedly received most of the messages the bigger ship had, and because he had heard her respond, knew she had too. Evans had been a Marconi employee for only six months- and had only been to sea four times- so his inexperience undoubtedly also factored into the equation.

But what would have happened if Phillips had taken down the message and taken it to the Captain? What would Smith have gathered from it? Again, we must resort to speculation. A ship, somewhere between fifteen and twenty miles north of *Titanic*'s course, as indicated by her given position, was stopped at the edge of the ice field. *Californian's* message may have convinced Captain Smith that the danger was still comfortably north of him.

However, one other possibility exists. If Phillips had taken down the message from the Californian, and delivered it to the bridge, he may have remembered the *Mesaba* message and taken it to the Captain too.

But when Evans shut down his set and went to bed, it didn't end the role of *Californian's* wireless in the story. Her third officer[207], Charles Groves, came off watch at midnight and decided to stop by the wireless shack before he turned in for the night. He was interested in wireless and sometimes when Evans was not busy, he would let Groves listen in on other ships.[208]

---

[207] Groves' actual position aboard the ship is a bit muddled. He's been identified as the First officer of *Californian* by some sources, but at the British hearing, he stated that while he was actually the second officer of the ship, he assumed the duties of third officer.

[208] Marconi operators, during their training at the Marconi school called the "Tin Tabernacle", had to sign an agreement that the privacy of messages sent by wireless would be protected. Technically, when Evans allowed Groves to listen, he was violating a Marconi regulation, but considering the primitive nature of radio- where anyone with a wireless set could listen in on anything their set could receive- it was a somewhat hollow rule.

The radio operator was already in bed and asleep. He roused when Groves entered.

"What ships have you got Sparks?" Groves asked.

Evans' reply was short- probably the result of fatigue and disinterest. "Only *Titanic*."

Groves pressed the headsets to one of his ears, listened for a few moments, but heard nothing. He returned them to the wireless table and left Evans' cabin.

Over the years, this abortive visit by Groves to the wireless cabin has been noted by many historians as yet another circumstance where a simple change in events could have led to the rescue of all aboard *Titanic*.

But let's examine what happened and what could have happened.

Groves was not an experienced radio operator, and it appears that he was more interested in eavesdropping on wireless traffic than understanding the device that made it possible. Had he been, he would have known that for the set to work, two things had to be done. One was obvious; the power had to be turned on.

The second would be the activation of the set's clockwork detector- a rudimentary tuner. It had to be wound up before any signals could be received. Groves was unaware of this.

Even had he managed to turn on the set, and the detector, Groves probably would have derived little from what he heard. He knew Morse code, but the rapid-fire speed of transmission used in wireless communication made it difficult for him to understand much of it- he later stated that if he was lucky if he could recognize one word in three. Like someone learning a foreign language, Groves could understand wireless Morse only if it were transmitted slowly.

Most, if not all, of the "shorthand" employed by the wireless operators eluded him too. It's almost certain that he could have recognized the three Morse letters "SOS" sent by *Titanic*, although it is unlikely that he would have understood their meaning. Although today virtually everyone knows what the three letters signify, few did in 1912. SOS was not a nautical signal- it was exclusive to the wireless system- and it was rarely transmitted- so Evans probably would have never have mentioned it. For the same reason, the older distress call- “CQD”- would have been meaningless too.[209]

Furthermore, he would have been unable to associate the call sign “MGY” with *Titanic*.

And, it appears that almost all of the above would have been rendered irrelevant. There were no

---

[209] While it is commonly thought that “SOS” has any one of a number of ingenious definitions- such as “Save Our Ship,” “Save Our Souls,” "Survivors On Ship," "Stop Other Signals," "Send Out Sailors," and even “Sink Or Swim,” it is not an acronym. It was selected because the series of letters- three dots, three dashes, three dots- was easy to transmit, was unlikely to be misunderstood, and could be read by almost anyone with a passing knowledge of Morse code- although it must have escaped everyone that the person who read the signal would have to know what the three letters meant.

“CQD”, the old signal- and the one originally sent by *Titanic*, did not have any designated meaning either. “CQ,” instead of meaning “Come Quick” as some believe, actually was a radio prefix for “All stations”- meaning that everyone transmitting at the time had to immediately stop and stand by for an important message. Because all radio activity was supposed to cease as soon as the signal was transmitted, “CQ” was also called the “silent” signal. The appended “D” was generally accepted as shorthand for “Danger” or “Disaster,” although, again, it had never been officially given either of these definitions.

Originally a German signal, “SOS” had been adopted internationally in 1906, and although there is debate about which ship actually was the first to send “SOS,” it was not *Titanic*. Most sources state that the most likely candidate for this “honor” was Cunard’s *Slavonia* on June 10, 1909.

transmissions from *Titanic* until almost forty-five minutes after the collision, and *Californian's* set lacked the range to receive anything more than messages from nearby stations. We must assume that Groves probably arrived in the wireless shack only a few minutes after his watch ended at midnight. Even if the wireless set had been operating, Groves would still have heard nothing, and assumed *Titanic*, which Evans had told him was the only ship within range, was not transmitting and would have quickly abandoned the radio.

Meanwhile, up on deck, Stone and Gibson, with little to do other than observe the ship to the south, saw her disappear- presumably steaming away. Again, Lord was advised. The Captain, as disinterested as before, sleepily listened to the news and told them to enter it in the log- the matter finished as far as he was concerned.

It was far from finished.

Early the next morning Evans was awakened by *Californian's* Chief Officer- George Stewart.

Stewart had come on duty at 0400. Stone told him about the ship that had been firing rockets.

Stewart immediately went below and knocked at the door of the wireless room- that doubled as Evans' cabin- heard no response, and finally entered to rouse the operator- who awoke with a start.

Stewart got right to the point, "Wireless, there is a ship that has been firing rockets in the night. Will you call and see if you can find out what is wrong - what is the matter?"

Evans rose from his bunk and switched on his set. He was surprised- and undoubtedly dismayed- to find the ether full of news of *Titanic*.

Carpathia had already arrived at the southern edge of the ice field and was in the process of picking up the survivors.[210] The ship was going to finish embarking those remaining in the boats and then steam through the area nearby to search for anyone who had been unable to board a lifeboat and somehow might be still alive in the frigid water.

---

[210] Stewart had observed *Carpathia* before he went below to wake Evans. He asked Stone if she was the ship they had seen firing rockets. Stone, who had not seen her before, indicated that she was a different ship.

Evans took the news to Lord, who must have finally put everything together. The times in *Californian's* scrap log almost perfectly coincided with what was learned over the wireless. It must have been *Titanic* that had steamed up and "stopped."

It had been she who fired the rockets.

It had been the dying *Titanic* frantically trying to signal to them by Morse Lamp.

It had been *Titanic* that went down under their noses while Captain Lord snoozed in the chartroom and Wireless operator Evans was literally asleep at the switch. While it could have been some other ship observed on the horizon, there was little debate about if it was.

Lord immediately ordered the engine started and a course set for *Titanic*'s last reported position. Finding nothing there, *Californian* steamed to join *Carpathia*. When she arrived, the small Cunarder had just completed the task of taking aboard all the survivors from the lifeboats- and Captain Rostron was doubtful about finding any more in the icy water.

Carpathia's crew had looked it over closely- finding only one dead crewman floating face down in the water, a barber pole, and a large quantity of cork, later determined to be insulation from *Titanic's* refrigerated stores, on the surface. Lord offered to continue the search. Rostron accepted and immediately ordered *Carpathia* to steer a course for New York.

Lord's examination was cursory. *Californian* made two passes through the area and found nothing more than a small amount of wreckage. Lord later stated that the amount of debris in the water looked as if something small like a "fishing boat" had gone down, and not a great liner. His observations confirmed his opinion that there was nothing further he or anyone else could do. *Californian* resumed her voyage to Boston.

It must have occurred to Captain Lord and his officers that they may have committed a grave error- or at least it might be construed in that way. They could all be in serious trouble if the word got out that they had allowed one of the greatest sea disasters the world had ever known to transpire within sight of their ship and had done little or nothing to investigate or assist. They would probably lose their jobs and maybe even their licenses. Perhaps it might be best for them to keep what they saw to themselves.

Apparently, there were some long, private discussions aboard the small ship before she reached Boston.[211] Lord asked each of his officers to give him written statements about what they observed the night *Titanic* sank.

Trouble has a way of eluding the most sophisticated precautions, and unfortunately for the officers of *Californian*, they did not think of everything- or everyone.

One of *Californian's* engine room crew, Ernest Gill, stated that he had been on deck, trying to get a little

---

[211] The investigations into the loss of *Titanic* revealed that none of the information concerning the observation of rockets contained in *Californian's* "scrap" log was transferred to the permanent log. The scrap log, which was somewhat like a child's rough writing tablet, was found to be missing the pages dealing with the night *Titanic* sank. The story given to the investigators was that pages of the scrap log were removed- and destroyed- as a matter of course when the information was transcribed to the permanent log. From the content of the questions directed to Captain Lord about this practice, it seems fairly clear that he was not believed.

relief from the heat of the engineering spaces on the night *Titanic* went down. He had also seen the rockets. Gill stated that he had gone on deck twice during the night of the 14th, the first time shortly before midnight. At that time, he reported observing a large steamer south of the ship. He made the comment that she was clearly visible from deck- so she also must have been evident from the bridge.[212]

Gill stated that he attempted to turn in after the conclusion of his watch, but found he could not sleep. He returned to the deck, and now observed the ship to the south firing rockets. The first rocket looked like a "falling star" to him, but as he watched, and additional rockets were fired, it became evident what they were. He also stated that he could not understand why nobody had thought "to wake up the wireless man" and find out what was happening.

---

[212] Unfortunately, it was never specified on which deck of *Californian* Gill was standing when he said he observed the rockets. Most likely he was standing on the main deck, which was twenty four feet above the waterline. The other deck on which he could have observed the other vessel was higher on the ship- on the same level as the bridge, so anything he observed from the main deck could have been also seen there.

However, oddly, it appears that Gill's indignation about the inaction of his crewmates was only expressed after the fact. He made no effort that night to find out if anyone *had* roused Evans. Gill did not visit the bridge- or make an attempt to wake the wireless operator himself. Instead, he went below and turned in for the night.

Almost as soon as *Californian* docked in Boston, Gill was giving his story to the press.[213] Within hours, the news of *Californian* was out. It seemed to be a clear case of dereliction of duty.

Or was it?

---

[213] Gill's revelation to the newspapers was not entirely altruistic. He was given five hundred dollars (an amount close to ten thousand dollars in today's money) for his story. This has led some historians to assert that it may have been, at the least, a gross exaggeration, and at the most- a lie. There has also been the suggestion that Gill fabricated the whole account from what he heard aboard the ship as she sailed toward Boston. Nevertheless, others aboard *Californian* testified later that his story was essentially correct. The rockets had been observed, and the Captain had done nothing.

Chapter Twenty Two – *Californian*- What really could she have done?

Over the years, there has been extensive, and exhaustive, discussion regarding the role of *Californian* in the *Titanic* disaster. Opinion about the smaller ship has diverged to opposite ends of the spectrum.

One group of historians stops just short of accusing the officers of *Californian* with criminal negligence in their failure to recognize and investigate the signals they sighted to their south.

Their contention is that had *Californian* immediately started her engine and moved toward the other ship, she would have instantly recognized her as *Titanic* in distress. The way the logic of their version progresses, *Californian* would have picked up everyone, and the loss of life would have been minimal.

The other side states that *Californian* was not even the ship involved. This faction has even been given a name by their detractors- "the Lordites." The Lordites staunchly maintain that there were other ships about that night, and any of a number of them could have been mistaken for the small Leyland liner.

They've even advanced the theory that *Titanic* may have even seen a Norwegian ship named *Samson* engaging in illegal seal poaching in the ice field. The crew of this ship understandably kept their presence to themselves to conceal their complicity in the disaster and their illegal activity.[214]

Neither version above is true.

The ship sighted on the horizon by *Californian* undoubtedly was *Titanic*. A comparison of signals reported as sent by *Titanic*, and the observations made

---

[214] Late in the 20th century, a man appeared who asserted that he had been aboard *Samson* on the night of April 14/15. He stated that *Samson* had observed the rockets fired from *Titanic*, but misinterpreted them as signals that *Samson* had been observed poaching and was about to be boarded and her crew arrested. Therefore, she extinguished her lights and sailed away. There is debate about the creditability of this man, but even had *Samson* come to the aid of *Titanic*, she was a tiny vessel, less than 550 tons, and would have been unable to save many of her passengers. But there are also some significant holes in this story too. The first is that the lights observed from *Titanic* continued to burn throughout the course of the night. One would think that *Samson* would have extinguished her lights- and thus disappeared- at the sighting of the first rocket. Other factors bearing on this discussion is that *Samson* would have been in international waters at the time she was sighted, and one may only "poach" where there are laws prohibiting hunting. The author can find no information about any treaties banning sealing in the Atlantic in 1912.

of the mystery ship by *Californian*- particularly the launching of the rockets- should convince most anyone that the two ships had each other within visual range. The assertion has been made that there was a ship in between *Titanic* and *Californian*- that the rockets observed on the smaller ship were beyond the ship they saw- but this would be largely irrelevant. Even if the Spanish Armada had been between the two ships, this still fails to address the reason for *Californian's* inaction.

Another factor unknown to many is that *Californian's* crew also noted green rockets being fired when *Carpathia* arrived at the scene of the disaster, plus the arrival of *Carpathia* herself.

Both the American and British investigations concluded that had *Californian* investigated and sailed south to the aid of *Titanic*, all aboard her would have been saved.

This idea has taken hold almost as readily as the notion that *Titanic* was unsinkable. It is just as wrong.

One of the unfortunate things in any examination of the *Titanic* disaster is an imprecise knowledge of many important factors. We have only an approximation of times- as many ships were using "apparent" time- based on their positions, and we may only estimate distances- particularly how far *Californian* actually was from *Titanic*.

The crewmen aboard *Titanic* who observed the smaller ship stated that they felt she was no farther than ten miles from them. In fact, as previously mentioned, Captain Smith believed her to be so close that he issued orders to some of the lifeboats to row to the other ship, discharge their occupants and then return to the sinking liner for more.[215]

---

[215] The theory has also been advanced that *Titanic* was visible from *Californian* because of a phenomenon called "superinversion"- where an atmospheric layer near the surface creates a mirror effect- somewhat like an inverted mirage, allowing the ships to see one another even though they were much farther away from each other than either believed. Even if this was the case, it still does not answer why the crew of *Californian* did not investigate.

Members of *Californian's* crew stated that they felt the other ship was even closer, estimating that the other ship was between three and eight miles away.

Captain Lord differed. In sworn testimony, he declared that the distance between his ship and *Titanic* was closer to twenty miles, but his estimate was based solely on the calculated positions of both ships, but since we have found that *Titanic*'s was seriously in error, it would be prudent to also suspect the accuracy of Californian's.

Lord maintained that at a distance of twenty miles, *Titanic* would have been out of sight, below the horizon, but that is not strictly correct. Simple calculations reveal that the bulk of *Titanic* would have been visible from the bridge of *Californian* up to a distance of 17 miles and her masthead light could have been seen from over 21 miles. In fact, given the combined sight distances of the two ships, *Californian* could have been anywhere in a circle around *Titanic* that totaled almost *1500 square miles* of sea. *Titanic* could also rig lights at the tops of her masts, and had she done so, she would have been visible that much further.[216]

Rockets fired from *Titanic* would obviously been visible at much longer ranges.

Since we know that unintelligible Morse lamp signals were observed on both ships, *Californian* had to be within 18 miles of *Titanic*, because that would be the maximum distance that her Morse lamp- which was mounted on top of her wheelhouse- would have been visible from *Californian's* bridge.

The extent and nature of the ice field that lay in between *Titanic* and Californian is unknown, but evidence suggests that both ships were east of the main body of the field.

If we average the accounts of the crews of both *Titanic* and *Californian* it appears that the ship they each observed was in all probability within a ten mile radius. Ten miles may seem like an insignificant distance, but

---

[216] It appears that someone aboard *Titanic* did hoist a kerosene lantern to the top of her after mast, as many survivors reported seeing a light in this position after the power failed, just before she sank.

when we talk about ships with a maximum speed of ten to thirteen knots such as *Californian*- it becomes important.

Additionally, we must remember that *Californian's* top speed would only be achieved under optimal conditions.[217] So, it becomes apparent that *Californian*- even at full speed- was at least one hour away from *Titanic*'s position. We already have seen that Smith wasted forty-five minutes before he ordered the first wireless distress call, and the first rocket was fired sometime between 00:45 and 01:00- at the earliest, one hour and fifteen minutes after the collision. *Titanic* sank at 02:20.

If the first rocket was fired at 00:45 and they were fired at an average rate of one every seven minutes, then it would have taken around an hour to fire

---

[217] It appears that Captain Lord himself was unsure of *Californian's* capabilities. The ship was not pressed to top speed the morning after the sinking because *Carpathia* was already on the scene and *Californian* was sailing though ice. Lord estimated that his ship probably could reach thirteen knots, but then qualified the answer by stating "at current rates of fuel consumption."

all eight. The time would have been around 01:40 when the last one was launched.

Titanic sank thirty-five minutes later.

If the crew of *Californian* had instantly recognized the rockets as distress signals, woke up Cyril Evans, received wireless confirmation, started the engine and headed south, *Californian* would have arrived- even under the most favorable reckoning- at 0145, giving her a window of only thirty-five minutes to rescue everyone before *Titanic* went down.

But we are not talking about sailing through an unobstructed sea on a sunny day aboard a ship that could instantly achieve her top speed. In fact, Captain Lord may not have ordered full speed, because he would have been sailing through a dangerous ice field in darkness.

Moreover, when Captain Lord decided to stop his engine (*Californian* only had one propeller) for the night, informing his engineers that he was not going to attempt a traverse through the field until daylight, they undoubtedly reduced power, producing just enough steam to run generators and heat the ship. In fact, they would have had little choice. Without the main engine to consume the steam, the safety valves would have lifted and quickly exhausted it overboard- as it did aboard the stopped *Titanic.*[218]

Unlike a motorboat, *Californian* could not simply crank up her engine, and achieve her top speed within seconds. If Lord had called down for propulsion, it would have taken some time to bring the boiler back to the point where it was able to generate enough steam to get the ship underway.[219] Then the ship would then have to work up to full speed. This would consume valuable time- perhaps as much as an hour or more.

---

[218] To a marine engineer, losing propulsion steam through safety valves is a cardinal sin.

[219] This subject is further complicated by the amount of "grating" area the boiler had. The larger the grating area, the more rapidly steam is able to be generated. *Californian*, given her primary role as a freighter, would not have needed a large amount of generation capability. It would have been, at best, average. Another factor would be how long it had been since her boiler had been washed of contaminants, such as the mineral scale that forms inside them. Contamination of her boiler would have required more time to generate steam and her top speed would have been unachievable. Accounts given by members of *Californian's* crew state that it took between fifteen and thirty minutes for her to get underway the next morning.

Lord told U.S. Senate investigators that his ship was surrounded by ice when he ordered her toward the site of *Titanic*'s sinking. It was slow going. Even with the advantage of daylight, it took *Californian* over two hours to reach the scene of the disaster. Obviously, darkness would have complicated any attempt at moving through the ice field.

Even if *Californian* had been able- despite the darkness- to make the voyage in two hours, she would have reached the scene of the disaster around thirty minutes *after Titanic* had gone down. Passengers cast into the icy water would have probably succumbed to hypothermia by that time or drowned.

Lord would have come as close to the site of *Titanic*'s sinking as he believed safe, but he would not have wanted to risk running down a lifeboat or anyone in the water. The almost impenetrable darkness would have only complicated his approach. Lord's only option would have been to stop in the vicinity and lower his boats to search the sea for survivors. Under these conditions, very few people in the water- if any- would have survived long enough to be rescued.

This is not speculation. Shortly after *Titanic* went down, Fifth officer Lowe had distributed the passengers from lifeboat 14 into other nearby boats and had returned to where the ship had gone down to search for any survivors in the water.[220]

He was only able to rescue four people- one who later died.

Californian's boats probably would have had no better luck. All the ship would have been able to do would have been little more than the *Carpathia* did- pick up the survivors in *Titanic*'s boats.

Had Cyril Evans observed Marconi regulations and stayed at his post, *Californian* may have been able to reach *Titanic* over an hour before she sank- but that again assumes the most favorable conditions. She may

---

[220] This rescue attempt is portrayed in James Cameron's *Titanic*. Lowe calls into the night "Can anyone hear me?" which echoes and dies. What was his voice echoing from?

have been able to make a significant difference in the number of people rescued- but again, this is speculation.

We must remember an additional detail- until *Titanic* began firing rockets; she had not exhibited any recognizable distress signals- to the men aboard *Californian* it looked merely as if she had stopped.

However, due to the darkness, and the ice field, we may make some assumptions. Captain Lord had already displayed caution when he had stopped for the night. No matter how heroic he wished to be, his nature would have dictated a slow, careful, traverse through the ice.

Knowing that they were the closest ship to the sinking *Titanic* undoubtedly would have added an air of urgency to the rescue, and Lord would have pushed his ship as swiftly as he thought safe.[221] However, no

---

[221] Captain Rostron of Carpathia testified at the American hearing that he had not known of the ice field at all until he was told of *Titanic* striking the iceberg. He also stated that had he been aware of the amount of ice he was sailing into during the rescue, he would have approached at a significantly slower speed. This is interesting, as the coordinates defined by the *Mesaba* ice message show that *Carpathia was also within the area of ice it defined* before she altered course to come to *Titanic*'s aid. However, either *Carpathia* did not intercept the *Mesaba* message, or as we have seen aboard *Titanic*, operator

matter how he felt about picking up *Titanic* survivors, his primary responsibility would have been the safety of *Californian*. He would not have wanted to jeopardize his vessel unnecessarily. Even if the ship arrived too late- Lord could not be criticized. He had done his best and nobody could fault him for that.

There is also a question of where Lord would have taken *Californian* had he received timely news of *Titanic*'s plight. If Evans had stayed at his post and relayed her first distress call to Lord, her need for assistance, and her reported location, Lord would have taken *Californian* to the wrong place. We now know that *Titanic's transmitted* position was seriously in error. Instead of taking *Californian* south, toward *Titanic's* actual location, *Titanic*'s indicated position would have led Lord to sail west- thirteen miles away from where she actually was. The position calculated by Boxhall was on the opposite side of the ice field from where *Californian* had stopped for the night.

Cotham did not deliver it to the bridge because it was not specifically addressed to his ship.

In fact, when the news of the disaster finally was received on *Californian*, Lord immediately ordered the ship to get underway and proceeded toward *Titanic*'s reported position, which required a traverse through the body of ice.[222] Finding nothing, he then sailed back through the ice field to the location provided to him by *Carpathia*.

Would Lord have done anything differently if he had been notified earlier? What if the observation of rockets being fired prompted *Californian's* watch officers to awaken the wireless operator? Would Lord have sailed toward the ship firing the rockets or instead proceed toward the position given by *Titanic*?

Would anyone on *Californian* have thought to have Evans ask *Titanic* if they had been firing rockets, or would they have continued to dismiss the observed rockets as company signals or even as another ship

---

[222] Apparently Captain Rostron believed he was at *Titanic*'s reported position when he began to recover the boats. There would have been no need to verify the coordinates transmitted by *Titanic*, as her lifeboats were the best evidence of all that he had arrived at the correct location.

trying to alert them to the disaster- or to the presence of an ice field? And if Evans *had* asked would Phillips have even known that *Titanic* was firing rockets?

We must now address the transfer of passengers between the two ships.

A common idea is that *Californian* could have gently come alongside *Titanic* and it would be a simple matter of allowing the passengers to step from one ship to the other.

Even if we dismiss the obvious disparity in deck levels on the two ships- no experienced mariner would have endorsed this. Even if *Californian* had arrived with time to spare, Lord would never have brought his ship that close to *Titanic*. The crush of passengers crowding to the side of the liner might affect her ability to remain on an even keel, particularly as she neared the end.

Additionally, *Titanic*'s stability would be impossible to predict as she went down. Conceivably, she could capsize, rolling over and taking the smaller ship with her. A more likely possibility would be that the weight of passengers leaving the larger ship may have destabilized the smaller ship- drawing *Californian* hard against the side of *Titanic*, and, again, the larger ship may have taken the smaller one with it.

And, yet again, we must address the idea that *Titanic* would generate a large area of "suction" as she left the surface. Lord may have feared that the larger ship might create such a powerful force that his ship might disappear too.

If the transfer of passengers could not be done directly, then the boats would have to be employed. Contrary to what most people seem to believe, moving passengers between the two ships would not have been simple or rapid. It may not have even been particularly safe.

Even if *Titanic*'s boats had been filled to capacity- each would have had to make at least two trips between the sinking liner and *Californian*. *Californian's* boats obviously could have supplemented the number, but she only had six boats, only four of which were considered as "lifeboats." The two smaller boats on *Californian* likely would have been pressed into service too, but all told, the boats aboard the smaller ship would only hold 218 people.[223] If *Californian's* boats were pressed into service and made two trips between their ship and *Titanic*, then the loss of life may have been diminished by about 400 people, but it's clear that everyone aboard would still have not been saved.

Conceivably, *Titanic* could have had her lifeboats filled and in the water at the time *Californian* arrived. However, what actually happened shows us that this would have been unlikely. Nevertheless, had it been possible it still would have taken a great deal of time to offload the passengers to the smaller ship then return to *Titanic* to embark more.

There are some additional factors which we must consider. The first is that boats of that era were not supplied with engines. They had to be rowed. It would have taken several minutes for the boats to traverse the distance between the two ships, and if their

---

[223] Unlike *Titanic*, *Californian* had an excess of lifeboat capacity- actually about *twice* the number of people who could be aboard at one time. She had a normal crew complement of fifty-five and was licensed to carry forty-seven passengers- a total of 103.

oars were manned by inexperienced people- such as passengers pressed into service- there would be a good chance that the boats might stray far from their intended destination.

Since the space between the two ships could vary considerably- determined by the boldness of Captain Lord as he approached *Titanic*- it is impossible to determine exactly how long it would have taken. However, even an optimistic estimate of a twenty minute trip between the two ships, gives us a forty minute round trip- and that does not factor loading and unloading.

This latter consideration also does not take into account that the boats probably still would have initially been filled with women and children- presenting obvious complications as they were boarding the smaller ship. It would have slowed down the process considerably. It might take thirty minutes or more for each boat to approach *Californian*, be made fast and unloaded. It's quite unlikely that there would be simultaneous unloading either- *Californian* obviously would not have enough personnel to accomplish this- perhaps two boats, at the most, could be unloaded at once. Boats would have to wait their turn, which would clearly delay their return to *Titanic*. So, even if we have two boats unloading at once, and we even cut the unloading time by half- to fifteen minutes- we find that it would take two and a half hours merely to unload the *first* group of passengers from *Titanic*.

The above estimate is optimistic. One of the most common complaints voiced by survivors in the lifeboats was that the rowing was uncoordinated and that most of the crewmen aboard, who were not seamen, did not know what they were doing. In some boats the women themselves took to the oars- mostly to keep warm.

Another factor we must consider is how many crewmen would be required to row the empty lifeboats back to the sinking liner. There would be an obvious shortage. Male passengers from *Titanic* could be enlisted to row the boats- or maybe seamen from *Californian*- but their presence would diminish the capacity of the boats when they were refilled and the inexperience of the former group in handling a small boat could obviously confuse the process.

We must also remind ourselves that filling the boats a second time as they returned to the sinking ship would be complicated by a lack of suitable boarding locations or any number of other unforeseen factors- such as hesitation on the part of the personnel manning the boats to approach the liner the second time because of fear of being drawn below by the ship.[224]

Although the sea state during the time *Titanic* was sinking was almost ideal for the transfer of passengers- with virtually no wind and the water's surface as smooth as glass- it still would have taken hours to move the passengers from one ship to the other. This is not conjecture; it has been illustrated by events.

---

[224] Although the fear of suction produced by the sinking liner was prevalent, evidence suggests that there was none. A baker, Charles Joughin, who was clinging to the aft rail of *Titanic* said he entered the water as the ship sank and did not even get his hair wet. However, there would be cases where people would have been swept into the ship in places where she had not completely flooded.

On the night of July 25, 1956, the Swedish liner *Stockholm* collided with the Italian liner *Andrea Doria* off the east coast of the United States- near the *Nantucket Lightship*. *Stockholm* was outbound and *Andrea Doria* was on an opposite course headed for New York. The area around the lightship was very busy and the danger of collision was compounded by high speeds, a night of thick fog, and miscalculation aboard both ships. There had a number of collisions in this area before, and in 1934, a liner- also running in fog- had actually collided with the lightship itself, sinking it.[225]

Stockholm, ironically, had a reinforced "ice breaker" type bow to enable her to punch through light ice. It made short work of the thin steel plating on the starboard side of *Andrea Doria*. The damage was quite

---

[225] *Olympic*. *Titanic*'s sister had a reputation for passing closely to the lightship at high speed- she was even photographed doing so, and the myth has grown that *Olympic* was at full throttle when the collision occurred. However, *Olympic* had significantly reduced speed prior to the accident- due to the thick fog- and drastically reduced speed after it was seen that she was on a collision course. The accident happened at a speed of less than three knots, but *Olympic's* bulk was sufficient to roll the smaller ship on her side and send her to the bottom. The other myth of the collision, that the lightship was cut in half, is also in error. Divers who have visited the wreck have reported that it has a massive gash in one side, but the hull is intact.

similar to what *H.M.S. Hawke* had done to *Olympic* years before.

However, there was one major difference- *Andrea Doria* was mortally wounded. She took on a severe list- the ship had always had a reputation for being somewhat unstable.

There has been debate- and conjecture- about why she failed to survive. One theory is that a key watertight door had never been fitted- allowing an adjacent undamaged compartment to fill with water and disable critical engineering functions. Another hypothesis concerns her inability to counter-flood deep tanks on the port side to trim the ship to a more even keel. No matter what the reason, the list rendered the lifeboats on her port side useless- and the lifeboats on her starboard side hard to fill.

She sent a distress call almost immediately, which was answered by several ships- including the French Line's *Ile De France*- a large liner equipped with more than enough lifeboats for the evacuation. The *Ile*, outbound, turned around and arrived at about 01:30.

She immediately launched ten of her motorized lifeboats- each having a capacity of 90 passengers. The *Doria's* crew had launched the eight boats on her starboard side. Two other ships arrived, an army transport, *PVT William Thomas*, and *Cape Ann*- a United Fruit Company Freighter. Even lifeboats from the heavily damaged *Stockholm* were eventually used to evacuate the Italian liner- once her Captain was certain she would not sink.[226] Accounts vary as to how many lifeboats these ships added to the small fleet- but, all in all, there were possibly as many as twenty five- of varying capacities- plying between *Andrea Doria* and the rescue ships scattered about her.

The sea conditions that night, like the night of April 14- 15, 1912, were also favorable for the evacuation- although there was some trouble with the boats becoming lost in the fog. *Ile De France* had a powerful whistle and searchlights that she used to

[226] *Stockholm* was not going anywhere anyway. The collision had released one of her anchors and she found herself moored to the sea bottom. Her crew eventually cut the chain with an acetylene torch and she was able to limp back to New York.

advantage. In that era, the French Line ships also had large lighted marquees mounted between their funnels- letting everyone know for miles around the name of the ship- and they were visible as well. It must have been heartening to the passengers of *Andrea Doria* to see the name *ILE DE FRANCE* looming out of the fog.

As with almost all incidents involving passenger ships, the numbers vary from account to account, but most state about 1700 people were aboard *Andrea Doria* that night. All who remained alive after the collision were evacuated- although some who were injured while leaving the ship later died.

Sailors say that their ships have souls. *Andrea Doria* may have had one. She seemed to struggle to stay afloat so her passengers could be saved- obliging the rescuers by refusing to die for almost eleven hours. The last person aboard *Andrea Doria*- her Captain- came off the ship less than an hour before she took her final plunge.

Titanic had 2207 people aboard that night- about 500 more than *Andrea Doria*. Even if *Californian* had arrived before *Titanic* sank- the total number of lifeboats available would have been twenty six- and that's if Captain Lord decided to commit all of his boats to the rescue. Moreover, the largest boat aboard *Titanic* had a capacity of only sixty-eight people. Even a cursory examination of the number of people involved and the time available to transfer them reveals that the presence of *Californian* would have made little difference.

In fact, if we consider human nature, the presence of *Californian* alongside the sinking ship may have even served as an *impediment* to evacuation. The sight of another ship nearby may have misled the passengers, falsely reassuring them. They may have not appreciated the urgency of leaving *Titanic*. It actually may have slowed her abandonment, leading to even greater loss of life.

Carpathia arrived at the scene about 0400. *Titanic* had been gone for almost two hours. Toward the end of her mad dash north, it had become somewhat hair-raising, with the little Cunarder dodging icebergs as she steered for green flares- fired by the occupants of the lifeboats- sighted in the distance.

The first survivor of *Titanic* came aboard at 0410- the last at around 0845. It took *Carpathia* over *four hours* to retrieve the people who had survived. Granted, at the time she arrived, the boats had become somewhat dispersed, but it gives us a general idea of how long it would have taken to transfer the passengers from *Titanic* to any rescue ship.

Even this timeline may not represent the actual time it would have taken *Californian* to board the passengers because *Carpathia* had made extensive preparations for the rescue of *Titanic's* survivors.[227]

Even if *Californian* had responded, and it took her *half* the time to gather the boats and unload the survivors, she would have made little difference. *Titanic* would have left the surface long before a significant number of survivors could have been brought aboard.

---

[227] Captain Rostron had a reputation for being a superior mariner, and he thought of almost everything required for the rescue. His crew called him the "Electric Spark."

The number of people who were rescued may have been slightly higher, but probably it would not have been substantial, and far less than “all” the passengers that both the American and British Inquiries assumed would have been saved had *Californian* arrived before *Titanic* left the surface.

Captain Lord spent the rest of his life trying to live down his involvement in the *Titanic* disaster. While he never faced any formal charges, public opinion was harsh toward him.

He was forced to resign from Leyland- and IMM- before the end of 1912 and had to take a berth commanding a nitrate ship- carrying guano- for the balance of his career. Lord felt that he had been unfairly singled out as a scapegoat and spent the rest of his life trying to clear his name, although after a few years, the public forgot about him and he was able to live a somewhat normal life.

However, Lord seemed to be one of those people who would be forever dogged by his involvement in the *Titanic* disaster. In 1955, a book about the event was published. Entitled *A Night to Remember*, it served to freshly present the controversy about *Californian* and Captain Lord's inaction to yet another generation. There were two ironies involving the publication of this book.

The author of *A Night to Remember* was also named Lord, Walter Lord. The other irony was that Stanley Lord was still alive in 1955, and because of the book, he had to begin defending himself all over again- and as in 1912- it was with limited success. Lord even asked his union to reopen the case and formally exonerate him. To his dying day, Captain Lord maintained that it was not *Titanic* that his officers observed.

Another irony of this series of events is that Captain Lord may have unjustly paid the price for the failures of others. There is little question that he was a competent mariner. His ship survived the ice field- without damage- and nobody has suggested that had he known of *Titanic*'s plight; he would have not come to her aid.

One of the biggest unknowns is the information Gibson gave him on the night of *Titanic*'s demise. We must remember that Gibson was an apprentice, twenty years old, and had probably never seen a ship firing *any* kind of rockets at night- much less knew that there was any difference in the types that might be used to signal distress or otherwise. Unfortunately, while the official investigations seemed obsessed in finding out how many rockets were fired, what color they were, and at what distance they could have been observed, it appears that nobody ever thought to ask Gibson if he knew what a distress rocket would have looked like.

It's unlikely that his companion on the bridge that night, Stone, had ever seen distress signals either. Had Gibson given Lord an accurate account of what had been observed, instead of merely telling him that they had seen a "ship firing rockets," Lord may have come on deck and seen to the matter himself.[228] His life could

[228] The story is a bit muddled here. Some accounts state that Gibson was the only one who talked to Lord about the rockets. Others say that Stone visited the Captain at least once and talked to him about the matter too.

have been much different if he had possessed the presence of mind to ask "what kind of rockets?"

Perhaps the biggest, and largely unpunished, culprit in the entire *Californian* affair was her Marconi operator, Cyril Evans, who botched sending the ice message to *Titanic* and then slept through the accident.

Evans, who either apparently did not appreciate the importance of the message Lord ordered him to send- or was somewhat intimidated at the brusque dismissal he received from Phillips and was unwilling to press the issue with a senior operator- should have assured himself that the message got through and was acknowledged, insisting that Phillips take it down, despite the latter's inconvenience and anger at being interrupted.

But as we have seen, even a timely and rapid reaction to the news of the *Titanic*'s distress may have made little to no difference.

Chapter Twenty Three- Was the Event Foretold?

Strangely, all the above discussion regarding ice warnings, inadequate lifeboat provision, lack of organization in evacuating the ship, and all the other factors which contributed to the great loss of life, would have been rendered irrelevant if people had merely paid attention to the seeming overabundance of premonitions, forebodings, omens, foreshadowings, augurs, portents, and funny feelings people claimed to have had about *Titanic* before she sailed.

The sea, and seafaring, has produced more than its share of superstitions and myths. Soon after men began to embark on the oceans, they realized that the safety of their fragile craft was often beyond their control, and- as they looked for meaning as to why one ship would survive and another would be lost- it seemed apparent to them that fate had more than a hand in it.

This led to the practice of christening ships and equipping them with figureheads, which were originally intended to ward off the evil spirits of the sea. Ships would often gain reputations as being lucky- or cursed.

And, in almost any disaster- whether it happened at sea or on dry land- there would be people who would assert that the event had been forecast.

There are many such incidents cited in the loss of *Titanic*- many more than her fair share. Some of these were the product of coincidence- some were the result of people stretching a non-event into something of perceived significance- and some were obvious products of overactive imaginations or invention.

Probably the most celebrated "foretelling" of the sinking of the *Titanic* was in a book. In 1890, an author named Morgan Robertson wrote a novel called *Futility*. As a work of fiction, it's somewhat of a failure- and a tedious read- but after *Titanic* went down, it gained a measure of notoriety that it had never achieved before. In fact, the book had a disappointing run and was out of print by 1912.[229] However, because of its connection to

---

[229] Another book that benefited from the loss of *Titanic* was survivor Archibald Gracie's *The Truth About Chickamauga*. Walter Lord gave it a rave review, calling it "an exercise in labored minutia."

the *Titanic* disaster, it was quickly set in type again, and continues to be available today.

The work has always been hailed as an astonishing- almost eerie- fictional foretelling of the actual event. But, as we have seen in much of this book, it's not entirely true.

Robertson's novel was set aboard a ship named *Titan*, a vessel roughly the same size as *Titanic*. *Titan* also sank on her maiden voyage in a collision with ice on a dark April night. *Titan* was also reputed to be unsinkable, so it was thought that there was no need to carry enough lifeboats for everyone aboard.

Were all these similarities an amazing coincidence, or did Robertson experience some kind of vision about the accident that he put to paper?

Robertson never claimed to have had any paranormal experience regarding his work, and the parallels between his story and the actual accident are not that striking if one examines them.

Robertson had been a sailor. He was more than aware that ships were becoming increasingly larger, and many of them were sailing without enough lifesaving equipment. He also knew what this combination would probably lead to a disaster, and even if it did not, he knew that it would make a good foundation for a work of fiction.

Ice would be a logical menace to a ship and it would permit a collision at any point in the ocean- allowing Robertson to imperil his characters out of reach of any assistance. One significant difference between *Titan* and *Titanic* concerned wireless. Because the book was published twenty-two years before the *Titanic* disaster, *Titan* was not equipped with wireless- it had not yet been invented, so Robertson's survivors are forced to cast away on an iceberg for a period before their rescue.

Morgan's uncannily accurate choice of the ship's name cements the idea that he was somehow aware of what was to come.[230]

---

[230] Robertson, who died in 1914, also wrote another novel called *Beyond the Spectrum*, which forecast a war between the United States and Japan, precipitated by a sneak attack on the United States Pacific Fleet. Again, it appears that Robertson had an uncanny ability to

But Morgan's work was not the only alleged harbinger of this event.

The loss of *Titanic*, like most major disasters, has always had its share of accompanying omens and premonitions- most mentioned, of course, after the fact.

One of these "omens" has already been discussed- the comment that "God himself could not sink this ship", which was uttered by a dockworker loading baggage.[231]

There were reportedly several instances of people who remarked to friends and/or loved ones that they did not feel safe aboard the big ship, or that they felt uneasy about sailing aboard her. There were also statements that people had told others that they felt they would not survive the voyage.

---

predict the future. However, when the book is examined, the similarities between what Robertson wrote and what actually happened are not that striking. The fleet is in the Philippines, and the war is decided by an infra-red "death-ray."

[231] And apparently a comment so appealing that James Cameron put the words into the mouth of character Cal Hockley prior to his boarding the ship.

There may have been individuals who made such remarks, but we will never know for certain. They may have decided that they had such feelings *after* they were rescued, or in the case of persons who did not survive, people may have "remembered" them making such statements.

Forebodings about disasters are common. People have reported them throughout history. They have also reported these same feelings in the *absence* of disaster, but since the ship did not sink, the airplane did not crash, or the volcano did not erupt, everyone either forgets about the odd premonition, or dismisses it as a manifestation of a character trait.

Anytime any untoward event occurs, there are people who are remembered as stating that something told them not to get aboard the airplane, or the train, or not to go to work that morning. People also have an odd need to link themselves to events, such as "my god, we flew that airline once."

Then, of course, there are people who wish to exploit an event for personal gain or a measure of notoriety.

A case somewhat related to the above statement involves a stoker (sometimes he's alternately identified as an "oiler") by the name of Frank Tower. Tower was cited for the remarkable achievement of not only surviving the sinking of *Titanic*, but also *Empress of Ireland*, and later, *Lusitania*. In most accounts he saved himself by swimming away from each liner just before she foundered- having done what he could to selflessly and heroically assist others in escaping the ship.

The story usually goes on to relate that Tower retired from his life at sea after the *Lusitania* disaster, either because he felt that his luck had been stretched too thin, or that an increasing number of other sailors refused to sail aboard any ship where he was employed, fearing the worst.

The story gained acceptance by being featured in Robert Ripley's *Believe it or Not* newspaper feature. In this case it would be prudent to select the "not" option.

The actual story is this; no record exists anywhere that proves Frank Tower was aboard *any* of the three ships when they went down. In fact, there is no proof that "Frank Tower" even existed.[232]

Oddly, there was a female crewmember, named Violet Jessup, who was aboard *Olympic* when she collided with *Hawke*, aboard *Titanic* when she foundered, and also, while working as a nurse, aboard *Britannic* when she sank, but Jessup never claimed to have had any paranormal experiences, and she never was regarded as a jinx, working out her career on several different ships.

One documented case of an actual person who *was* uneasy about sailing aboard *Titanic* was the mother of passenger Eva Hart. Hart was a young girl at the time of the sinking.[233] Her family was aboard because her father intended to open a tobacco store in Winnipeg.

---

[232] In some incarnations, Tower is referred to as "Lucky" Tower. I'm sure that if he really had been aboard three ships that encountered disaster, his "luck" would be a matter of debate.

[233] Many of the last few survivors of *Titanic* were infants- or even newborns at the time of the sinking, and so therefore their recollections

Hart stated that her mother was troubled about the ocean voyage and had asked her father about the safety of *Titanic*. He told her that the ship was perfectly safe- said to be unsinkable.

This comment apparently did not have the soothing effect desired. Hart said her mother was shocked by this assertion- responding that saying such a thing "was flying in the face of God." It was almost an invitation of trouble.

Eva's mother reportedly acted on her concerns. She insisted on remaining awake throughout each night her family was aboard *Titanic*. She would sit, fully dressed, reading, almost as if guarding her loved ones against the calamity she was sure was to come. The night the ship struck the iceberg, what her family regarded as her odd behavior was vindicated.

Hart and her mother survived the sinking- her father did not.

---

would be of little value- undoubtedly they, although well intentioned, were repeating what they had heard from others over the years.

As may well be imagined, Hart suffered psychological scars from her voyage on *Titanic* and sought professional help afterward. Her doctor's solution was for her to make a voyage on *Olympic*- in the same cabin that she had occupied on the night of the disaster.

She improved afterward. However, unlike Violet Jessop, Hart gained a reputation as a jinx later in her life, being aboard *Olympic* when the ship suffered minor damage from an abnormally large wave (referred to erroneously in most texts as a "tidal" wave) that smashed several of her portholes and stained-glass panels just inside, leading to some passenger injuries.

Hart was also aboard White Star's *Majestic* (not the *Majestic* commanded by Captain Smith, but a liner originally built as the German *Bismarck*) in 1923 when the ship developed a serious stress crack in her hull.

Eva Hart's mother is not the only documented case of someone who had forebodings about the fate of *Titanic* before her sailing.

Chief officer Wilde was said to have expressed uneasiness about his post aboard the new ship. In a letter to his sister, mailed in Queenstown just before the ship left for New York, he told her that the ship seemed "queer" to him and that he would be glad when his assignment was over and he could return to *Olympic*.

There are also reports that he expressed his uneasiness about *Titanic* to some of his fellow officers. Since Wilde reported to *Titanic* only a few hours before she sailed from Southampton, we may only speculate as to what caused this feeling in him. In fact, it may have not been the ship at all- but the somewhat strange circumstances that resulted in his posting to her, and how the other officers aboard the ship- two of who had been demoted one rank because of his last minute assignment- were acting toward him.

Archibald Butt, President Taft's military advisor, was also said to have experienced uneasiness about his voyage, but it appears that it did not specifically involve *Titanic*, but instead his entire trip abroad.

Butt had been under considerable stress for several months. He was a close friend of both Teddy Roosevelt and William Howard Taft, who had become bitter political and personal enemies. Butt's divided loyalty had taken a toll on him.

Artist Frank Millet, who also went down on *Titanic*, suggested that Butt accompany him on a short sabbatical to Europe. The intent was to allow Butt to take some time to clear his mind and relax.

Butt wired his sister that he had stored all his personal papers and she would find everything in good order in the event that "the old ship went down." While this may seem ominous, Butt was said to have had a habit of making such statements before he embarked on *any* voyage.

Shortly before he was to leave for Europe, Butt suddenly cancelled all his travel plans, citing his feeling that he needed to be on hand for the President. Taft dismissed this idea, assuring his aide that he deserved the excursion and insisted that Butt go. Taft assigned a few diplomatic chores to Butt to give him a better feeling about his trip.

Butt was said to have had bad feelings on the voyage over, and during his stay abroad. He availed himself of a tour of Westminster Abbey, stating that if he did not see it then, he would never get another chance to do so.

Millet had made arrangements for the pair to return to America aboard *Titanic*. It appeared as if Butt was more than happy with this arrangement- if not actually relieved- and his forebodings had been wrong. He stated that he would gladly board the ship, because he knew her to be perfectly safe.

Charles Hays, president of the Grand Trunk railroad, did not claim to have any premonition of disaster, but just before he retired to his cabin aboard *Titanic* on the night of the collision, he expressed to Colonel Gracie his concern about the increasing competition between the major shipping lines on the North Atlantic. Hays forecast that "the time will soon come when the greatest and most appalling of all disasters at sea will be the result." Hays found out that his forecast had been correct- his name soon appeared on the roster of those lost.

W. T. Stead, another prominent passenger, was the editor of an influential and widely read British magazine called *Review of Reviews*. In 1893 he had published a piece of fiction foretelling an event similar to the one he would eventually experience. His story is remarkable in the fact that it took place aboard White Star's *Majestic*. *Majestic* was the line's flagship at the time and her commander was Edward J. Smith.

The story diverges here in that *Majestic* does not strike an iceberg, but instead finds survivors of another shipwreck floating on an ice floe. There is no evidence that Stead ever believed that *Titanic* was standing into danger, and in fact, had he made such a statement it probably would have been dismissed.

Toward the end of his life Stead had developed an odd fascination with spiritualism, as had Sir Arthur Conan Doyle- the creator of Sherlock Holmes. Although spiritualism had become somewhat of a craze in the late

19th and early 20th century, Stead's passionate interest embarrassed many of his friends. Several had even begun to question whether the old editor was losing his grip on reality because of it. In fact, in Stead's story, *Majestic* is drawn to the survivors by "thought transmissions."

There is also a story of a young man who stated that he had had a premonition of Stead's death prior to the sailing. Stead was walking with the man, apparently excitedly extolling how wonderful his voyage aboard *Titanic* was to be. The younger man said he was struck by the overwhelming feeling that Stead would soon die. However, there is no way to verify this story, as it was told after the fact, and the younger man stated that when he had the feeling, he did not associate it with *Titanic*.

There were also stories- again after the fact- that *Titanic* had been viewed as an unlucky ship and that some crewmen refused to sail aboard her. Considering that the ship's entire career prior to that point had been less than eight hours of sea trials and an overnight voyage from Ireland, it's a matter of conjecture as to how she could have obtained this reputation in such a short span of time.

However, as evidence of this perceived curse, sources cite a number of crewmen who failed to report for her sailing and were replaced by last minute substitutes- only one who was saved. The obvious inference is that these missing crewmen had second thoughts and intentionally avoided boarding the ship.

However, there is nothing ominous about this, most of the crewmen who missed the ship were having a last drink in nearby pubs, guests of the local constabulary, overslept, or were otherwise detained. A crewmember missing a sailing- particularly of a ship that carried a crew the size of *Titanic*- was so common that the lines kept crewmen in reserve who would board just before departure to take the place of anyone who failed to report.

Apparently, the uneasiness about the ship did not stop with the crew. There were also stories that a few passengers were spooked by *Titanic*, advising others to leave her in Cherbourg as they were planning to do or cancelled their passage at the last moment. There is no evidence that any passengers- other than those who had bought tickets to Cherbourg or Queenstown left the ship before she departed for America.

Obviously, one could reasonably expect that a ship with over 2,000 people aboard, one or two might express forebodings. It would be much more persuasive if everyone aboard- or a large majority- either stated feeling these same forewarnings, or deserted the ship before she embarked on her voyage.

Most of the cancelled bookings could obviously be attributed to a simple change in plans or circumstances- only taking on the ominous connotations after the passage of years. Good examples of this exist. Two prominent passengers that had booked aboard *Titanic*, Marconi and Milton Hershey, who invented the Hershey bar, both decided independently that they could not wait until *Titanic* sailed and embarked on ships leaving earlier.

It's also more than likely that more than a few of these stories were total fiction, told in later years to garner attention or make a few dollars, which would also serve to explain the several instances of reported *Titanic* "survivors" who were later proven to never have sailed on her.[234]

There are also many other stories that have been told over the years regarding dreams, paranormal experiences, and even "feelings" people had about the voyage of *Titanic*.

There were even a few "Captain Smith sightings" after the disaster. One report stated that one of E.J.'s old shipmates had encountered him on the streets of Baltimore several weeks *after Titanic*'s demise. The person said that the Captain had conversed with him, called him by name, and after being pressed about it, admitted that he- indeed- was Smith,

---

[234] A good example is Alvin Clarence Thomas, aka "*Titanic* Thompson," a golf hustler, gambler, and scam artist who maintained for years that he survived the sinking, and has been so reported by several authors. Thompson did survive the disaster, saved from almost certain death by being in Missouri when *Titanic* went down.

but asked the man to keep their meeting "to himself." The Captain was last seen boarding a train to Washington D.C.

There is also the account of a man named "Silent Smith" who appeared in Lima, Ohio about three years after the disaster. He was presumed to be an Irish seaman, but would only utter his name- "Smith" when any question was posed to him. Silent Smith soon died, and nobody stepped forward to claim the body. He was roughly the same height and weight as E.J., and because he had the same extremely rare last name, he had to be the Captain.

Either of these could have happened. There are several different accounts of Captain Smith's final moments aboard *Titanic*, and although they disagree in important details, none conclusively shows that he died in the accident.

One account portrays the Captain roaming the decks with a revolver, supervising the loading of each boat and threatening to shoot any man who attempted to seek refuge in one, stating "I want every man to act like a man- for manhood's sake, and if they don't- a bullet awaits the coward." He must have been somewhere else when Ismay left the ship.

Another account states that he told his crew- during *Titanic*'s final moments- to "Be British." What he meant is unknown- I will leave it up to the reader. Apparently he decided that his last words should be as ambiguous as some of his orders.

Several stories concern his demise. He was seen several different places- on the bridge, clinging to a ladder on the side of the ship, and in the water. One account states that a wave washed him from the ship and he found himself near a lifeboat. The occupants of the boat attempted to rescue him but he refused, swimming back to the ship. Another story says that he approached a lifeboat with a baby in his arms, handed it over and then swam away. Others state that he attempted to climb aboard the capsized collapsible, but was driven off by other survivors.

However, no story ever stated that he was seen dead, and his body was never recovered.

However, he may have been found alive. In its September 10, 1991 edition, the incisive and now unfortunately defunct supermarket checkout line tabloid *The Weekly News of the World* reported that Captain Smith had been found "242 miles southwest of Iceland." According to the account, Smith, who had apparently not aged a day since 1912, was found sitting in a lifeboat clad in a fresh White Star Uniform and smoking his pipe prior to his rescue by a "Navy research ship." According to the account, he was under the impression that it was still April 14, 1912 and was last seen being taken to a psychiatric hospital in Oslo. Amazingly no other members of the news media reported this story.

If this wasn't enough, the story also related that a *Titanic* passenger named Winnie Coutts (who actually was aboard) had been rescued from an iceberg in the same general area the previous September. She, like Smith, was also under the impression that it was 1912. After her rescue she rapidly aged and died.

Here we must relate that *The Weekly News of the World* was allegedly a humor publication, but apparently this was lost on some readers.

In fact, it appears that this story may have grown legs and taken on a life of its own. In 1998, a book entitled *Strange But True*, written by Thomas Sleman, reported essentially the same story about the female passenger, with a few minor variations. The "Navy" ship was Soviet, the body was lifeless (except for an eerie incident during the post rescue examination where the eyes allegedly "popped open," leading to a failed resuscitation attempt) and the name of the victim-despite the recovery of numerous documents on the body- was never revealed.

The above book has no bibliography or citations, so there is no way to verify or trace the origin of the story, but the similarities are very close.[235]

---

[235] The reader must be aware by now that there are no citations in this book either, but if the reader examines the sources listed in the bibliography, the facts will emerge. The author may be different than the average reader, but I have never found any advantage to slogging through endless footnotes citing sources.

What about the "omens" that supposedly foretold the end of the liner?

One of these events has already been mentioned, the near collision with the liner *New York* in Southampton.

Another "omen" that supposedly foretold the end of *Titanic* has also been discussed- the simple act of a stoker climbing to the top of the forth funnel and poking his head out from the inside, either with the intent to surprise the passengers below or seek some relief from the heat in the bowels of the ship.

Interpreting either of these two events as an "evil portent" would put a severe strain on the imagination, but after the fact they were accepted as valid without debate.

Then we come to what we could term "non-events," or things that *did not* happen that people thought either foreshadowed the disaster or contributed to its cause.

One of these, again mentioned after the fact, was the failure to christen *Titanic* before she was launched. Many dignitaries from both White Star and Harland and Wolff were on hand to witness the ship slide down the ways, but there was no bottle of champagne broken over her stem and nobody recited the traditional words of "God bless her and all that sail in her."[236]

At first glance this appears to be an unbelievable oversight, but in Harland and Wolff's Belfast yard it was the practice not to christen ships. As one shipyard worker summed it up, "they just builds them and shoves them in."

The origin of this is unclear, but at least one author has attributed it as an attempt to avoid inciting or inflaming religious conflict within the shipyard, which has always been a volatile subtext to life in Belfast. The premise is that the Catholic and Protestant workers

---

[236] There are a number of people who believe that *Titanic* had a traditional launching, because the event is depicted in *A Night to Remember*. The sequence shows the bottle of champagne being broken over the bow, and the ship moving down the ways. At least four different ships are shown sliding into the water- one being the original *Queen Elizabeth*! Filmmakers believe that all ocean liners look alike, so they commonly substitute one ship, usually the *Queen Mary*, for another. Since her permanent mooring in Long Beach, the *Queen Mary* has become an almost continuous movie set, and has stood in for *Titanic* many times.

would have had very different ideas about how a christening should be conducted and so the yard avoided the whole problem by not performing them. *Olympic* was never christened, nor was *Britannic*.

In the same vein, there is also the oft repeated story that *Titanic*'s hull number, when it was read as an upside down mirror image- a stretch of some significance- said "NOPOPE," which was interpreted as an obvious slap at the Catholic workers in the Belfast shipyard. The story then relates that these deeply offended employees intentionally did substandard work on *Titanic* to get even for this insult.

The idea, of course, is that had the labor been properly accomplished, the berg would have bounced off the ship, leaving little more than some paint scratches to mark its passage. Unfortunately for the story, *Titanic*'s actual hull number was 401.

Another "omen" that has achieved a measure of acceptance is that *Olympic*, which was the only one of the sisters who served out her career, was painted white- or light gray- for her launch, while *Titanic* and

Britannic were painted black. This actually meant nothing, as it was an accepted practice to paint the first ship of a series in lighter colors so the details of her hull would photograph better.[237]

There were invented stories too. There was the tale of a Harland and Wolff employee who had been entombed in the ship while she was under construction. Various reasons are given for this error- one being that the employee died in an accident on the job and his co-workers, not wishing to have to explain it, left him where he was. Another says that the worker fell asleep- or passed out from alcohol- of course everyone believes that the Irish are perpetually inebriated- and was unintentionally sealed in. Neither explains why this worker was never missed- either by his family or the shipyard.

---

[237] This "omen" also was applied *Mauritania* (painted white) and *Lusitania* (painted black). It was even applied to the original *Queen Mary* and *Queen Elizabeth*. *Queen Mary* was painted white for her launch, *Elizabeth* black. *Queen Mary* is now a hotel, *Queen Elizabeth* was destroyed by fire- but only after she had served out her entire career as a North Atlantic liner. Additionally, the original Queens were not sister ships.

This story, in different forms, appears over and over in the history of construction. Essentially the same story is cited in the building of Hoover dam where the tempo of work was allegedly so frenzied that workers who were unfortunate to fall into freshly poured concrete were supposedly covered over instead of being rescued- although one engineer dismissed this idea as ludicrous. In his words (recited with his tongue firmly in cheek), leaving a body entombed in the concrete would "weaken the structure."

There are also similar stories of workers being sealed inside the Brooklyn, Golden Gate, and Verrazano-Narrows bridges.

Possibly the most ingenious legend regarding the demise of *Titanic* involves the supernatural. In this tale, a stolen Egyptian mummy- endowed with the obligatory curse of death- was spirited aboard the ship as cargo in Southampton and loaded in the forward hold on the starboard side. Amazingly, the location where the mummy was stowed happened to be the exact spot where the ship first struck the iceberg.

As the ship began to sink, the mummy's owner[238] descended into the hold and retrieved it. He then bribed an officer to get it- and himself- into a lifeboat- one that was apparently filled with passengers so unobservant that they could not detect the presence of a mummy in their midst. Of course, we do not know if the mummy was still in its sarcophagus, boarded the boat in its bandages, or changed into a sport coat and slacks, and it *was* dark.

It appears that the mummy was off-duty, curse-wise, at the time *Titanic* was going down, because it neglected to exploit a perfect opportunity to work its evil magic. The owner was allowed to escape *Titanic*, but the mummy apparently soon clocked in again, reactivating the curse to allow all manner of bad luck to befall him once he arrived ashore.

The tale usually ends with the mummy thief ending his life by his own hand. The mummy ends up as

---

[238] In some incarnations of the story, the mummy's owner is W.T. Stead. Stead is a source of all manner of spurious stories involving the shipwreck. He was supposed to have returned from the spirit world several times at séances where he related some of these tales.

an exhibit at any of a number of different museums- usually the Smithsonian. Of course, none of the museums in question will acknowledge having the mummy in their collection- for fear that the curse will become active again.[239]

There is even a story that *Californian* misinterpreted the rockets fired from *Titanic* as a "party" going on aboard. Apparently the smaller ship failed to investigate the observed signals because the crew was miffed at not having received an invitation.

Then there is matter of the names selected for this trio of large ships. After *Titanic* went down, many people cited her name as a deliberate tempting of fate. But, in fact, the ship we know as the *Titanic* was not the first one to bear that name. A British freighter had carried the name over forty years earlier. She served out her career. There was a sailing ship, of American

---

[239] In one version of this story, the mummy does not sink *Titanic*, but is instead responsible for the demise of *Empress of Ireland*. However, in another variation, it sinks *both* ships. Clearly, this was a mummy with a serious attitude.

registry, with the name of *Olympic* that co-existed with her larger namesake. She served out her career too.[240]

Amazingly, the ship we know as the *Titanic* was not the *last* to bear the name either. Obviously we may dismiss the large number of pleasure boats that have born the name- clearly labored attempts at wit.

However, there have been at least two seagoing ships with that name since 1912 and at the time of this writing; the U.S. Coast Guard register lists an active *passenger* ship named *Titanic*. Naming a ship *Titanic* would seem more than odd given the somewhat superstitious nature of seamen. However, none of these ships met any untoward end.

As an aside, it appears unusual that this idea of tempting fate with the name of the ship seems to have receded into the background today. One wonders how a

---

[240] There are some sources that state that any ship name that begins with the letter "O" is unlucky. Apparently White Star did not share this superstition, not just with *Olympic*, but also with one of their earlier flagships named *Oceanic*. It also doesn't account for the fact that *Olympic* gained a reputation as being an extraordinarily lucky ship during her career and she developed a loyal clientele who would sail aboard her even when newer and faster ships were available.

ship named *Sovereign of the Seas* would have been accepted in 1912 after *Titanic* went down.

And what would the legend of *Titanic* be without a conspiracy theory? According to this one, the identities of *Olympic* and *Titanic* were switched during the time the two sisters were in Belfast after *Olympic* dropped the propeller blade and had returned for repairs.

The driving force behind this idea is that *Olympic* had sustained such extensive and serious damage during her short career, that White Star (a.k.a. Ismay and/or Morgan) decided that the best course would be to dispose of her and collect the insurance money.

The case for the switch is incredibly thin, the reasons for making it are even thinner, and the obstacles to actually making such an exchange are enormous.

First, outside of the fact that virtually everyone in Belfast would have known of the scheme, the whole plot would make little sense if the ship had not been insured by an outside party. As we have mentioned, International Mercantile Marine was largely self-insured, so sinking *Olympic/Titanic* would have achieved little, as most of the cost of replacement would have come out of their pocket- and in fact, a replacement for *Titanic* was never built.[241]

White Star's own regulations belabor the self-insurance angle. One states: "The Company assumes the entire risk of insurance on its vessels, their freights, and on a considerable portion of the cargoes carried by them; whilst the large sum which is paid annually to it's officers as a bonus for absolute immunity from accident is additional evidence of anxiety to subordinate all other considerations to the paramount one of *safety in navigation*." (Emphasis in the original.) A second regulation reaffirms this: "Commanders are reminded that the steamers are to a great extent uninsured, and that their own livelihood, as well as the Company's success, depends upon immunity from accident; no

---

[241] White Star announced, shortly before the First World War, that they intended to build a new liner, larger than those of the *Olympic* class, to be named *Ceric*. She was to be over 1,000 feet long and displace more than 50,000 tons. However, nothing ever came of the idea. The odd name of this planned ship was derived from the element Cerium, which is a rare earth and corrodes so quickly that it will ignite spontaneously if scratched. Even a casual observer would have to admit that this name would seem to be more likely to provoke a disaster.

precaution which ensures safe navigation is to be considered excessive."

Another item of which we must be aware is that barratry- the intentional destruction of a ship for the purpose of collecting compensation- is considered a serious crime- with severe consequences.[242]

Whomever authorized the sinking of *Olympic/Titanic* would have taken the grave risk of being sent to prison for an extensive time- and in 1912, British prisons were not noted for their four star service. This assumes that the offense was not accompanied by any loss of life- then the crime would obviously escalate to mass murder.

Then there is the question of why anyone would have suggested, given serious consideration to, or approved such an idea. What possible advantage could be achieved by *switching the identities* of the two ships? Why not just destroy *Olympic*, by sinking or otherwise, and be done with her?

---

[242] In fact, only a few years earlier, hanging was the preferred method of punishment.

Why also would Ismay, who undoubtedly would have had knowledge of the switch, have agreed to accompany the ship on her fatal voyage? Was Captain Smith asked to sacrifice his reputation, and ultimately his life, for this scheme? Would there be other- more controllable, and far more desirable- ways to dispose of the unwanted ship?

Fire has always been a reliable way to end the career of most any structure, be it a building or a ship. As stated above, the French Liner *Normandie* was effectively destroyed by fire during World War II.

The original *Queen Elizabeth*, undergoing conversion to a floating school in Hong Kong harbor and renamed the *S.S. Seawise University*, was also lost in this same fashion.[243] In the case of *Normandie*, the cause was found to be accidental, but in the latter, arson was strongly suspected- particularly because the fire

---

[243] She was then owned by Tung Chao Yung, who went by "C.Y." Tung. The name "SEAWISE" was an obvious pun on his initials. All ships owned by his company, the Orient Overseas Container Line, had SEAWISE in their names. To this day, responsibility for the fire has never been officially determined. Motives ranging from insurance fraud to political retribution have been offered.

was traced to at least three simultaneous ignition sources- located in widely separated parts of the ship.

As we have just observed, ships are often the most vulnerable when they are undergoing refit or repair. *Olympic* could have easily been "accidentally" set ablaze while she was in Belfast following her collision with *Hawke*. If it were properly done, there would have been no loss of life at all. The fire could have been set at night, when the yard was largely inactive, and the small number of people aboard could have been easily evacuated.

If the intent was to dispose of the ship in a location where its loss could not be practically investigated, why not just sink her as she made the voyage to Belfast for repairs? There would be no more than a skeleton crew aboard her, and since diving equipment in the early 20th century was inefficient and clumsy- and the waters around the British Isles are not noted for their clarity- a detailed inspection of any wreck would have been next to impossible.

This leads us to another question. Why would dispatching the marked ship with innocent passengers- and insufficient lifesaving equipment- be an attractive option?

We know that Ismay had a complex personality, but nobody ever accused him of being insane.

Another question begging an answer regards the “arrangement” of the accident. How did the perpetrators manage to accomplish it?

Was the decision made to plow the ship into the ice field and hope she would sustain enough damage to sink her? Did Smith and his officers receive detailed instructions on where the ship was to sail, her required velocity, and even what emergency maneuvers she was to make when the ice was sighted?

What if, despite all the “arranged” negligence that would have brought her to the ice, she failed to strike the ice at the proper angle, or speed, or her watertight bulkheads had done their job?

Now White Star would have had more repairs to deal with, and- because they switched the names of the ships- the perception would be that they had another accident-prone liner in their fleet. People might begin to believe that maybe there was something wrong with the way they were operated. In fact, the second collision may have persuaded people that these new ships were unmanageable and dangerous.

One last question that the theorists who embrace this preposterous idea fail to address is that *Olympic*, after she arrived in Belfast, could have been surveyed and declared either "beyond repair" or the cost of the repairs could be estimated as exceeding the cost of replacing the liner. It would be somewhat akin to "totaling" the ship.

Harland and Wolff could have officially recommended to White Star that the ship be scrapped and never be allowed to sail again. In the collision with the *Hawke*, nobody was injured. There was no way to predict how another collision- particularly one in the middle of the Atlantic- would have transpired.

White Star may have even come out ahead- both from a monetary standpoint and also from a public relations angle. Instead of trying to patch up a seriously damaged ship, they made the hard, but sensible, decision to remove her from service and scrap her.

Chapter Twenty Four- The Myths Live On

Perhaps the most enduring legend- up until Robert Ballard found the wreck in 1986- was that *Titanic* had gone down in one piece, and that she had drifted slowly to the bottom of the ocean and settled softly to the ocean floor. It was thought that her eventual discovery would reveal her to be in near perfect condition- possibly in such an exceptional state of preservation that it would be possible to raise her.

There were more than a few people who proposed schemes for doing so, one even suggesting that tennis balls be employed as the flotation medium for bringing her back to the surface. Many of those who had ideas about raising *Titanic* had no idea what they would do with her afterward. Some indicated that they would repair and sail her again. Others felt that she would be a sure draw as a museum. Of course, none of these schemes ever progressed beyond talk.

Shortly after the disaster, John Jacob Astor's family made an announcement that they were investigating the feasibility of raising *Titanic*. Astor had been presumed to have been trapped inside the ship and had gone down with her. It was important to his family that his body be recovered, both for personal and legal reasons. When Astor's body was found by one of the ships White Star had chartered to recover victims, the idea was abandoned.[244] However, the scheme would not have lasted long anyway. It would have been impossible to even locate the ship with the technology available at the time and, as we now know- they would have been looking in the wrong place.

Although several survivors had stated that they were certain that the ship split in two before she sank, most people refused to believe them.[245] Even the thunderous noises caused by her fracturing were attributed to the sounds of her boilers and engines

---

[244] Astor's body was badly mutilated. There was speculation that he may have died when one of the forward funnels collapsed. The identification of his body was aided by the presence of over a thousand dollars in his pocket.

[245] Survivor Jack Thayer, who jumped into the sea, and was near the ship when she made her descent, later drew a series of pictures that depicted *Titanic*'s demise. The drawings clearly indicate that the ship broke in two, but they also show the bow of the ship briefly resurfacing, which tended to cast doubt on his account.

breaking loose and crashing forward through the ship as she went down. It was almost as if people wished to believe that although *Titanic* was proven not to be unsinkable, she still was somehow superior- able to resist the forces that would have destroyed a lesser ship.

It was thought that not only her structure would be in near pristine condition when and if she was ever discovered, but almost everything that had been aboard would be too. The belief was that at her depth, the temperature of the ocean was so low that it would be as if the ship had been placed in cold storage. It was also thought that there was insufficient oxygen in the water at the bottom to support either corrosion or life, both of which were known to devastate wrecks in shallow water, and that the salinity of the seawater would be much lower as well.

It was held that in such an environment the absence of these destructive agents would not only allow the steel and wooden components of the ship to endure, but it might even allow even some foodstuffs aboard the ship to survive, as well as most of the soft items- such as furnishings, carpets and bedding. There was even a possibility that intact bodies of victims who went down with the ship might be recovered.

Prior to the time the wreck was found, people envisaged *Titanic* resting on the bottom of the Atlantic like a time capsule, her funnels still towering over her deserted decks in the inky darkness. When and if she were found, it might be a simple matter of patching the hole and re-floating her.

Discovery of the wreck quickly dispelled these notions. *Titanic* had broken into two sections before she went to the bottom, and her hull had been twisted and crushed by the breakup and impact with the ocean floor. She did remain upright, but her pieces were several hundred feet from each other. Her funnels were never found- they presumably were swept away and lost to corrosion.

Of the two sections, *Titanic*'s bow seemed to be in better shape, apparently having planed through the water to its final resting place and burrowing into the ocean floor. It still resembled a ship in most respects, although it had been shorn of the bridge structure, leaving only the brass telemotor- to which the ship's wheel had been affixed- standing alone on the deck.

The stern was in much worse condition. The upper deck had been peeled aft by hydrodynamic forces, and instead of coming to a relatively soft landing like the bow, the stern hit hard. It looked like a wreck.

Aquatic life, instead of being absent, seemed to have thrived on the wreckage. It appeared that undersea creatures had ravished the ship and her contents, then moved on, only leaving formations caused by iron eating bacteria, that Robert Ballard christened "rustcicles," clinging to the exposed steel of the ship, slowly consuming it.

Anything made of wood or cloth was long gone, the only articles of clothing found being shoes and boots, apparently the chemicals used in treating the leather did not agree with the residents of the deep. The sole items that seemed to survive unscathed were made of glass, porcelain, ceramic, or copper-based alloys such as bronze or brass.

Since the wreck was discovered, and particularly since the Cameron movie was released, many people have asked me why the stern did not stay afloat after it separated from the bow section. They ask why when the remaining part of the ship settled back into the sea, the watertight compartments didn't furnish enough buoyancy to allow it to survive.

While it is impossible to make a definitive statement about why this did not occur, we may make some informed assumptions.

First, the ship split at its weakest point, just above the reciprocating engine room which was the largest watertight compartment, and open space, in the ship. The area above the engine room was largely non-structural, meaning that it added nothing to the strength of the ship. The construction here was designed to be comparatively easy to remove in the event that major components of the engines had to be repaired or replaced. So, structurally, the ship had a large void within it.

Below this essentially empty space were the heaviest parts of the entire ship, the two reciprocating engines, which unfortunately remained in the stern section when the ship broke apart.

Below the engines were the strongest structural members in the ship- the reinforced bed plates on which they rested, and the keel. The keel undoubtedly was the last part of the ship to break, and as the bow sank, the keel- still attached to the rear section, must have dragged the stern down with it until it finally separated.

The weight of the engines, in now what was an almost completely flooded compartment, simply dragged the stern below as they plummeted to the ocean floor, so swiftly that several refrigerated spaces aft apparently imploded before the pressure equalized. These compartments were the source of the large amount of cork found floating at the scene of the sinking on the morning after the ship went down.

Titanic has deteriorated significantly since her discovery. The decks are slowly collapsing into the hull. Some have attributed this to the inevitable ravages of time, but others have cited the irresponsible activities of those visiting the wreck, if not actually causing the damage- at least accelerating it.[246]

When it became apparent that the ship was not worth raising, plans quickly sprang up to build exact replicas of her and sail them with paying passengers.

However, it soon became apparent to the dreamers- and schemers- that they were facing insurmountable problems- most having to do with the fact that nobody- nobody with money- was interested in building a ship that, if it remained true to the original in all respects, might cost in the neighborhood of a half billion dollars plus.

This price may sound odd, as we have already noted that *Titanic* was, by today's standards, not a large

---

[246] Robert Ballard attempted to establish the site of the *Titanic* wreck as an internationally protected place- and he tried to keep her exact location secret. However, there were too many people involved in her discovery and soon a French company called RMS *TITANIC* (also called Premier Exhibitions) secured the salvage rights to the ship and began to recover artifacts from her. They originally stated that they were going to retrieve items only from *Titanic*'s extensive debris field, but it appears that artifacts from the wreck itself, like the bell on the crow's nest, were also recovered.

ship. However, when one sets out to build a "replica" there are some difficult choices that have to be made.

First, shipbuilding has changed significantly since *Titanic* was constructed. Ships are no longer built by laying a keel, working up, and then launching the hull into the water. Welding has supplanted riveting and vessels are built in prefabricated modules that are joined in a dry dock.

Some choices would be dictated by simple economics. Almost all her fittings would have to be custom made- most having gone out of production years ago, so modern- less expensive- equivalents would most probably be used.

It would be quite unlikely that her owners would be able to find anyone willing to work in the primitive conditions of the original *Titanic*'s stokehold- which included working in extreme heat shoveling coal into the massive fireboxes beneath her boilers, and she would likely have to sail under a waiver that would allow the great amount of pollution she would produce. If that was not enough, present work safety laws would prohibit a number of the practices common in 1912.

Even if all these problems could be resolved, functional coaling facilities are long gone, and it often took several days to refuel a ship the size of *Titanic* when they were available.

It would also be an expensive choice to equip the ship with exact replicas of the original *Titanic*'s engines too, which required giant steel castings and extensive machining.

So, our intrepid builders might decide to opt for more modern construction methods, and probably would also decide to equip the ship with a more modern and efficient mode of propulsion.

There would be other problems too. An "exact" duplicate of *Titanic* would be illegal, except as a static display.[247]

---

[247] Even as a static display an exact replica would likely be illegal. The original *Titanic* had crude waste disposal facilities. Human and kitchen wastes were discharged directly into the sea.

A seagoing *Titanic* replica would require modern navigation equipment, such as radar, and internal modifications- such as improved collision protection, marked evacuation routes, and a public address system.

Obviously, she would also require many more lifeboats, and because those she carried do not meet today's regulations, these would have to be of modern design. Even the extensive and lavish woodwork featured aboard *Titanic* would not conform to modern fireproofing standards, which also requires sprinklers in passenger spaces. A replica would also require fire doors to isolate sections of the ship should a blaze occur.

Today's passenger would likely be disappointed with the ship's outmoded amenities too. Although *Titanic* was considered a floating palace in 1912, her appointments, if judged by modern standards, would appear stodgy, dated, and in some cases, primitive.

Many of her cabins would be viewed as gloomy, crowded with furniture, over-decorated, and most of them would be surprisingly tiny- even in first class. The largest first class cabins (excepting the suites) were smaller than an average modern hotel room, and the single cabins were almost claustrophobic- many had only a narrow bunk, a small dressing table, and a window seat- if they even had a window. Only a few cabins had private bathrooms.

Second class was even more cramped than first and it's difficult to envision anyone today willingly paying to travel in the spartan and crowded steerage spaces of the ship. In fact, modern regulations make such congested areas unlawful.

Then there's the problem of where she would sail. The North Atlantic has now become the realm of jet aircraft, and only a few people travel the route by ship. The real *Titanic* was very unwieldy, requiring tugs everywhere she was berthed, and although a *Titanic* replica would easily be able to traverse the Panama Canal, any tropical voyage would likely be miserable as the real *Titanic* lacked air-conditioning.

All in all, a replica would likely be an expensive venture, with little prospect of any return on investment.

Although the ship would undoubtedly be a novelty- for a time- once the people in the tweed coats and snap-brim hats disappeared, it's unlikely that her popularity could be sustained.

Chapter Twenty Five- Afterword

As previously noted, both the governments of the United States and Britain conducted investigations into the loss of *Titanic*. Both hearings were criticized. The American hearings were viewed by many- particularly those in Britain- as the largely inept satisfaction of Senator Smith's political agenda against J. P. Morgan. The British inquiry was labeled a "whitewash."

However, despite their differences in method and objective, each investigation reached a similar conclusion. Both cited *Titanic*'s speed in an area of ice danger as the primary cause of the disaster.

And, in the great tradition of investigative bodies, they looked for individuals on which to hang the blame. Captain Smith was singled out as the primary culprit. Bruce Ismay and Captain Lord were also found culpable for their roles in the disaster.

Both investigations were critical of the Board of Trade regulations that failed to require an adequate number of boats for all those aboard.

Each made recommendations to prevent a similar event from ever occurring again. Many were implemented, and some were deemed to be so important that they were enacted into law.

Lifeboat regulations were quickly revised, and simplified. If a ship was rated to carry a specific number of people- then there had to be a space for that person in either a lifeboat or a raft- a real raft.

Regulations regarding watertight subdivision of ships were revised. Soon new construction would be mandated to have a double hull which extended above the water line, and interior bulkheads would have to reach higher.

Then there was the problem of what to do about icebergs. The most commonly suggested solution was to dispatch warships to the area of ice danger and destroy them with gunfire. It would give the gun crews much needed target practice and eliminate the hazard with one stroke. However, when the plan was put into practice, the results quickly revealed that even large caliber guns would only scar an iceberg. It has been estimated that it would require over 1,000 tons of TNT to demolish an iceberg of the size that sank *Titanic*, which is the equivalent explosive power of the atomic bomb that destroyed Hiroshima.

The next option was to establish a system of charting and reliably relating the location of the danger.

Since leaving the reporting of ice to ship's masters had been so dramatically found to be lacking, navy ships were dispatched to the area east of Newfoundland and tasked with the duty of accurately locating and warning ships of icebergs and growlers. It came to be called the International Ice Patrol, and eventually fell to the Canadian and American Coast Guards to implement. Today during the ice season, aircraft keep a constant watch for ice and their reports may be found online.[248]

---

[248] The NOAA charts may be found at: *http://weather.noaa.gov/fax/marsh.shtml* and the Canadian charts at: *http://www.ice-glaces.ec.gc.ca*

No ship has been lost to ice in the North Atlantic since the patrol was instituted.[249]

An alarm was invented that would sound when an SOS was keyed into the air- allowing ships with only one operator to participate in rescues.

Laws were passed to regulate wireless and operators were required to obtain licenses.[250]

Regulations regarding distress signals were revised and "company signals" became a thing of the past.

Obviously, the *Titanic* disaster also wrought drastic personal changes for many people, but surprisingly some were positive.

Perhaps the person who benefited the most was the Captain of *Carpathia*, Arthur Rostron. His

---

[249] This doesn't mean that ships have not been lost to ice since the patrol began. One notable example was a Canadian Ferry named *William Carson*, which struck ice in June 1977 between Newfoundland and Labrador. The ice patrol is not responsible for this stretch of water.

[250] This reduced, but did not eliminate, the type of wireless hoaxing that was thought to have occurred when *Titanic* sank. When Amelia Earhart disappeared, there were also bogus radio messages sent, many long after her fuel would have been exhausted.

participation in the rescue brought him renown and honor throughout the world. Within a few years he was Commodore of Cunard, in command of *Mauritania*. He received the Congressional Medal from a grateful United States Congress.[251] He also was the recipient of numerous other awards and honorariums, one being a knighthood.

Carpathia's Second officer, James Bissett, was also knighted later in his career and finished out his service in command of the original *Queen Mary*.

Margaret Brown finally found acceptance into the circles of society that she had always craved. Through this was able to further many of her personal causes, such as obtaining the right to vote for women.[252]

Phillip Franklin, White Star's representative in New York, eventually became chairman of IMM.

---

[251] Many sources state that Rostron received the "Congressional Medal of Honor" for his participation in the *Titanic* rescue, but his award was not the one given for heroism in combat.

[252] She was also later the subject of a Broadway musical and movie which christened her the "Unsinkable" Molly Brown. However, according to her family, she was never called "Molly" during her life.

There were others who benefitted less directly from the sinking of the *Titanic*.

The Cunard Line's business increased for a while, particularly after they adopted the advertising slogan, "We've never lost a human life."

Olympic finished out the 1912 travel season and then returned to Belfast to undergo a radical upgrading. Shipyard workers at Harland and Wolff received an unexpected amount of bonus work, rebuilding her to new safety standards and incorporating these same improvements into the last of the three sisters, now renamed *Britannic*.

When *Olympic* resumed her career early in 1913, she enjoyed an odd distinction for a time, as people booked aboard her to vicariously live out the *Titanic* disaster again. She was advertised as the "*New Olympic*," and her improved safety was stressed. She was possibly the safest ship now afloat, able to easily survive the accident that had claimed her younger sister. But nobody would ever say- even in the small print- that she, or any other ship, was unsinkable.

Bibliography

Books

A Journey into the Heart of the Titanic- Ghosts of the Abyss Don Lynch and Ken Marschall 2003 Da Capo Press/Madison Press Toronto

Analysis of Three Mile Island- Unit 2 Accident Nuclear Safety Analysis Center 1980

A Night to Remember Walter Lord 1955 Holt, Rinehart and Winston New York

A Titanic Hero- Thomas Andrews Shipbuilder (Reprint) Shan F. Bullock 19127 C's Press Riverside,Conneticut

Atlantic- The Last Great Race of Princes Scott Cookman 2002 John Wiley New York

Battleship Texas Hugh Power 1993 Texas A&M University Press College Station, Texas

Beyond Reach- The Search for the Titanic William Hoffman and Jack Grimm 1982 Beaufort Books New York

Castles of Steel- Britain, Germany, and the Winning of the Great War at Sea Robert K. Massie 2003 Random House New York

Challenger Launch Decision, The- Risky Technology, Culture and Deviance at NASA Diane Vaughan 1996 The University of Chicago Press Chicago

Collision Course Alvin Moscow 1959 Grosset and Dunlap New York

Darkest Hours- A narrative encyclopedia of worldwide disasters from ancient times to the present Jay Robert Nash 1977 Nelson Hall Chicago

Deathless Story of the Titanic, The Reprint from Lloyds Weekly news 1912 Lloyds Weekly News London

Devil in the White City, The Eric Larson 2003 Vintage Books New York

Discovery of the Titanic, The Dr. Robert Ballard 1987 Warner/Madison Press
New York

Empire of the Air- The men who made radio Tom Lewis 1991 Harper Collins
New York

Falling Star- Misadventures of White Star Line Ships John P. Eaton and Charles A. Haas 1989 Crown Publishing New York

Fourteen Minutes- The Last Voyage of the Empress of Ireland James Croall 1978 Stein and Day New York

Futility- the Wreck of the Titan (Reprint) Morgan Robertson 1898 7 C's Press Riverside,Conneticut

Great Bridge, The- The Epic Story of the Building of the Brooklyn Bridge David McCullough 1972 Simon and Shuster New York

Great Liners, The Melvin Maddocks 1978 Time Life New York

Her Name, Titanic Charles Pellegrino 1988 McGraw Hill New York

Hershey- Milton S. Hershey's Extraordinary Life of Wealth, Empire and Utopian Dreams Michael D'Antonio 2006 Simon and Shuster New York

James Cameron's Titanic Ed Marsh 1997 Harper Perennial New York

Ken Marschall's Art of Titanic Rick Archbold 1998 Hyperion New York

Loss of the S.S. Seawise University Report of the Marine Court 1972 7 C's Press Riverside,Conneticut

Lost Liners-From the Titanic to the Andrea Doria, the Ocean Floor Reveals its Greatest Lost Ships Rick Archbold and Dr. Robert Ballard 1997 Hyperion New York

Lost Moon Jim Lovell and Jeffrey Kluger 1994 Houghton Mifflin Boston

Lulu in Hollywood Louise Brooks 1974 Alfred A. Knopf New York

Lusitania- An Epic Tragedy Diana Preston 2002 Walker and Company New York

Maiden Voyage, The- The Titanic Epic- From the embarkation to the disaster and the dramatic courtroom aftermath Geoffrey Marcus 1969 Viking Press New York

Making of the Atomic Bomb, The Richard Rhodes 1986 Simon and Shuster
New York

Night Lives on, The- New Thoughts, Theories and Revelations about the Titanic Walter Lord 1986 William Morrow New York

No Downlink- A dramatic Narrative about the Challenger Accident and our Time
Claus Jensen 1996 Farrar Straus Giroux New York

Normandie- Her Life and Times Harvey Ardman 1985 Franklin Watts
New York

Normandie- France's Legendary Art Deco Ocean Liner
John Maxtone Graham 2007 W.W. Norton New York

Ocean Liners of the Past- Lusitania and Mauritania- a Reprint of the Souvenir Shipbuilder and Marine Engine Builder 1970 Patrick Stephens Ltd Letchworth, U.K

Ocean Liners of the Past- Normandie- a Reprint of the Souvenir Shipbuilder and Marine Engine Builder 1972 Patrick Stephens Ltd Letchworth, U.K

Ocean Liners of the Past- Olympic and Titanic- a Reprint of the Souvenir Shipbuilder and Marine Engine Builder 1970 Patrick Stephens Ltd Letchworth, U.K

Ocean Liners of the Past- Queen Mary- a Reprint of the Souvenir Shipbuilder and Marine Engine Builder 1972 Patrick Stephens Ltd Letchworth, U.K

Odyssey of C.H. Lightoller, The Patrick Stenson 1984 W.W. Norton New York

Only Way to Cross, The John Maxtone Graham 1972 Macmillan Publishing New York

Path Between the Seas, The- The Creation of the Panama Canal 1870-1914 David McCullough 1977 Simon and Shuster New York

Perfect Machine- The Building the Palomar Telescope Ronald Florence 1995 Harper Perennial New York

Picture History of the SS United States William H. Miller Jr. 2003 Dover Maritime New York

Report of the Wreck Commissioners' Court (British Inquiry) 1912

Return to Titanic- A new look at the world's most famous lost ship Dr. Robert Ballard with Michael S. Sweeney 2004 National Geographic Washington, D.C.

RMS Olympic- Titanic's Sister Mark Chirnside 2004 Tempus Publishing Gloucester, UK

Saved- The Story of the Andrea Doria- the Greatest Sea Rescue in History William Hoffer 1979 Summit Books New York

Story of the Titanic as Told by its survivors, The Lawrence Beesley, Archibald Gracie, Charles Lightoller, Harold Bride- edited by Jack Winocour 1960 Dover Publications New York

Strange But True- Mysterious and Bizarre People Thomas Sleman 1998 Barnes and Noble

Thunderstruck Eric Larson 2006 Crown Publishing New York

Total Titanic Marc Shapiro 1998 Pocket Books New York

True Tales of the Great Lakes Dwight Boyer 1971 Freshwater Press

Titanic - The Death and Life of a Legend Michael Davie 1986 Alfred A. Knopf New York

Titanic- An Illustrated History Don Lynch and Ken Marschall 1992 Hyperion New York

Titanic and Her Sisters Olympic and Brittanic Tom McCluskie, Michael Sharpe, Leo Marriot 1998 PRC Publishing New York

Titanic Conspiracy, The - Cover ups and Mysteries of the World's most famous Sea Disaster Robin Gardiner and Dan Van Der Vat 1995 Birch Lane Press New York

Titanic- Destination Disaster John P. Eaton and Charles A. Haas 1987 W.W. Norton New York

Titanic Disaster Hearings-The: The Official Transcript of the 1912 Senate Investigation Edited by Tom Kunz 1998 Pocket Books New York

Titanic-The Last Great Images Dr. Robert Ballard and Ian Coutts 2007 Running Press Philadelphia

Titanic Survivor- the newly discovered memoirs of Violet Jessop who survived both the Titanic and Brittanic Disasters John Maxtone Graham 1997 Sheridan House Dobbs Ferry, New York

Titanic- The Story of the Disaster in the Newspapers of the Day Collected by Eric Caren and Steve Goldman 1998 Castle Books Edison, New Jersey

Titanic, The - End of a Dream Wyn Craig Wade 1979 Rawson Wade New York

White Hurricane- A Great Lakes November Gale and America's Deadliest Maritime Disaster David G. Brown 2002 McGraw Hill New York

Periodicals

Popular Science February 1995 "What Really Sank the *Titanic*."

Popular Mechanics September 1998 "*Titanic* Reborn"

National Geographic December 2004 "What's Destroying *Titanic*?"

The Weekly News of the World September 10, 1991

26012629R00348

Printed in Great Britain
by Amazon